INTELLASTIC
SUCCESS READING PROGRAM
FOR OLDER STUDENTS

Learn to Read English With Directions In Chinese

Answer Key
Classwork
Color Edition

Classwork

ISBN 978-1-947984-77-6
© 2022 – Wendy A. Charles & Alexander J. Charles
All Rights Reserved
Baldwin, New York
www.intellastic.com

All rights reserved. No portion of this book may be reproduced, stored in a retrieval system, or transmitted in any form or by any means – electronic, mechanical, photocopy, recording, video presentation, private instruction, scanning or other – except for brief quotations in critical reviews or articles, without the prior written permission of the writers.

All Rights Reserved. Printed in the USA.

Answer Key

Table of Contents

Unit A

Lesson 1.1	Reading Words with the Letter A/a	1
Lesson 1.2	Reading Words with the Short Vowel "a" Sound	2
Lesson 1.2	Reading & Writing Words with the Short Vowel "a" Sound	3
Lesson 1.3	Reading Words with the Long Vowel "a" Sound	4
Lesson 1.3	Reading & Writing Words with the Long Vowel "a" Sound	5
Lessons 1.2 & 1.3	Reading Short Vowel and Long Vowel Words	6
Lesson 1.4	Reading Words with the "age" Letter Combination	7
Lesson 1.5	Reading Words with the "ai" Vowel Pair	8
Lesson 1.6	Reading Letter "a" Words with the Schwa Sound	9
Lesson 1.7	Reading Words with the "ar" Letter Combination	10
Lesson 1.7	Reading Words with the "ar" Letter Combination	11
Lesson 1.8	Reading Words with a Silent Letter "a"	12
Unit Review	Reading Words with Vowel "a" Sounds: /ă/,/ā/,/ə/ & Silent	13
Lesson 1.9	Reading Multisyllable Words	14
Lesson 1.9	Reading Multisyllable Words	15
Lesson 1.10	Proper and Common Nouns and Adjectives	16

Unit B

Lesson 2.1	Reading Words with the Letter B/b	17
Lesson 2.2	Reading Words with the "br" Letter Combination	18
Lesson 2.3	Reading Words with the "bl" Letter Combination	19
Lesson 2.3	Reading Words with the "ble" Letter Combination	20
Lesson 2.4	Reading Words with the "mb" Letter Combination	21
Lesson 2.4	Reading Words with the "bt" Letter Combination	22
Lesson 2.5	Reading Words with a Silent Letter "b"	23
Lesson 2.6	Reading Multisyllable Words	24
Lesson 2.6	Reading Multisyllable Words	25
Lesson 2.7	Proper and Common Nouns and Adjectives	26

Classwork

Unit C

Lesson 3.1	Reading Words with the Letter C/c	27
Lesson 3.1	Reading Words with the Hard Letter "c"	28
Lesson 3.2	Reading Words with the Soft Letter "c"	29
Lessons 3.1 & 3.2	Reading Hard Letter "c" and Soft Letter "c" Words	30
Lesson 3.3	Reading Words with the "cr" Letter Combination	31
Lesson 3.4	Reading Words with the "cl" Letter Combination	32
Lesson 3.4	Reading Words with the "cle" Letter Combination	33
Lesson 3.5	Reading Words with the "ct" Letter Combination	34
Lesson 3.6	Reading Soft Letter "c" Words	35
Lesson 3.6	Reading Soft Letter "c" Words	36
Lesson 3.7	Reading Words with the "ch" Letter Combination	37
Lesson 3.8	Reading Words with the "cc" Letter Combination	38
Lesson 3.9	Reading Words with a Silent Letter "c"	39
Lesson 3.10	Reading Multisyllable Words	40
Lesson 3.10	Reading Multisyllable Words	41
Lesson 3.11	Proper and Common Nouns and Adjectives	42

Unit D

Lesson 4.1	Reading Words with the Letter D/d	43
Lesson 4.2	Reading Letter "d" Words with the /d/ Sound & /j/ Sound	44
Lesson 4.2	Reading Words with the "dr" Letter Combination	45
Lesson 4.3	Reading Words with the "ed" Suffix/ Past Tense Verbs	46
Lesson 4.4	Reading Words with a Silent Letter "d"	47
Lesson 4.5	Reading Multisyllable Words	48
Lesson 4.5	Reading Multisyllable Words	49
Lesson 4.6	Proper and Common Nouns and Adjectives	50

Unit E

Lesson 5.1	Reading Words with the Letter E/e	51
Lesson 5.2	Reading Words with the Short Vowel "e" Sound	52
Lesson 5.2	Reading & Writing Words with the Short Vowel "e" Sound	53

Answer Key

Lesson 5.3	Reading Words with the Long Vowel "e" Sound	54
Lesson 5.3	Reading & Writing Words with the Long Vowel "e" Sound	55
Lessons 5.2 & 5.3	Reading Short Vowel and Long Vowel Words	56
Lesson 5.4	Reading Words with Letter "e" Vowel Pairs	57
Lesson 5.5	Reading Words with the Final Letter "e"	58
Lesson 5.6	Reading Letter "e" Words with the Schwa Vowel Sound	59
Lesson 5.7	Reading Words with the "er" Letter Combination	60
Lesson 5.8	Reading Words with the "eu" and "ew" Letter Combinations	61
Lesson 5.9	Reading Words with the "ey" Letter Combination	62
Lesson 5.10	Reading Words with a Silent Letter "e"	63
Unit Review	Reading Words with Vowel "e" Sounds: /ĕ/, /ē/, /ə/ & Silent	64
Lesson 5.11	Reading Multisyllable Words	65
Lesson 5.11	Reading Multisyllable Words	66
Lesson 5.12	Proper and Common Nouns and Adjectives	67

Unit F

Lesson 6.1	Reading Words with the Letter F/f	68
Lesson 6.2	Reading Words with the "fr" Letter Combination	69
Lesson 6.3	Reading Words with the "fl" Letter Combination	70
Lesson 6.3	Reading Words with the "fle" Letter Combination	71
Lesson 6.4	Reading Words with the "ft," "lf" and "ff" Letter Combinations	72
Lesson 6.5	Reading Words with a Silent Letter "f"	73
Lesson 6.6	Reading Singular and Plural forms of Words Ending in "-f" & "-fe"	74
Lesson 6.7	Reading Multisyllable Words	75
Lesson 6.7	Reading Multisyllable Words	76
Lesson 6.8	Proper and Common Nouns and Adjectives	77

Unit G

Lesson 7.1	Reading Words with the Letter G/g	78
Lesson 7.1	Reading Words with the Hard Letter "g"	79
Lesson 7.2	Reading Words with the Soft Letter G/g	80
Lessons 7.1 & 7.2	Reading Hard Letter "g" and Soft Letter "g" Words	81

Classwork

Lessons 7.1 & 7.2	Reading Hard Letter "g" and Soft Letter "g" Words	82
Lesson 7.3	Reading Words with the "gr" Letter Combination	83
Lesson 7.4	Reading Words with the "gl" Letter Combination	84
Lesson 7.4	Reading Words with the "gle" Letter Combination	85
Lesson 7.5	Reading Words with the "gh" Letter Combination	86
Lesson 7.6	Reading Words with the "gn" Letter Combination	87
Lesson 7.7	Reading Words with a Silent Letter "g"	88
Lesson 7.8	Reading Multisyllable Words	89
Lesson 7.8	Reading Multisyllable Words	90
Lesson 7.9	Proper and Common Nouns and Adjectives	91

Unit H

Lesson 8.1	Reading Words with the Letter H/h	92
Lesson 8.2	Reading Words with the Letter "h" Combinations: "sh," "wh," "ch," "th," "rh," "ph" and "gh"	93
Lesson 8.2	Reading Words with the Letter "h" Combinations: "sh," "wh," "ch," "th," "rh," "ph," "gh" and "sch"	94
Lesson 8.3	Reading Words with a Silent Letter "h"	95
Lesson 8.4	Reading Multisyllable Words	96
Lesson 8.4	Reading Multisyllable Words	97
Lesson 8.5	Proper and Common Nouns and Adjectives	98

Unit I

Lesson 9.1	Reading Words with the Letter I/i	99
Lesson 9.2	Reading Words with the Short Vowel "i" Sound	100
Lesson 9.2	Reading & Writing Words with the Short Vowel "i" Sound	101
Lesson 9.3	Reading Words with the Long Vowel "i" Sound	102
Lesson 9.3	Reading & Writing Words with the Long Vowel "i" Sound	103
Lessons 9.2 & 9.3	Reading Short Vowel and Long Vowel Words	104
Lesson 9.4	Reading Words with Letter "i" Vowel Pairs	105
Lesson 9.5	Reading Words with the Final Letter "i"	106
Lesson 9.6	Reading Letter "i" Words with the Schwa Vowel Sound	107

Lesson 9.7	Reading Words with the "ir" Letter Combination	108
Lesson 9.8	Reading Letter "i" Words with the Long Vowel "e" Sound	109
Lesson 9.9	Reading Words with a Silent Letter "i"	110
Unit Review	Reading Words with Vowel "i" Sounds: /ĭ/, /ī/, /ə/ & Silent	111
Lesson 9.10	Reading Multisyllable Words	112
Lesson 9.10	Reading Multisyllable Words	113
Lesson 9.11	Proper and Common Nouns and Adjectives	114

Unit J

Lesson 10.1	Reading Words with the Letter J/j	115
Lesson 10.2	Reading Multisyllable Words	116
Lesson 10.2	Reading Multisyllable Words	117
Lesson 10.3	Proper and Common Nouns and Adjectives	118

Unit K

Lesson 11.1	Reading Words with the Letter K/k	119
Lesson 11.2	Reading Words with the Letter "k" and "ck" Letter Combination	120
Lesson 11.3	Reading Words with the "kle" Letter Combination	121
Lesson 11.4	Reading Words with a Silent Letter "k"	122
Lesson 11.5	Reading Multisyllable Words	123
Lesson 11.5	Reading Multisyllable Words	124
Lesson 11.6	Proper and Common Nouns and Adjectives	125

Unit L

Lesson 12.1	Reading Words with the Letter L/l	126
Lesson 12.2	Reading Words with the Letter "l" Combinations: "fl," "pl" & "sl"	127
Lesson 12.3	Reading Words with a Silent Letter "l"	128
Lesson 12.4	Reading Multisyllable Words	129
Lesson 12.4	Reading Multisyllable Words	130
Lesson 12.5	Proper and Common Nouns and Adjectives	131

Classwork

Unit M

Lesson 13.1	Reading Words with the Letter M/m	132
Lesson 13.2	Reading Words with a Silent Letter "m"	133
Lesson 13.3	Reading Multisyllable Words	134
Lesson 13.3	Reading Multisyllable Words	135
Lesson 13.4	Proper and Common Nouns and Adjectives	136

Unit N

Lesson 14.1	Reading Words with the Letter N/n	137
Lesson 14.2	Reading Words with the "ng" Letter Combination	138
Lesson 14.3	Reading Words with a Silent Letter "n"	139
Lesson 14.4	Reading Multisyllable Words	140
Lesson 14.4	Reading Multisyllable Words	141
Lesson 14.5	Proper and Common Nouns and Adjectives	142

Unit O

Lesson 15.1	Reading Words with the Letter O/o	143
Lesson 15.2	Reading Words with the Short Vowel "o" Sound	144
Lesson 15.2	Reading & Writing Words with the Short Vowel "o" Sound	145
Lesson 15.3	Reading Words with the Long Vowel "o" Sound	146
Lesson 15.3	Reading & Writing Words with the Long Vowel "o" Sound	147
Lessons 15.2 & 15.3	Reading Short Vowel and Long Vowel Words	148
Lesson 15.4	Reading Words with Letter "o" Vowel Pairs	149
Lesson 15.5	Reading Words with the Final Letter "o"	150
Lesson 15.6	Reading Letter "o" Words with the Schwa Vowel Sound	151
Lesson 15.7	Reading Words with Vowel "o" Sounds: /ŏ/, /ō/ & /$\overline{oo}$/	152
Lesson 15.8	Reading Words with the "or" Letter Combination	153
Lesson 15.8	Reading Words with the "or" Letter Combination	154
Lesson 15.9	Reading Words with a Silent Letter "o"	155
Unit Review	Reading Words with Vowel "o" Sounds: /ŏ/, /ō/, /ə/ & Silent	156
Lesson 15.10	Reading Multisyllable Words	157
Lesson 15.10	Reading Multisyllable Words	158

Answer Key

| Lesson 15.11 | Proper and Common Nouns and Adjectives | 159 |

Unit P

Lesson 16.1	Reading Words with the Letter P/p	160
Lesson 16.2	Reading Words with the "ph" Letter Combination	161
Lesson 16.3	Reading Words with the "pr" Letter Combination	162
Lesson 16.4	Reading Words with the "pl" Letter Combination	163
Lesson 16.4	Reading Words with the "ple" Letter Combination	164
Lesson 16.5	Reading Words with a Silent Letter "p"	165
Lesson 16.6	Reading Multisyllable Words	166
Lesson 16.6	Reading Multisyllable Words	167
Lesson 16.7	Proper and Common Nouns and Adjectives	168

Unit Q

Lesson 17.1	Reading Words with the Letter Q/q	169
Lesson 17.2	Reading Words with the Letter "q" and "qu" Letter Combination	170
Lesson 17.2	Reading Words with the "qu" Letter Combination	171
Lesson 17.3	Reading Multisyllable Words	172
Lesson 17.3	Reading Multisyllable Words	173
Lesson 17.4	Proper and Common Nouns and Adjectives	174

Unit R

Lesson 18.1	Reading Words with the Letter R/r	175
Lesson 18.2	Reading Words with the Letter "r" Combinations: "br," "cr," "dr," "fr," "gr," "pr" and "tr"	176
Lesson 18.3	Reading Multisyllable Words	177
Lesson 18.3	Reading Multisyllable Words	178
Lesson 18.4	Proper and Common Nouns and Adjectives	179

Unit S

| Lesson 19.1 | Reading Words with the Letter S/s | 180 |
| Lesson 19.1 | Reading Words with the Letter S/s | 181 |

Classwork

Lesson 19.2	Reading Words with the "sion," "sial" & "scious" Suffixes	182
Lesson 19.3	Reading Words with the "sch" Letter Combination	183
Lesson 19.4	Reading Words with the "scr," "shr," "spr" & "str" Letter Combinations	184
Lesson 19.5	Reading Words with the "sl" & "sle" Letter Combinations	185
Lesson 19.5	Reading Words with the "sle" Letter Combination	186
Lesson 19.6	Reading Words with the "sm" Letter Combination	187
Lesson 19.7	Reading Words with the "ss" Letter Combination	188
Lesson 19.8	Reading Words with a Silent Letter "s"	189
Lesson 19.9	Reading Multisyllable Words	190
Lesson 19.9	Reading Multisyllable Words	191
Lesson 19.10	Proper and Common Nouns and Adjectives	192

Unit T

Lesson 20.1	Reading Words with the Letter T/t	193
Lesson 20.2	Reading Words with the "thm" Letter Combination	194
Lesson 20.3	Reading Words with the "tion," "tial" & "tious" Suffixes	195
Lesson 20.4	Reading Words with the "tr" Letter Combination	196
Lesson 20.5	Reading Words with the "tle" Letter Combination	197
Lesson 20.6	Reading Words with the Letter "t" Sounds	198
Lesson 20.7	Reading Words with a Silent Letter "t"	199
Lesson 20.8	Reading Multisyllable Words	200
Lesson 20.8	Reading Multisyllable Words	201
Lesson 20.9	Proper and Common Nouns and Adjectives	202

Unit U

Lesson 21.1	Reading Words with the Letter U/u	203
Lesson 21.2	Reading Words with the Short Vowel "u" Sound	204
Lesson 21.2	Reading & Writing Words with the Short Vowel "u" Sound	205
Lesson 21.3	Reading Words with the Long Vowel "u" Sound	206
Lesson 21.3	Reading & Writing Words with the Long Vowel "u" Sound	207
Lessons 21.2 & 21.3	Reading Short Vowel and Long Vowel Words	208
Lesson 21.4	Reading Words with Letter "u" Vowel Pairs	209

Answer Key

Lesson 21.5	Reading Words with the Final Letter "u"	210
Lesson 21.6	Reading Letter "u" Words with the Schwa Vowel Sound	211
Lesson 21.7	Reading Words with the "ur" Letter Combination	212
Lesson 21.8	Reading Words with a Silent Letter "u"	213
Unit Review	Reading Words with Vowel "u" Sounds: /ŭ/, /o͞o/, /ə/ & Silent	214
Lesson 21.9	Reading Multisyllable Words	215
Lesson 21.9	Reading Multisyllable Words	216
Lesson 21.10	Proper and Common Nouns and Adjectives	217

Unit V

Lesson 22.1	Reading Words with the Letter V/v	218
Lesson 22.2	Reading Multisyllable Words	219
Lesson 22.2	Reading Multisyllable Words	220
Lesson 22.3	Proper and Common Nouns and Adjectives	221

Unit W

Lesson 23.1	Reading Words with the Letter W/w	222
Lesson 23.2	Reading Words with a Vowel before the Letter "w"	223
Lesson 23.3	Reading Words with a Silent "w" and "wr" Letter Combination	224
Lesson 23.3	Reading Words with a Silent Letter "w"	225
Lesson 23.4	Reading Multisyllable Words	226
Lesson 23.4	Reading Multisyllable Words	227
Lesson 23.5	Proper and Common Nouns and Adjectives	228

Unit X

Lesson 24.1	Reading Words with the Letter X/x	229
Lesson 24.1	Reading Words with the Letter X/x	230
Lesson 24.2	Reading Multisyllable Words	231
Lesson 24.2	Reading Multisyllable Words	232
Lesson 24.3	Proper and Common Nouns and Adjectives	233

Classwork

Unit Y

Lesson	Title	Page
Lesson 25.1	Reading Words with the Letter Y/y	234
Lesson 25.1	Reading Words with the Letter Y/y	235
Lesson 25.2	Reading Words with a Vowel before the Letter "y"	236
Lesson 25.3	Reading Words with the "cy" Letter Combination	237
Lesson 25.4	Reading Words with the Final Letter "y"	238
Lesson 25.5	Reading Words with the "yr" Letter Combination	239
Lesson 25.6	Reading Letter "y" Words with the Schwa Sound	240
Lesson 25.7	Reading Words with a Silent Letter "y"	241
Lesson 25.8	Reading Multisyllable Words	242
Lesson 25.8	Reading Multisyllable Words	243
Lesson 25.9	Proper and Common Nouns and Adjectives	244

Unit Z

Lesson	Title	Page
Lesson 26.1	Reading Words with the Letter Z/z	245
Lesson 26.1	Reading Words with the Letter Z/z	246
Lesson 26.2	Reading Words with a Silent Letter "z"	247
Lesson 26.3	Reading Multisyllable Words	248
Lesson 26.3	Reading Multisyllable Words	249
Lesson 26.4	Proper and Common Nouns and Adjectives	250

Appendix

Appendix	Title	Page
Appendix 1.0	Introduction of the Letter A/a	251
Appendix 2.0	Introduction of the Letter B/b	252
Appendix 2.0	Letter Recognition B/b	253
Appendix 3.0	Introduction of the Letter C/c	254
Appendix 3.0	Letter Recognition C/c	255
Appendix 4.0	Introduction of the Letter D/d	256
Appendix 4.0	Letter Recognition D/d	257
Appendix 5.0	Introduction of the Letter E/e	258
Appendix 6.0	Introduction of the Letter F/f	259
Appendix 6.0	Letter Recognition F/f	260

Appendix 7.0	Introduction of the Letter G/g	261
Appendix 7.0	Letter Recognition G/g	262
Appendix 8.0	Introduction of the Letter H/h	263
Appendix 8.0	Letter Recognition H/h	264
Appendix 9.0	Introduction of the Letter I/i	265
Appendix 10.0	Introduction of the Letter J/j	266
Appendix 10.0	Letter Recognition J/j	267
Appendix 11.0	Introduction of the Letter K/k	268
Appendix 11.0	Letter Recognition K/k	269
Appendix 12.0	Introduction of the Letter L/l	270
Appendix 12.0	Letter Recognition L/l	271
Appendix 13.0	Introduction of the Letter M/m	272
Appendix 13.0	Letter Recognition M/m	273
Appendix 14.0	Introduction of the Letter N/n	274
Appendix 14.0	Letter Recognition N/n	275
Appendix 15.0	Introduction of the Letter O/o	276
Appendix 16.0	Introduction of the Letter P/p	277
Appendix 16.0	Letter Recognition P/p	278
Appendix 17.0	Introduction of the Letter Q/q	279
Appendix 17.0	Letter Recognition Q/q	280
Appendix 18.0	Introduction of the Letter R/r	281
Appendix 18.0	Letter Recognition R/r	282
Appendix 19.0	Introduction of the Letter S/s	283
Appendix 19.0	Letter Recognition S/s	284
Appendix 20.0	Introduction of the Letter T/t	285
Appendix 20.0	Letter Recognition T/t	286
Appendix 21.0	Introduction of the Letter U/u	287
Appendix 22.0	Introduction of the Letter V/v	288
Appendix 22.0	Letter Recognition V/v	289
Appendix 23.0	Introduction of the Letter W/w	290
Appendix 23.0	Letter Recognition W/w	291

Classwork

Appendix 24.0	Introduction of the Letter X/x	292
Appendix 24.0	Letter Recognition X/x	293
Appendix 25.0	Introduction of the Letter Y/y	294
Appendix 25.0	Letter Recognition Y/y	295
Appendix 26.0	Introduction of the Letter Z/z	296
Appendix 26.0	Letter Recognition Z/z	297

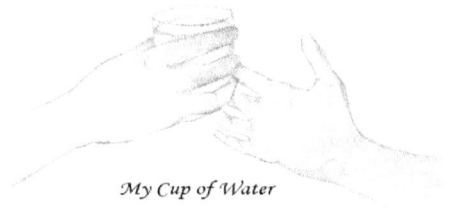

My Cup of Water

Answer Key

 Name: _____ Date: ___/___/_____ Score: _____

Lesson 1.1

Reading Words with the Letter A/a

 Lesson Check Point

Directions: Read each target word. Find the letter "a" and put a check (✓) in the column that identifies its position: beginning, within or end.
路线：读每个目标词。找出字母 a 在栏中打勾 (✓) 示意： 开 始，中间 或末尾。

Target Words	Beginning (First Letter)	Within	End (Last Letter)
1. taxicab		✓	
2. black		✓	
3. anklet	✓		
4. opera			✓
5. above	✓		

 Directions: Read each target word. Read the words in the row and circle the word that has a different vowel "a" sound.
路线：读每个目标词。阅读这一行的词，圈出元音 a 发不同的 词。

Target Words				
6. am	cat	sand	(pail)	bank
7. apple	cab	(sofa)	back	sad
8. happy	band	ant	sank	(cake)
9. pants	(zebra)	sat	cap	man
10. thanks	cash	(bake)	map	pan

Classwork

 Name: _____ Date: ___/___/_____ Score: _____

Lesson 1.2

Reading Words with the Short Vowel "a" Sound

✓ **Lesson Check Point**

 Directions: Read the words in the four boxes. Circle two words with the short vowel /ă/ sound. The anchor word for the short vowel /ă/ sound is <u>apple</u>.

路线：读四个框中的词。圈出含短元音/ă/的两个词。锚点词词含短元音/ă/为英语单词，apple。

day	(hat)
(cap)	sofa

(grass)	(nap)
tuna	lake

agree	(yam)
(sand)	paint

Asia	(pad)
ago	(back)

walk	father
(flap)	(map)

(flag)	(man)
grape	bake

 Directions: Read the words in the four boxes. Circle two words that rhyme. Rhyming words have the same ending sound, such as <u>tap</u> and <u>map</u>.

路线：读四个框中的词。圈出押韵的两个词。押韵词有同样尾音，如单词 tap 和 map。

(had)	tax
(dad)	zap

(nap)	cake
cape	(map)

(camp)	(lamp)
spa	alike

away	plane
(ran)	(man)

game	(cat)
(sat)	lane

take	(tan)
ate	(ran)

Answer Key

Name: _____ Date: ___/___/_____ Score: _____

Lesson 1.2

Reading & Writing Words with the Short Vowel "a" Sound

✓ **Lesson Check Point**

Directions: Read each sentence and underline three words with the short vowel /ă/ sound. Then, write the underlined words on the lines below. The anchor word for the short vowel /ă/ sound is apple.

路线：读每个句子，划出含短元音/ă/的三个词。然后，在下面的划线处写上带下划线的词。锚点词为短元音/ă/的英语单词，apple。

Model

<u>Ann</u> raised her <u>hand</u> in <u>class</u>.

    Ann   hand   class
  _____   _____   _____

1. <u>Pam's</u> <u>tan</u> <u>hat</u> is faded.

    Pam's   tan   hat
  _____   _____   _____

2. My father <u>asked</u> for <u>apples</u> <u>and</u> grapes.

    asked   apples   and
  _____   _____   _____

3. <u>Sam</u> <u>and</u> <u>Dan</u> walked by the lake.

    Sam   and   Dan
  _____   _____   _____

4. David <u>planted</u> the <u>flag</u> in the <u>sand</u>.

    planted   flag   sand
  _____   _____   _____

5. My music teacher plays the <u>sax</u> in a large <u>jazz</u> <u>band</u>.

    sax   jazz   band
  _____   _____   _____

Classwork

 Name: _____ Date: ___/___/_____ Score: _____

Lesson 1.3

Reading Words with the Long Vowel "a" Sound

✓ Lesson Check Point

 Directions: Read the words in the four boxes. Circle two words with the long vowel /ā/ sound. The anchor word for the long vowel /ā/ sound is <u>ape</u>.

路线：读四个框中的词。圈出带长元音/ā/的两个词。锚点词为含长元音/ā/的英语单词 ape。

cap	(sale)		alike	cat		(ate)	sofa
talk	(nail)		(gain)	(pace)		(wave)	tap

rat	(lake)		(page)	(mate)		(stay)	above
(male)	ago		pan	about		alone	(sail)

 Directions: Read the words in the four boxes. Circle two words that rhyme. Rhyming words have the same ending sound, such as <u>wait</u> and <u>date</u>.

路线：读四个框中的词。圈出押韵的两个词。押韵的词含同样的尾音。如，英语单词 wait 和 date。

mama	(wake)		tuna	(lane)		land	puma
(take)	ban		dad	(cane)		rate	(late)

(came)	man		(tale)	Asia		(pave)	(gave)
(same)	panda		bran	(mail)		villa	have

Answer Key

Name: _____ Date:___/___/_____ Score: _____

Lesson 1.3

Reading & Writing Words with the Long Vowel "a" Sound

✓ Lesson Check Point

Directions: Read each sentence and underline three words with the long vowel /ā/ sound. Then, write the underlined words on the lines below. The anchor word for the long vowel /ā/ sound is <u>ape</u>.
路线：读每个句子，给带长元音/ā/的三个词加下划线。然后，在下面的划线处写上带下划线的词。锚点词为长元音/ā/的英语单词，ape。

Model

Ann has <u>grapes</u> and <u>cake</u> on her <u>plate</u>.

grapes	cake	plate

1. <u>Dain</u> can't <u>wait</u> to <u>paint</u> the chair.

Dain	wait	paint

2. The <u>skates</u> and <u>sails</u> are packed in the <u>basement</u>.

skates	sails	basement

3. Alvin did not <u>take</u> the large slice of <u>cake</u> from the <u>plate</u>.

take	cake	plate

4. <u>Dale</u> Anderson said, "Beware of garter <u>snakes</u> by the <u>lake</u>."

Dale	snakes	lake

5. Jackson and Andrew sold chocolate <u>cupcakes</u> at Annie's <u>bake</u> <u>sale</u>.

cupcakes	bake	sale

Classwork

Name: _____ Date: ___/___/_____ Score: _____

Review Lessons 1.2 & 1.3
Reading Short Vowel and Long Vowel Words

✓ **Lesson Check Point**

Directions: Read the target words in the word box. In the first column, write the words that have the short vowel /ă/ sound, as in the word <u>apple</u>. In the second column, write the words that have the long vowel /ā/ sound, as in the word <u>ape</u>.

路线：读框中的目标词。在第一栏写上含短元音/ă/的词。如，英语单词 apple。在第二栏写上含长元音/ā/的单词。如，英语单词 ape。

Target Word Box				
bagel	grass	glad	clan	basic
trap	came	taken	grapes	hat
fame	maps	sand	stay	gain
slaps	bake	train	flag	brand

Letter "a" has the /ă/ sound as in the word <u>apple</u>

Letter "a" has the /ā/ sound as in the word <u>ape</u>

hat	gain
glad	stay
clan	came
trap	bake
flag	train
grass	fame
sand	basic
slaps	bagel
maps	taken
brand	grapes

Unit A — Review Lessons 1.2 & 1.3

Answer Key

 Name: _____ Date: ___/___/_____ Score: _____

Lesson 1.4

Reading Words with the "age" Letter Combination

✓ Lesson Check Point

 Directions: Read each target word. Find the "age" letter combination and put a check (✓) in the column that correctly identifies its sounds.
路线：读每个目标词。找到"age"字母组合，并在栏中打勾(✓)示意。

Target Words	"age" has the /ā/ + /j/ sounds as in the word <u>stage</u>	"age" has the /ĭ/ + /j/ sounds as in the word <u>package</u>	"age" has the /ä/ + /j/ or /ä/ + /zh/ sounds as in the word <u>massage</u>
1. camouflage			✓
2. Anchorage		✓	
3. enrage	✓		
4. baggage		✓	
5. teenagers	✓		

 Directions: Read each sentence and underline the word that has an "age" letter combination that has the /ĭ/ + /j/ sounds, as in the word <u>package</u>.
路线：读每个句子，给含"age"字母组合且发/ĭ/+/j/音的词加下划线。如，英语单词 package。

6. The teenager's albums and books are in the <u>cottage</u>.

7. The teenager's <u>luggage</u> set was stolen from the airport.

8. My large boxes from <u>Anchorage</u>, Alaska are on the stage.

9. The backstage <u>manager</u> ate apple pie and drank lemonade.

10. Everyone in the entourage had massages after their long <u>voyage</u>.

Classwork

 Name: _____ Date:___/___/_____ Score: _____

Lesson 1.5

Reading Words with the "ai" Vowel Pair

✓ Lesson Check Point

 Directions: Read each target word. Circle the word in the column that has the same "ai" sound as the target word.
路线：读每个目标词。在栏中圈出与目标词含相同 "ai" 音的单词。

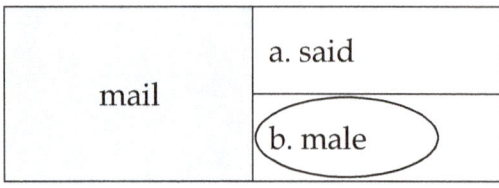
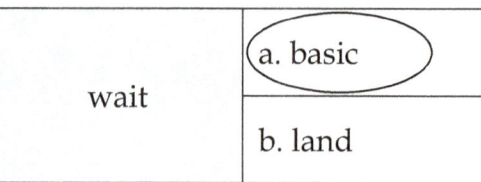

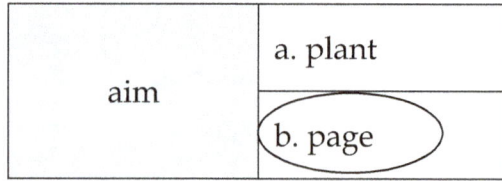

 Directions: Read each target word.   Put a check (✓) under the correct column heading.
路线：读每个目标词。在符合要求的栏下打勾 (✓)。

Target Words	Words have the long "a" sound as in the word <u>sail</u>	Words do not have the long "a" sound
1. tail	✓	
2. trait	✓	
3. plaid		✓
4. pain	✓	

Unit A Lesson 1.5

Learn To Read English With Directions In Chinese

Answer Key

 Name: _____ Date:___/___/_____ Score: _____

Lesson 1.6

Reading Letter "a" Words with the Schwa Vowel Sound

✓ Lesson Check Point

 Directions: Read each target word. Circle the word in the column that has the same "a" sound as the target word.
路线：读每个目标词。圈出栏中与目标词含相同 a 音的单词。

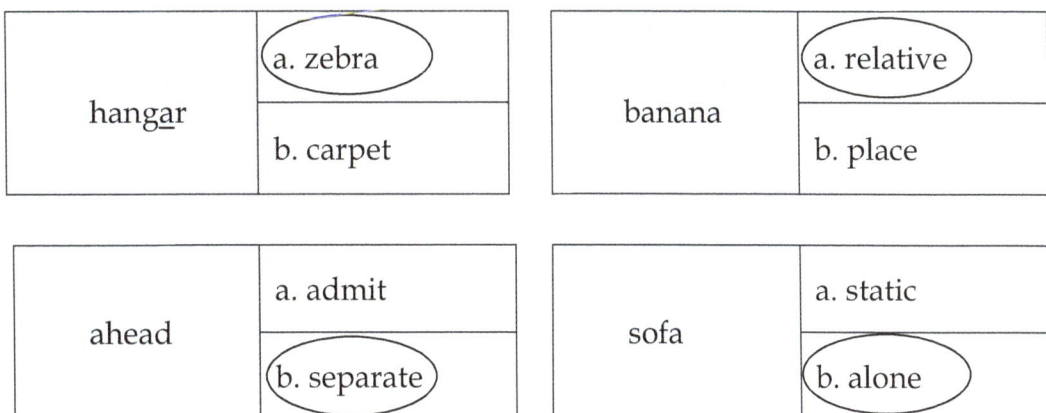

 Directions: Read each sentence and underline the letter "a" word that has the schwa vowel /ə/ sound. The anchor word for the letter "a" schwa vowel sound is sofa.
路线：读每个句子。给含字母 a 且发施瓦 /ə/ 音的单词加下划线。锚点词为含字母 a 且发施瓦音的英语单词，sofa。

1. The class is going to the <u>opera</u>.

2. The Erie <u>Canal</u> is an awesome place.

3. On Saturday, Ann ate two large <u>bananas</u>.

4. This year, I have an <u>amazing</u> math teacher.

5. Dr. Anderson paid the cab driver three <u>dollars</u>.

6. Andrew ate whole wheat <u>spaghetti</u> with white sauce.

Classwork

 Name: _____ Date: ___/___/_____ Score: _____

Lesson 1.7

Reading Words with the "ar" Letter Combination

✓ Lesson Check Point

 Directions: Read each target word. Circle the word in the column that has the same "a" + "r" sounds as the target word.
路线：读每个目标词。圈出栏中与目标词含相同 a + r 音的单词。

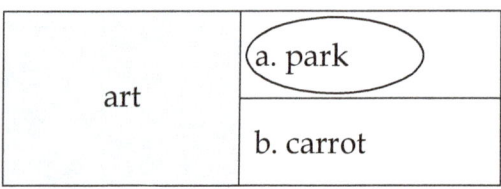 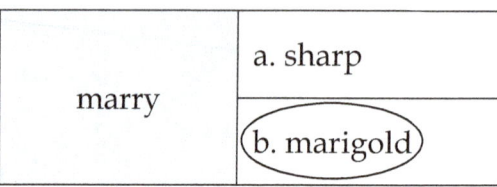

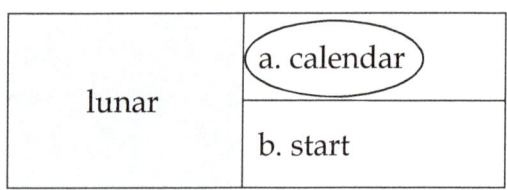 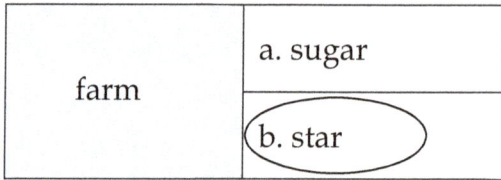

 Directions: Read each target word. Put a check (✓) under the correct column heading.
路线：读每个目标词。在符合要求的栏下打勾 (✓)。

Target Words	"ar" has the /ă/ + /r/ sounds as in the word <u>baron</u>	"ar" has the /ə/ + /r/ sounds as in the word <u>dollar</u>	"ar" has the /ä/ + /r/ sounds as in the word <u>car</u>	"ar" has the /ô/ + /r/ sounds as in the word <u>war</u>
1. art			✓	
2. marry	✓			
3. lunar		✓		
4. farm			✓	

Answer Key

Name: _____ Date: ___/___/_____ Score: _____

Lesson 1.7

Reading Words with the "ar" Letter Combination

Dictionary Skills/ Vocabulary

 Lesson Check Point

 Directions: Read each target word and its definition. Write the target word on the line in front of its meaning. Use a dictionary or the Internet to check your answers.

路线：读每个目标词及其定义。在其意思前的线上写出目标词。用词典或通过互联网检查你的答案。

Target Word Box				
Oscar	narrator	party	paramedics	garlic

1. __party__ a fun gathering where people socialize
2. __paramedics__ medical professionals
3. __Oscar__ a boy or man's name
4. __garlic__ an edible plant that looks like a bulb
5. __narrator__ a person who tells the events of the story

 Directions: Read each sentence and write the target word that correctly completes the sentence.

路线：读每个句子和并在划线处填上合适的词。

6. Baroness invited all her friends to the ___party___.

7. __Oscar__ registered for classes at the registrar's office.

8. The dynamic __narrator__ dramatically read the play's stage directions.

9. I enhanced the flavor of the soup by adding vinegar and ___garlic___.

10. The skilled ___paramedics___ saved Arty's life by administering CPR.

Classwork

 Name: _____ Date:___/___/_____ Score: _____

Lesson 1.8

Reading Words with a Silent Letter "a"

✓ Lesson Check Point

 Directions: Read the target words in the word box. Write the words that have a silent letter "a" in the first column. Write the words that do not have a silent letter "a" in the second column.

路线：读单词框中的目标词。在第一栏中写上含不发音a的词。在第二栏中写上不带不发音 a 的词。

Target Word Box				
floats	pain	dragon	aisle	goats
games	broad	oasis	sandy	anthills
beauty	oats	days	raining	crash
central	gloating	bread	bureau	boating

Letter "a" is silent	Letter "a" has a letter "a" sound
oats	pain
aisle	crash
goats	days
broad	oasis
beauty	sandy
floats	games
bread	anthills
bureau	raining
boating	dragon
gloating	central

Learn To Read English With Directions In Chinese

Name: _____ Date:___/___/_____ Score:_____

Unit Review - A/a

Reading Words with Vowel "a" Sounds: /ă/, /ā/, /ə/ & Silent

 Lesson Check Point

Directions: Read each target word. Circle the word in the column that has the same "a" sound as the target word.
路线：读每个目标词。圈出栏中与目标词含相同 a 音的单词。

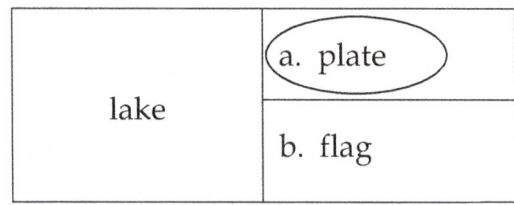
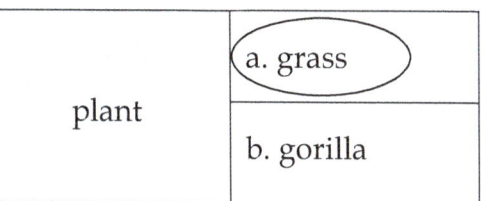
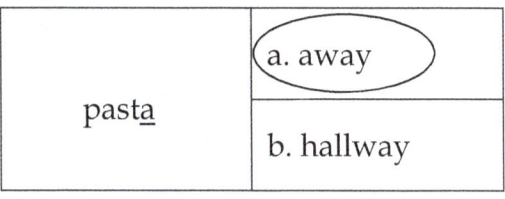
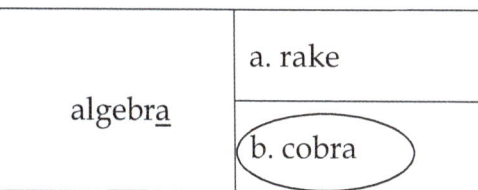

 Directions: Read each target word. Put a check (✓) under the correct column heading.
路线：读每个目标词。在符合要求的栏下打勾 (✓)。

Target Words	"a" has the /ă/ sound as in the word <u>apple</u>	"a" has the /ā/ sound as in the word <u>ate</u>	"a" has the /ə/ sound as in the word <u>sofa</u>	"a" is silent as in the word <u>boat</u>
1. l<u>a</u>ke		✓		
2. pl<u>a</u>nt	✓			
3. past<u>a</u>			✓	
4. algebr<u>a</u>			✓	

Classwork

Name: _____ Date: ___/___/_____ Score: _____

The Reading Challenge

Lesson 1.9

Reading Multisyllable Words

✓ **Lesson Check Point**

Directions: Read and divide each target word into syllables. Write each word and place a hyphen (-) between the syllables in the second column. Write the number of syllables in the third column. Use a dictionary or the Internet to check your answers.

路线：读目标词后，划分音节。写下每个词，在第二栏中写上音 节，用 (-) 连接。在第三栏写上音节数。用词典或通过互联网检 查你的答案。

Target Words	Words Divided into Syllables	Number of Syllables
1. payback	pay-back	2
2. slogan	slo-gan	2
3. turban	tur-ban	2
4. abdomen	ab-do-men	3
5. batman	bat-man	2
6. husband	hus-band	2
7. Alaskan	A-las-kan	3
8. Scotland	Scot-land	2
9. embanking	em-bank-ing	3
10. migrated	mi-grat-ed	3

Answer Key

Name: _____ Date: ___/___/_____ Score: _____

The Reading Challenge

Lesson 1.9

Reading Multisyllable Words

 Lesson Check Point

 Directions: Read each target word. Circle the word in the row that is divided correctly into syllables. Use a dictionary or the Internet to check your answers.

路线：读每个目标词。圈出行中音节划分正确的词。用词典或通过互联网检查你的答案。

Model

| important | **a. im-por-tant** (circled) | b. im-port-ant | c. im-porta-nt |

1. diploma	**a. di-plo-ma** (circled)	b. di-plom-a	c. dip-lom-a
2. absolute	a. a-bso-lute	b. a-bsol-ute	**c. ab-so-lute** (circled)
3. admonish	a. adm-o-nish	b. a-dmon-ish	**c. ad-mon-ish** (circled)
4. magistrate	**a. mag-is-trate** (circled)	b. mag-i-strate	c. ma-gis-trate
5. kilogram	a. ki-lo-gram	b. ki-log-ram	**c. kil-o-gram** (circled)
6. caravan	a. ca-rav-an	**b. car-a-van** (circled)	c. car-av-an
7. admiral	a. ad-mir-al	**b. ad-mi-ral** (circled)	c. a-dmir-al
8. monogram	a. mo-no-gram	b. mo-nog-ram	**c. mon-o-gram** (circled)

Unit A Lesson 1.9

Learn To Read English With Directions In Chinese

Classwork

Name: _____ Date: ___/___/_____ Score: _____

Lesson 1.10

Reading and Writing

Proper and Common Nouns and Adjectives

✓ **Lesson Check Point**

Directions: Read the words in the word box. Put an (X) on the line next to each word that is written incorrectly. Remember that all proper nouns and proper adjectives are capitalized. Use a dictionary or the Internet to check your answers.

路线：读单词框中的词。在书写错误的单词旁边的线上打叉(X)。记得合适的名词和形容词需要大写。用词典或通过互联网检查你 的答案。

Word Box					
__	August	__	Argentina	X	Author
X	Achievers	__	advanced	__	adventure
X	apollo	X	athens	__	America
__	airmail	X	alaska	X	ArubA

Directions: Read each unedited sentence and underline the word that is written incorrectly. Write each sentence correctly on the line.

路线：读每个未经编辑的句子，并给书写错误的词加下划线。在线 上写上正确的句子。

Model

Andrew has a view of the <u>atlantic</u> Ocean from his apartment.
<u>Andrew has a view of the Atlantic Ocean from his apartment.</u>

1. Anne and <u>alex</u> are from Australia.
<u>Anne and Alex are from Australia.</u>

2. The <u>Author's</u> article, "Awaken," is amazing.
<u>The author's article, "Awaken," is amazing.</u>

3. Mr. <u>aaron</u> got a lot of cash from the ATM.
<u>Mr. Aaron got a lot of cash from the ATM.</u>

4. In <u>august</u>, Ashley will attend Ace Academy.
<u>In August, Ashley will attend Ace Academy.</u>

Answer Key

 Name: _____ Date: ___/___/_____ Score: _____

Lesson 2.1

Reading Words with the Letter B/b

✓ Lesson Check Point

 Directions: Read each target word. Find the letter "b" and put a check (✓) in the column that identifies its position: beginning, within or end.
路线：读每个目标词。找出字母b在栏中打勾(✓)示意： 开始，中间 或末尾。

Target Words	Beginning (First Letter)	Within	End (Last Letter)
1. cab			✓
2. bit	✓		
3. table		✓	
4. tab			✓
5. bottom	✓		

 Directions: Read each sentence and underline the words that begin with the letter "b." Write all the underlined words in alphabetical order on the lines below.
路线：读每个句子，并给首字母为 b 的词加下划线。在下面的线上按照字母顺序写出所有下划线标记的单词。

6. Andy's <u>bat</u> is <u>black</u>.

7. He has a <u>belt</u> and a <u>billfold</u>.

8. There is a cat on the <u>baby's</u> <u>bib</u>.

9. Abe and Andy are in the <u>big</u> <u>band</u>.

10. Annie and Aaron have the <u>best</u> <u>books</u>.

baby's   band   bat
belt   best   bib
big   billfold   black
              books

Classwork

Name: _____ Date: ___/___/_____ Score: _____

Lesson 2.2

Reading Words with the "br" Letter Combination

Dictionary Skills/ Vocabulary

✓ **Lesson Check Point**

Directions: Read each target word and its definition. Write the letter of the definition on the line of each target word. Use a dictionary or the Internet to check your answers.

路线：读每个目标词及其定义。在目标词前线上写上正确定义的 字母编号。用词典或通过互联网检查你的答案。

Target Words	Definitions
1. _c_ brags	a. a large country on the South American continent
2. _a_ Brazil	b. a physical injury without an open cut
3. _d_ broccoli	c. to say something in a boastful way
4. _e_ bridal	d. a green vegetable with densely clustered flower buds
5. _b_ bruise	e. something or someone pertaining to a wedding

Directions: Read each sentence. Underline the word in the parentheses that correctly completes each sentence. Then, write the underlined word on the line.

路线：阅读每个句子。在括号中选择符合句子的词，并添加下划 线。然后，在线上写出下划线单词。

6. The bride has a nice _____bridal_____ dress. (<u>bridal</u>, brags)

7. The _____bruise_____ on Betsy's back is black. (Brazil, <u>bruise</u>)

8. I ate _____broccoli_____ and bread for breakfast. (bruise, <u>broccoli</u>)

9. Brenda _____brags_____ about her brand new boat. (<u>brags</u>, broccoli)

10. Do you know that _____Brazil_____ is a big country? (bruise, <u>Brazil</u>)

Name: _____ Date: ___/___/_____ Score: _____

Lesson 2.3

Reading Words with the "bl" Letter Combination

Dictionary Skills/ Vocabulary

✓ Lesson Check Point

  Directions: Read each target word and its definition. Write the target word on the line in front of its meaning. Use a dictionary or the Internet to check your answers.

路线：读每个目标词及其定义。在目标词前线上写上正确定义的 字母编号。用词典或通过互联网检查你的答案。

Target Word Box				
blanket	blasted	bleed	blender	blinks

1. <u>bleed</u>   the flow of blood out of a blood vessel
2. <u>blender</u> a machine that mixes things together
3. <u>blinks</u>   the quick closing and opening movement of eyes
4. <u>blasted</u> to have shot something out with great force
5. <u>blanket</u> a large cloth covering used to cover a bed

 Directions: Read each sentence. Underline the word in the parentheses that correctly completes each sentence. Then, write the underlined word on the line.

路线：阅读每个句子。在括号中选择符合句子的词，并添加下划 线。然后，在线上写出下划线单词。

6. My big rocket ___<u>blasted</u>___ off. (blinks, <u>blasted</u>)

7. Bill blends bananas in his <u>blender</u>. (blanket, <u>blender</u>)

8. Bethany <u>blinks</u> her big, brown eyes. (bleed, <u>blinks</u>)

9. Betty puts a big, blue <u>blanket</u> on her bed. (<u>blanket</u>, blender)

10. The big blade cut Bill and made him <u>bleed</u>. (<u>bleed</u>, blasted)

Classwork

 Name: _____ Date:___/___/_____ Score:_____

Lesson 2.3

Reading Words with the "ble" Letter Combination

✓ Lesson Check Point

 Directions: Read each target word. Find the "ble" letter combination and put a check (✓) in the column that identifies its position: beginning, within or end.

路线：读每个目标词。找到"ble"字母组合，并在栏中打勾(✓)示意：开始，中间，结尾。

Target Words	Beginning (First 3 Letters)	Within	End (Last 3 Letters)
1. table			✓
2. problem		✓	
3. bleach	✓		
4. adorable			✓
5. scribbler		✓	

 Directions: Read each target word. Put a check (✓) in the "yes" column if the "ble" letter combination has the /b/ + /ə/ + /l/ sounds. Put a check (✓) in the "no" column if the "ble" letter combination does not have the /b/ + /ə/ + /l/ sounds.

路线：读每个目标词。如果"ble"字母组合发/b/ + /ə/ + /l/的音，在"是"栏中打勾 (✓)。如果"ble"字母组合不发/b/ + /ə/ + /l/的音，在"没有"栏中打勾(✓)。

Target Words	Yes	No
6. bleed		✓
7. bleach		✓
8. babble	✓	
9. agreeable	✓	
10. collectible	✓	

Name: _____ Date: ___/___/_____ Score: _____

Answer Key

Lesson 2.4

Reading Words with the "mb" Letter Combination

✓ Lesson Check Point

 Directions: Read each target word. Circle the word in the column that has the same "mb" sound(s) as the target word.

路线：读每个目标词。圈出栏中与目标词含相同"mb"音的单词。

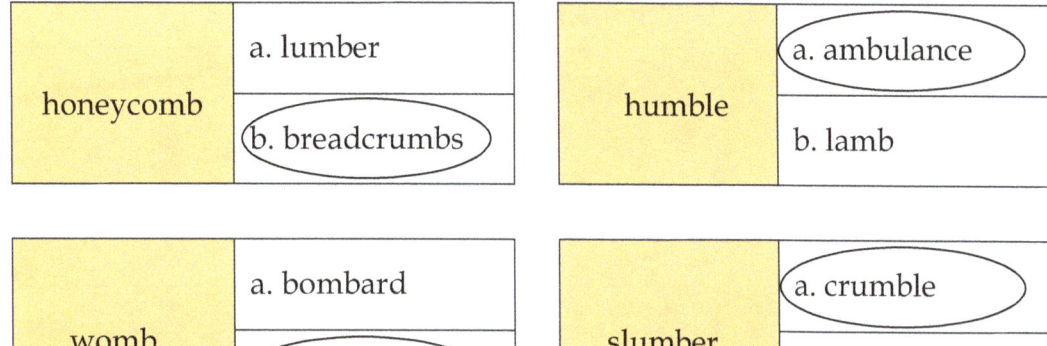

 Directions: Read each target word. In the second column, write the number of letters in the word. In the third column, write the number of letters heard in the word.

路线：读每个目标词。在第二栏中，写上单词所含字母数。在第 三栏，写下这个单词发音的字母数。

Target Words	Number of letters in the word	Number of letters heard
1. combat	6	6
2. climber	7	6
3. limbs	5	4
4. lumber	6	6

Classwork

 Name: _____ Date:___/___/_____ Score:_____

Lesson 2.4

Reading Words with the "bt" Letter Combination

✓ Lesson Check Point

 Directions: Read each target word. Circle the word in the column that has the same "bt" sound(s) as the target word.
路线：读每个目标词。圈出栏中与目标词含相同 "bt" 音的单词。

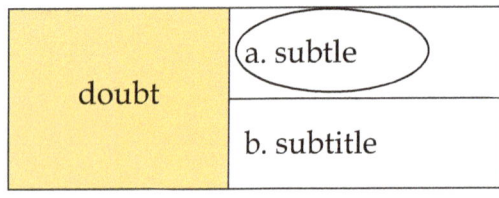
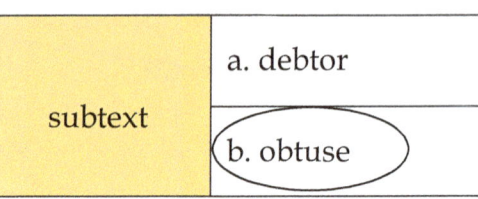
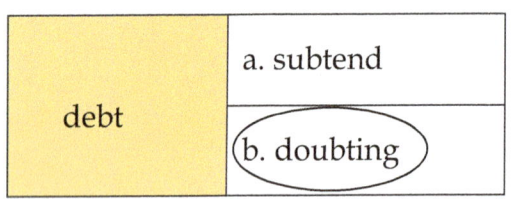
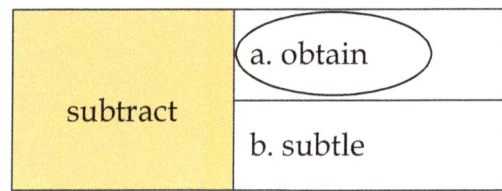

 Directions: Read each target word. In the second column, write the number of letters in the word. In the third column, write the number of letters heard in the word.
路线：读每个目标词。在第二栏中，写上单词所含字母数。在第三栏，写下这个单词发音的字母数。

Target Words	Number of letters in the word	Number of letters heard
1. doubt	5	4
2. subtext	7	7
3. debt	4	3
4. subtract	8	8

Answer Key

 Name: _____ Date: ___/ ___/ _____ Score: _____

Lesson 2.5

Reading Words with a Silent "b"

✓ Lesson Check Point

 Directions: Read the target words in the word box. Write the words that have a silent letter "b" in the first column. Write the words that do not have a silent letter "b" in the second column.

路线：读单词框中的目标词。在第一栏中写上含不发音 b 的词。 在第二栏中写上不带不发音 b 的词。

Target Word Box				
labels	climbing	bread	zebra	subpoena
thumbs	bugs	debt	crumb	lamb
abandon	plumbers	basement	ability	bedroom
combs	brother	entomb	books	limbs

Letter "b" is silent	Letter "b" has the /b/ sound
debt	labels
crumb	books
limbs	bugs
lamb	ability
thumbs	bread
entomb	zebra
combs	brother
climbing	abandon
plumbers	basement
subpoena	bedroom

Learn To Read English With Directions In Chinese

Classwork

 Name: _____ Date: ___/___/_____ Score: _____

The Reading Challenge

Lesson 2.6

Reading Multisyllable Words

✓ Lesson Check Point

 Directions: Read and divide each target word into syllables. Write each word and place a hyphen (-) between the syllables in the second column. Write the number of syllables in the third column. Use a dictionary or the Internet to check your answers.

路线：读目标词后，划分音节。写下每个词，在第二栏中写上音 节，用 (-) 连接。在第三栏写上音节数。用词典或通过互联网检 查你的答案。

Target Words	Words Divided into Syllables	Number of Syllables
1. balance	bal-ance	2
2. submit	sub-mit	2
3. sublet	sub-let	2
4. bigwig	big-wig	2
5. banana	ba-nan-a	3
6. obstacle	ob-sta-cle	3
7. biceps	bi-ceps	2
8. tablet	tab-let	2
9. beckon	beck-on	2
10. blanket	blan-ket	2

Unit B Lesson 2.6

Answer Key

 Name: _____ Date: ___/___/_____ Score: _____

The Reading Challenge

Lesson 2.6

Reading Multisyllable Words

✓ Lesson Check Point

 Directions: Read each target word. Circle the word in the row that is divided correctly into syllables. Use a dictionary or the Internet to check your answers.

路线：读每个目标词。圈出行中音节划分正确的词。用词典或通过互联网检查你的答案。

Model

| because | (a. be-cause) | b. beca-use | c. b-ecause |

| 1. bachelor | a. bac-he-lor | (b. bach-e-lor) | c. ba-ch-elor |

| 2. backpack | (a. back-pack) | b. ba-ckpa-ck | c. ba-ckp-ack |

| 3. bellboy | a. be-llboy | b. bellb-oy | (c. bell-boy) |

| 4. blackout | a. bla-ckout | (b. black-out) | c. bl-ackout |

| 5. bicycle | a. bi-cycle | (b. bi-cy-cle) | c. bicy-cle |

| 6. baritone | a. ba-ri-tone | b. ba-rit-one | (c. bar-i-tone) |

| 7. bracelet | a. bracel-et | b. bra-celet | (c. brace-let) |

| 8. bumblebee | (a. bum-ble-bee) | b. bumb-le-bee | c. bu-mbleb-ee |

Classwork

Name: _____ Date: ___/___/_____ Score: _____

Lesson 2.7

Reading and Writing
Proper and Common Nouns and Adjectives

✓ **Lesson Check Point**

Directions: Read the words in the word box. Put an (X) on the line next to each word that is written incorrectly. Remember that all proper nouns and proper adjectives are capitalized. Use a dictionary or the Internet to check your answers.

路线：读单词框中的词。在书写错误的单词旁边的线上打叉(X)。记得合适的名词和形容词需要大写。用词典或通过互联网检查你的答案。

Word Box					
__	Bolivia	X	BuBBle	__	absent
__	barber	__	bottom	X	BarBados
X	Bread	__	bread	__	bridges
X	buckingham	X	bulB	X	bahamas

Directions: Read each unedited sentence and underline the word that is written incorrectly. Write each sentence correctly on the line.

路线：读每个未经编辑的句子，并给书写错误的词加下划线。在线上写上正确的句子。

Model

<u>brandon's</u> books are about big boats.
Brandon's books are about big boats.

1. The black <u>Bat</u> is really big.
   The black bat is really big.

2. <u>bob</u> has a brown bag.
   Bob has a brown bag.

3. The blue <u>taBle</u> is too big.
   The blue table is too big.

4. <u>benjamin's</u> baked bread is in his bag.
   Benjamin's baked bread is in his bag.

Answer Key

Name: _____ Date: ___/___/_____ Score: _____

Lesson 3.1

Reading Words with the Letter C/c

✓ Lesson Check Point

Directions: Read each target word. Find the letter "c" and put a check (✓) in the column that identifies its position: beginning, within or end.
路线：读每个目标词。找出字母 c 在栏中打勾(✓) 示意： 开 始，中间或末尾。

Target Words	Beginning (First Letter)	Within	End (Last Letter)
1. clog	✓		
2. toxic			✓
3. tackle		✓	
4. basic			✓
5. picture		✓	

Directions: Read each sentence and underline the words that begin with the letter "c." Write all the underlined words in alphabetical order on the lines below.
路线：读每个句子，并给首字母为 c 的词加下划线。在下面的线上按照字母顺序写出所有下划线标记的单词。

6. The big <u>cows</u> are <u>cute</u>.

7. The black <u>car</u> is very <u>clean</u>.

8. The <u>child</u> is in the blue <u>crib</u>.

9. Bobby has a <u>cap</u> and a big <u>coat</u>.

10. The boys are <u>chasing</u> the <u>chicken</u>.

cap	car	chasing
chicken	child	clean
coat	cows	crib
	cute	

Unit C Lesson 3.1

Classwork

Name: _____ Date: ___/___/_____ Score: _____

Lesson 3.1

Reading Words with the Hard Letter "c"

✓ Lesson Check Point

Directions: Read each target word. Put a check (✓) under the correct column heading.

路线：读每个目标词。在符合要求的栏下打勾 (✓)。

Target Words	Hard "c" has the /k/ sound as in the word cat	Soft "c" has the /s/ sound as in the word cell
1. school	✓	
2. cleaning	✓	
3. cement		✓
4. civilized		✓
5. character	✓	

Directions: Read each sentence and underline the words that have the hard "c" sound, as in the word cat. Write all the underlined words in alphabetical order on the lines below.

路线：读每个句子，并给含硬 c 音的词加下划线。如，英语单 词cat。在下面的线上按照字母顺序写出所有下划线标记的单词。

6. Ms. <u>Clarke's</u> big chips are <u>crunchy</u>.

7. The <u>cake</u> has a <u>caramel</u> apple center.

8. Andrew is chewing <u>cranberry</u> <u>candy</u>.

9. Cindy is <u>counting</u> the <u>crabs</u> in the bowl.

10. Everyone in my <u>class</u> had a bowl of ice <u>cream</u>.

cake _____   candy _____   caramel _____

Clarke's _____   class _____   counting _____

crabs _____   cranberry _____   cream _____

crunchy _____

Answer Key

 Name: _____ Date: ___/___/_____ Score: _____

Lesson 3.2

Reading Words with the Soft Letter "c"

✓ Lesson Check Point

 Directions: Read each target word. Put a check (✓) under the correct column heading.

路线：读每个目标词。在符合要求的栏下打勾(✓)。

Target Words	Hard "c" has the /k/ sound as in the word cat	Soft "c" has the /s/ sound as in the word cell
1. face		✓
2. curl	✓	
3. cast	✓	
4. city		✓
5. clue	✓	

 Directions: Read each sentence and underline the words that have the soft "c" sound, as in the word cell. Write all the underlined words in alphabetical order on the lines below.

路线：读每个句子，并给含软 c 音的词加下划线。如，英语单词cell。在下面的线上按照字母顺序写出所有下划线标记的单词。

6. <u>City</u> Hall is in the <u>center</u> of Clarkston.

7. <u>Lucy</u> said, "The comedian is a <u>cynic</u>."

8. Caleb said, "We live in a <u>civilized</u> <u>society</u>."

9. The baby in the crib ate cranberry and <u>cinnamon</u> <u>cereal</u>.

10. I stored my <u>bicycles</u> and <u>ceramic</u> casserole dishes in the den.

bicycles _____   center _____   ceramic _____

cereal _____   cinnamon _____   City _____

civilized _____   cynic _____   Lucy _____

                         society _____

Classwork

Name: _____ Date: ___/___/_____ Score: _____

Review Lessons 3.1 & 3.2

Reading Hard Letter "c" and Soft Letter "c" Words

✓ **Lesson Check Point**

Directions: Read the target words in the word box. In the first column, write the words with the letter "c" that have the /k/ sound, as in the word <u>cat</u>. In the second column, write the words with the letter "c" that have the /s/ sound, as in the word <u>cell</u>.

路线：读框中的目标词。在第一栏中，写上 c 发/k/音的单词。 如，英语单词 cat。在第二栏中，写上字母 c 发/s/音的词。 如，英语单词 cell。

Target Word Box				
cause	cook	citizen	city	curb
curve	mice	cute	code	citrus
cedar	cube	cake	call	spicy
coil	cysts	place	cease	cent

Hard letter "c" has the /k/ sound as in the word <u>cat</u>

- call
- coil
- code
- cook
- cube
- cute
- curb
- cake
- curve
- cause

Soft letter "c" has the /s/ sound as in the word <u>cell</u>

- cent
- city
- mice
- cysts
- cedar
- place
- cease
- citrus
- spicy
- citizen

Answer Key

 Name: _____ Date:___/___/_____ Score:_____

Lesson 3.3

Reading Words with the "cr" Letter Combination

Dictionary Skills/ Vocabulary

✓ Lesson Check Point

 Directions: Read each target word and its definition. Write the letter of the definition on the line of each target word. Use a dictionary or the Internet to check your answers.
路线：读每个目标词及其定义。在目标词前线上写上正确定义的 字母编号。用词典或通过互联网检查你的答案。

Target Words	Definitions
1. _d_ cranberry	a. to really want something, such as food
2. _a_ craving	b. to move along the ground on hands and knees
3. _b_ crawls	c. a thick dairy product made from milk
4. _c_ cream	d. a small, tart, red berry-like fruit
5. _e_ crumbs	e. small pieces of bread or other baked goods

 Directions: Read each sentence. Underline the word in the parentheses that correctly completes each sentence. Then, write the underlined word on the line.
路线：阅读每个句子。在括号中选择符合句子的词，并添加下划线。然后，在线上写出下划线单词。

6. The cats ate the cookie ___crumbs___. (crawls, <u>crumbs</u>)

7. Cindy's ice ___cream___ is very cold. (<u>cream</u>, craving)

8. The baby ___crawls___ on the carpet. (<u>crawls</u>, cream)

9. I have a ___craving___ for cotton candy. (<u>craving</u>, cranberry)

10. Chad likes to drink ___cranberry___ juice. (crumbs, <u>cranberry</u>)

Classwork

Name: _____ Date:___/___/_____ Score:_____

Lesson 3.4

Reading Words with the "cl" Letter Combination

Dictionary Skills/ Vocabulary

✓ Lesson Check Point

Directions: Read each target word and its definition. Write the target word on the line in front of its meaning. Use a dictionary or the Internet to check your answers.

路线：读每个目标词及其定义。在目标词前线上写上正确定义的 字母编号。用词典或通过互联网检查你的答案。

Target Word Box				
cleared	cliff	clipped	clock	closet

1. cliff   the overhanging of a mountain

2. clock   a device used to display time

3. closet   a small inner room used for clothing and storage

4. cleared   to have moved something out of the way

5. clipped   to fasten or grip with a firm metal or plastic clamp

Directions: Read each sentence. Underline the word in the parentheses that correctly completes each sentence. Then, write the underlined word on the line.

路线：阅读每个句子。在括号中选择符合句子的词，并添加下划线。然后，在线上写出下划线单词。

6. Chad cleaned out his bedroom ____closet____. (closet, cliff)

7. Charles ____cleared____ the clogged drain. (cleared, closet)

8. Yesterday, we climbed up the steep ____cliff____. (clipped, cliff)

9. I ____clipped____ my index cards on the clipboard. (clipped, clock)

10. This morning, my alarm ____clock____ woke me up. (clock, cleared)

Answer Key

 Name: _____ Date:___/___/_____ Score:_____

Lesson 3.4

Reading Words with the "cle" Letter Combination

✓ Lesson Check Point

 Directions: Read each target word. Find the "cle" letter combination and put a check (✓) in the column that identifies its position: beginning, within or end.

路线：读每个目标词。找到"cle"字母组合，并在栏中打勾(✓) 示意：开始，中间，结尾。

Target Words	Beginning (First 3 Letters)	Within	End (Last 3 Letters)
1. article			✓
2. cleaning	✓		
3. inclement		✓	
4. particle			✓
5. cleverly	✓		

 Directions: Read each target word. Put a check (✓) in the "yes" column if the "cle" letter combination has the /k/ + /ə/ + /l/ sounds. Put a check (✓) in the "no" column if the "cle" letter combination does not have the /k/ + /ə/ + /l/ sounds.

路线：读每个目标词。如果"cle"字母组合发/k/ + /ə/ + /l/的音，在"是"栏中 打勾 (✓)。如果"cle"字母组合不发/k/ + /ə/ + /l/的音，在"没有"栏中打勾(✓)。

Target Words	Yes	No
6. article	✓	
7. cleaning		✓
8. inclement		✓
9. particle	✓	
10. cleverly		✓

Classwork

 Name: _____ Date: ___/___/_____ Score: _____

Lesson 3.5

Reading Words with the "ct" Letter Combination

✓ Lesson Check Point

 Directions: Read each target word. Circle the word in the column that has the same "ct" sound(s) as the target word.
路线：读每个目标词。圈出栏中与目标词含相同"ct"音的单词。

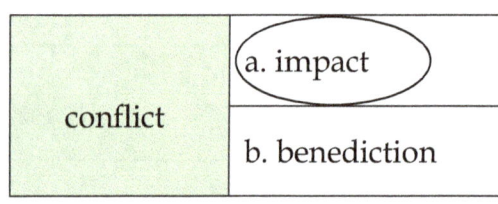

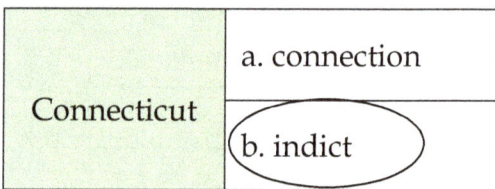

 Directions: Read each target word. Put a check (✓) under the correct column heading.
路线：读每个目标词。在符合要求的栏下打勾 (✓)。

Target Words	"ct" has the /k/ + /t/ sounds as in the word <u>fact</u>	"ct" has the silent "c" + /t/ sound as in the word <u>indict</u>
1. conflict	✓	
2. predict	✓	
3. electric	✓	
4. Connecticut		✓

Answer Key

Name: _____ Date: ___/___/_____ Score: _____

Lesson 3.6

Reading Soft Letter "c" Words

 Lesson Check Point

Directions: Read each target word. Circle the word in the column that has the same "cean," "cian," "cial," "cious," or "cient" sound as the target word.

路线：读每个目标词。圈出栏中含与目标词一样的"cean,""cian,""cial,""cious,"或"cient"音的词。

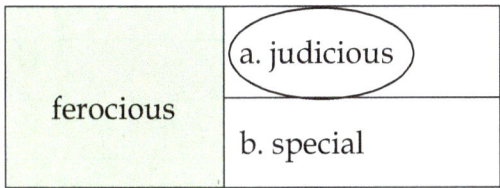
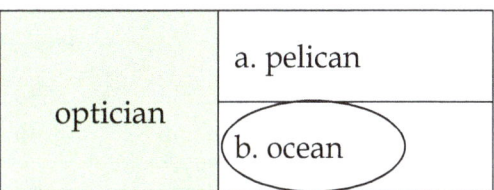
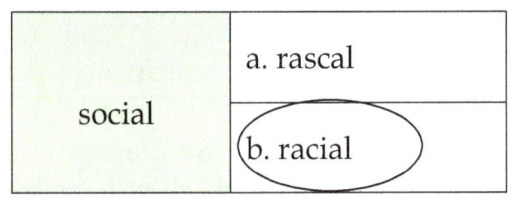
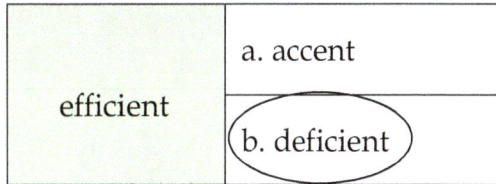

Directions: Read each target word. Put a check (✓) in the column that identifies the same "cean," "cian," "cial," "cious," or "cient" sound within the target word.

路线：读每个目标词。在栏中打勾(✓)若该词有与目标词一样的"cean","cian," "cial," "cious," 或 "cient" 音。

Target Words	"cean" has the /sh/+/ə/+/n/ sounds as in the word ocean	"cial" has the /sh/+/ə/+/l/ sounds as in the word special	"cious" has the /sh/+/ə/+/s/ sounds as in the word delicious	"cient" has the /sh/+/ə/+/n/+/t/ sounds as in the word ancient
1. ferocious			✓	
2. optician	✓			
3. social		✓		
4. efficient				✓

Classwork

 Name: _____ Date: ___/___/_____ Score: _____

Lesson 3.6

Reading Soft Letter "c" Words

✓ Lesson Check Point

 Directions: Read the target words in the word box. In the first column, write the words with the letter "c" that have the /s/ sound, as in the word <u>cell</u>. In the second column, write the words with the letter "c" that have the /sh/ sound, as in the word <u>ocean</u>.

路线：读框中的目标词。在第一栏中，写上字母 c 发/s/音的 词。如，英语单词 cell。在第二栏中，写上字母 c 发/sh/音的 词。如，英语单词 ocean。

Target Word Box				
commercial	delicious	office	place	lacy
technician	gallinacean	spices	cement	artificial
circus	proficient	prince	race	decided
omniscient	twice	optician	conscious	socialize

Soft letter "c" has the /s/ sound as in the word <u>cell</u>

- lacy
- race
- place
- twice
- circus
- office
- spices
- prince
- cement
- decided

Soft letter "c" has the /sh/ sound as in the word <u>ocean</u>

- socialize
- optician
- artificial
- delicious
- conscious
- proficient
- omniscient
- gallinacean
- technician
- commercial

Answer Key

 Name: _____ Date: ___/___/_____ Score: _____

Lesson 3.7

Reading Words with the "ch" Letter Combination

✓ Lesson Check Point

 Directions: Read each target word. Circle the word in the column that has the same "ch" sound as the target word.
路线：读每个目标词。圈出栏中与目标词含相同"ch"音的单词。

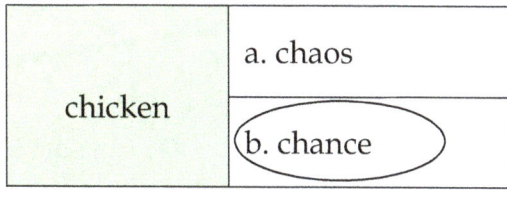
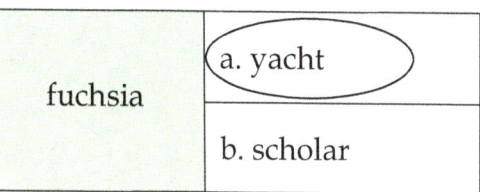

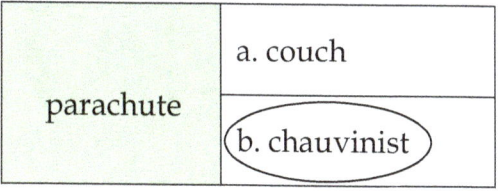

 Directions: Read each target word. Put a check (✓) under the correct column heading.
路线：读每个目标词。在符合要求的栏下打勾 (✓)。

Target Words	"ch" has the /ch/ sound as in the word <u>chain</u>	"ch" has the /sh/ sound as in the word <u>chef</u>	"ch" has the /k/ sound as in the word <u>chaos</u>	"ch" is silent as in the word <u>yacht</u>
1. chicken	✓			
2. fuchsia				✓
3. anchor			✓	
4. parachute		✓		

Classwork

 Name: _____ Date: ___/ ___/ _____ Score: _____

Lesson 3.8

Reading Words with the "cc" Letter Combination

 Lesson Check Point

Directions: Read each target word. Circle the word in the column that has the same "cc" sound(s) as the target word.
路线：读每个目标词。圈出栏中与目标词含相同"cc"音的单词。

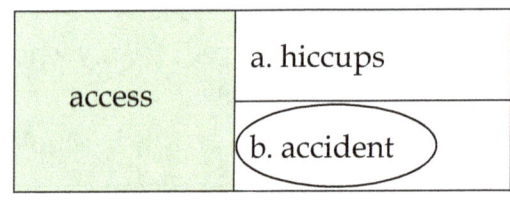
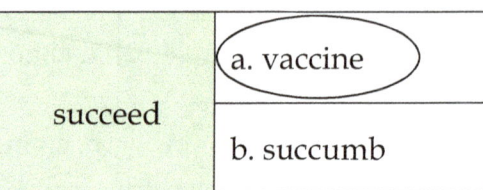
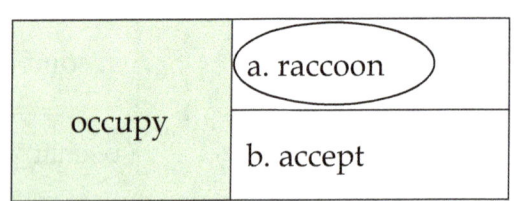
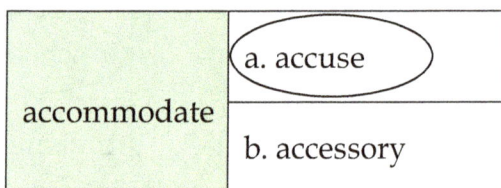

 Directions: Read each target word. Put a check (✓) under the correct column heading.
路线：读每个目标词。在符合要求的栏下打勾 (✓)。

Target Words	"cc" has the /k/ sound as in the word <u>soccer</u>	"cc" has the /k/ + /s/ sounds as in the word <u>accept</u>
1. access		✓
2. succeed		✓
3. occupy	✓	
4. accommodate	✓	

Answer Key

 Name: _____ Date: ___/___/_____ Score: _____

Lesson 3.9

Reading Words with a Silent Letter "c"

✓ Lesson Check Point

 Directions: Read the target words in the word box. Write the words that have a silent letter "c" in the first column. Write the words that do not have a silent letter "c" in the second column.

路线：读单词框中的目标词。在第一栏中写上含不发音 c 的词。 在第二栏中写上不带不发音 c的词。

Target Word Box				
czar	scent	scalp	cake	acquit
occupy	corpuscle	muscle	excited	scissors
citizens	produce	congress	scenery	ascend
classic	yacht	increase	court	scale

Letter "c" is silent	Letter "c" has the /k/, /s/ or /sh/ sound

Letter "c" is silent	Letter "c" has the /k/, /s/ or /sh/ sound
czar	cake
scent	court
yacht	scale
acquit	scalp
ascend	classic
occupy	citizens
scissors	excited
muscle	produce
scenery	increase
corpuscle	congress

Classwork

Name: _____ Date:___/___/_____ Score:_____

The Reading Challenge

Lesson 3.10

Reading Multisyllable Words

✓ Lesson Check Point

Directions: Read and divide each target word into syllables. Write each word and place a hyphen (-) between the syllables in the second column. Write the number of syllables in the third column. Use a dictionary or the Internet to check your answers.

路线：读目标词后，划分音节。写下每个词，在第二栏中写上音节，用 (-) 连接。在第三栏写上音节数。用词典或通过互联网检 查你的答案。

Target Words	Words Divided into Syllables	Number of Syllables
1. climber	climb-er	2
2. cleaner	clean-er	2
3. climbing	climb-ing	2
4. crayons	cray-ons	2
5. construction	con-struc-tion	3
6. cereal	ce-re-al	3
7. crocodile	croc-o-dile	3
8. creditors	cred-i-tors	3
9. crackers	crack-ers	2
10. camping	camp-ing	2

Answer Key

 Name: _____ Date: ___/___/_____ Score: _____

The Reading Challenge

Lesson 3.10

Reading Multisyllable Words

✓ Lesson Check Point

 Directions: Read each target word. Circle the word in the row that is divided correctly into syllables. Use a dictionary or the Internet to check your answers.

路线：读每个目标词。圈出行中音节划分正确的词。用词典或通过互联网检查你的答案。

Model

| calculus | a. calcu-lus | b. cal-cu-lus ⭕ | c. cal-culus |

1. chipmunk	a. chip-munk ⭕	b. chip-mu-nk	c. ch-ipmu-nk
2. calendar	a. ca-lend-ar	b. cal-en-dar ⭕	c. ca-le-ndar
3. circuit	a. cir-cu-it	b. circu-it	c. cir-cuit ⭕
4. compound	a. com-pound ⭕	b. co-mpou-nd	c. com-po-und
5. cereal	a. ce-re-al ⭕	b. cer-e-al	c. c-ere-al
6. charisma	a. char-isma	b. cha-rism-a	c. cha-ris-ma ⭕
7. cinema	a. cin-e-ma ⭕	b. cine-ma	c. ci-ne-ma
8. cylinder	a. cy-lin-der	b. cyl-in-der ⭕	c. cylin-der

Learn To Read English With Directions In Chinese   Copyrighted Material

Classwork

Name: _____ Date: ___/___/_____ Score: _____

Lesson 3.11

Reading and Writing

Proper and Common Nouns and Adjectives

 Lesson Check Point

 Directions: Read the words in the word box. Put an (X) on the line next to each word that is written incorrectly. Remember that all proper nouns and proper adjectives are capitalized. Use a dictionary or the Internet to check your answers.

路线：读单词框中的词。在书写错误的单词旁边的线上打叉(X)。记得合适的名词和形容词需要大写。用词典或通过互联网检查你 的答案。

Word Box					
__	China	X	cliniC	__	camp
X	cleveland	X	College	__	Colombia
__	cities	__	castle	X	charles
X	chicago	X	chinese	__	cherry

 Directions: Read each unedited sentence and underline the word that is written incorrectly. Write each sentence correctly on the line.

路线：读每个未经编辑的句子，并给书写错误的词加下划线。在线 上写上正确的句子。

Model
The <u>Camp</u> in Cleveland is closed.
<u>The camp in Cleveland is closed.</u>

1. The crickets chirp loudly on <u>clement</u> Cliff.
<u>The crickets chirp loudly on Clement Cliff.</u>

2. Do you like <u>cindy's</u> corn and chili?
<u>Do you like Cindy's corn and chili?</u>

3. The City of Chicago is cold and <u>Chilly</u>.
<u>The City of Chicago is cold and chilly.</u>

4. The <u>coyotes</u> is the name of our chess team.
<u>The Coyotes is the name of our chess team.</u>

Answer Key

 Name: _____ Date: ___/___/_____ Score: _____

Lesson 4.1

Reading Words with the Letter D/d

✓ Lesson Check Point

 Directions: Read each target word. Find the letter "d" and put a check (✓) in the column that identifies its position: beginning, within or end.
路线：读每个目标词。找出字母 d 在栏中打勾 (✓) 示意： 开 始，中间或末尾。

Target Words	Beginning (First Letter)	Within	End (Last Letter)
1. calendar		✓	
2. dusting	✓		
3. garden		✓	
4. hard			✓
5. dictionary	✓		

 Directions: Read each sentence and underline the words that begin with the letter "d." Write all the underlined words in alphabetical order on the lines below.
路线：读每个句子，并给首字母为 d 的词加下划线。在下面的 线上按照字母顺序写出所有下划线标记的单词。

6. Brandon has a <u>dark</u> blue <u>drum</u>.

7. The barking <u>dogs</u> are on the <u>deck</u>.

8. The <u>driver</u> is <u>driving</u> a big blue bus.

9. My <u>daughter</u> ate the biggest <u>drumstick</u>.

10. Candice <u>designed</u> a beautiful black <u>dress</u>.

dark_____   daughter_____   deck_____
designed_____   dogs_____   dress_____
driver_____   driving_____   drum_____
                   drumstick_____

Classwork

 Name: _____ Date:___/___/_____ Score:_____

Lesson 4.2

Reading Letter "d" Words with the /d/ Sound & /j/ Sound

✓ Lesson Check Point

 Directions: Read each target word. Circle the word in the column that has the same "d" sound as the target word.
路线：读每个目标词。圈出栏中与目标词含相同 d 音的单词。

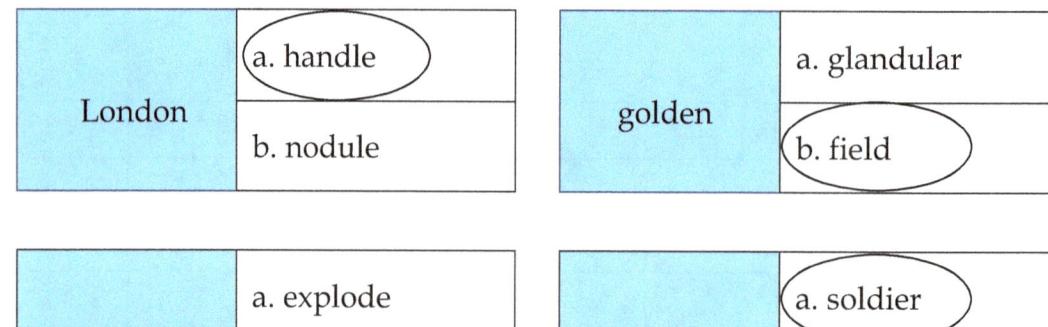

 Directions: Read each target word. Put a check (✓) under the correct column heading.
路线：读每个目标词。在符合要求的栏下打勾 (✓)。

Target Words	"d" has the /d/ sound as in the word doctor	"d" has the /j/ sound as in the word educate
1. London	✓	
2. golden	✓	
3. education		✓
4. modulate		✓

Name: _____ Date: ___/___/_____ Score: _____

Lesson 4.2

Reading Words with the "dr" Letter Combination

Dictionary Skills/ Vocabulary

 Lesson Check Point

 Directions: Read each target word and its definition. Write the letter of the definition on the line of each target word. Use a dictionary or the Internet to check your answers.

路线：读每个目标词及其定义。在目标词前线上写上正确定义的 字母编号。用词典或通过互联网检查你的答案。

Target Words	Definitions
1. _c_ dreams	a. to have fallen unintentionally
2. _d_ driveway	b. the cooked leg of a chicken, duck or turkey
3. _e_ driving	c. visualizing events that happen during sleep
4. _a_ dropped	d. a short path that leads to a house or garage
5. _b_ drumstick	e. the process of operating a vehicle

 Directions: Read each sentence. Underline the word in the parentheses that correctly completes each sentence. Then, write the underlined word on the line.

路线：阅读每个句子。在括号中选择符合句子的词，并添加下划线。然后，在线上写出下划线单词。

6. I drove the blue car into the ____driveway____. (dreams, <u>driveway</u>)

7. The boy ____dropped____ his big chocolate donut. (<u>dropped</u>, driving)

8. At night, Dan ____dreams____ about big animals. (<u>dreams</u>, driveway)

9. I am ____driving____ my car to Denver, Colorado. (<u>driving</u>, drumstick)

10. At dinner, David ate a delicious ____drumstick____. (dropped, <u>drumstick</u>)

Classwork

 Name: _____ Date: ___/__/_____ Score: _____

Lesson 4.3

Reading Words with the "ed" Suffix/ Past Tense Verbs

✓ **Lesson Check Point**

Directions: Read each target word. Circle the word in the column that has the same "ed" sound(s) as the target word.

路线：读每个目标词。圈出栏中与目标词含相同"ed"音的单词。

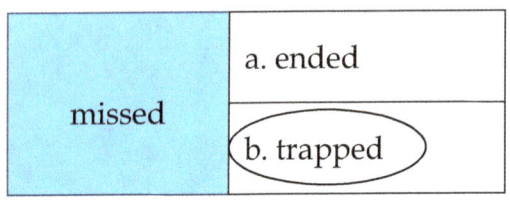

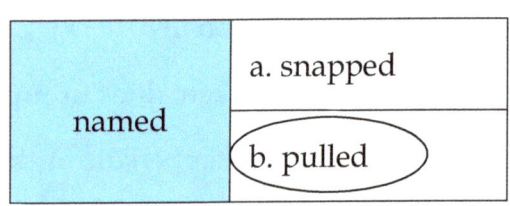

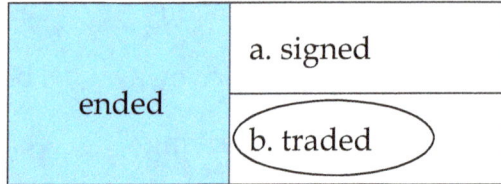

 Directions: Read each target word. Put a check (✓) under the correct column heading.

路线：读每个目标词。在符合要求的栏下打勾 (✓)。

Target Words	"ed" has the /ĭ/ + /d/ sounds as in the word <u>rested</u>	"ed" has the /d/ sound as in the word <u>hugged</u>	"ed" has the /t/ sound as in the word <u>tipped</u>
1. missed			✓
2. burned		✓	
3. named		✓	
4. ended	✓		

Answer Key

 Name: _____ Date: ___/___/_____ Score: _____

Lesson 4.4

Reading Words with a Silent Letter "d"

✓ Lesson Check Point

 Directions: Read the target words in the word box. Write the words that have a silent letter "d" in the first column. Write the words that do not have a silent letter "d" in the second column.

路线：读单词框中的目标词。在第一栏中写上含不发音 d 的词。 在第二栏中写上不带不发音 d 的词。

Target Word Box				
handicap	Cambridge	dock	Windsor	elder
does	conduct	handsome	adjourn	adjustment
judge	adjacent	director	handkerchief	discuss
padlock	doctor	footbridge	Wednesday	depend

Letter "d" is silent

- judge
- adjacent
- adjourn
- Windsor
- footbridge
- handsome
- Wednesday
- Cambridge
- adjustment
- handkerchief

Letter "d" has the /d/ sound

- does
- dock
- doctor
- elder
- discuss
- padlock
- conduct
- depend
- director
- handicap

Unit D Lesson 4.4

Learn To Read English With Directions In Chinese

Classwork

 Name: _____ Date:___/___/_____ Score:_____

The Reading Challenge

Lesson 4.5

Reading Multisyllable Words

✓ Lesson Check Point

 Directions: Read and divide each target word into syllables. Write each word and place a hyphen (-) between the syllables in the second column. Write the number of syllables in the third column. Use a dictionary or the Internet to check your answers.

路线：读目标词后，划分音节。写下每个词，在第二栏中写上音节，用 (-) 连接。在第三栏写上音节数。用词典或通过互联网检查你的答案。

Target Words	Words Divided into Syllables	Number of Syllables
1. demonstrate	dem-on-strate	3
2. duplicate	du-pli-cate	3
3. diagram	di-a-gram	3
4. decimal	dec-i-mal	3
5. descendent	de-scen-dent	3
6. digital	dig-i-tal	3
7. disengaged	dis-en-gaged	3
8. doormat	door-mat	2
9. discomfort	dis-com-fort	3
10. driver	driv-er	2

Answer Key

 Name: _____ Date: ___/___/_____ Score: _____

The Reading Challenge

Lesson 4.5

Reading Multisyllable Words

✓ Lesson Check Point

 Directions: Read each target word. Circle the word in the row that is divided correctly into syllables. Use a dictionary or the Internet to check your answers.

路线：读每个目标词。圈出行中音节划分正确的词。用词典或通过互联网检查你的答案。

Model

dictionary	a. di-ction-ary	(b. dic-tion-ar-y)	c. dic-tiona-ry

1. disciple	a. di-sci-ple	b. dis-cip-le	(c. dis-ci-ple)
2. deceptive	(a. de-cep-tive)	b. dec-ep-tive	c. de-cept-ive
3. Dakota	a. Dako-ta	b. Da-kot-a	(c. Da-ko-ta)
4. disgruntle	(a. dis-grun-tle)	b. di-sgrun-tle	c. dis-grunt-le
5. dimension	a. dim-e-nsion	b. dim-en-sion	(c. di-men-sion)
6. domino	(a. dom-i-no)	b. do-min-o	c. dom-in-o
7. decelerate	a. decel-er-ate	b. dec-el-er-ate	(c. de-cel-er-ate)
8. distribute	a. dist-rib-ute	b. dis-tri-bute	(c. dis-trib-ute)

Classwork

Name: _____ Date:___/___/_____ Score:_____

Lesson 4.6

Reading and Writing

Proper and Common Nouns and Adjectives

✓ **Lesson Check Point**

Directions: Read the words in the word box. Put an (X) on the line next to each word that is written incorrectly. Remember that all proper nouns and proper adjectives are capitalized. Use a dictionary or the Internet to check your answers.

路线：读单词框中的词。在书写错误的单词旁边的线上打叉(X)。记得合适的名词和形容词需要大写。用词典或通过互联网检查你 的答案。

Word Box					
X	Daughter	X	denmark	__	Dutch
__	Dana	X	detroit	__	director
__	Denver	__	diner	X	danish
X	dakota	__	door	X	Detective

Directions: Read each unedited sentence and underline the word that is written incorrectly. Write each sentence correctly on the line.

路线：读每个未经编辑的句子，并给书写错误的词加下划线。在线 上写上正确的句子。

Model
Dan said, "My daughter's name is donna."
Dan said, "My daughter's name is Donna."

1. Drake's Dictionary is not on his desk.
   Drake's dictionary is not on his desk.

2. The dark blue Doormat has one big dot.
   The dark blue doormat has one big dot.

3. The diploma belongs to doctor Davis.
   The diploma belongs to Doctor Davis.

4. The danish pastries, pancakes, and donuts cost five dollars.
   The Danish pastries, pancakes, and donuts cost five dollars.

Name: _____ Date: ___/___/_____ Score: _____

Answer Key

Lesson 5.1

Reading Words with the Letter E/e

✓ **Lesson Check Point**

Directions: Read each target word. Find the letter "e" and put a check (✓) in the column that identifies its position: beginning, within or end.
路线：读每个目标词。找出字母 e 在栏中打勾 (✓) 示意： 开 始，中间或末尾。

Target Words	Beginning (First Letter)	Within	End (Last Letter)
1. eating	✓		
2. belong		✓	
3. cake			✓
4. father		✓	
5. embark	✓		

Directions: Read each target word. Read the words in the row and circle the word that has a different vowel "e" sound.
路线：读每个目标词。阅读这一行的词，圈出元音 e 发不同的 词。

Target Words				
6. beds	leg	(she)	check	pet
7. men	(be)	ten	vet	hen
8. decks	yet	pen	(we)	set
9. stem	hem	(me)	net	fled
10. them	(he)	send	less	test

Classwork

 Name: _____ Date: ___/___/_____ Score: _____

Lesson 5.2

Reading Words with the Short Vowel "e" Sound

✓ **Lesson Check Point**

 Directions: Read the words in the four boxes. Circle two words with the short vowel /ĕ/ sound. The anchor word for the short vowel /ĕ/ sound is <u>egg</u>.

路线：读四个框中的词。圈出含短元音 /ĕ/ 的两个词。 锚点词词含元音 /ĕ/ 为英语单词，egg。

cake	(web)	bead	(speck)	ease	choose
(check)	theme	bee	(fed)	(dwelt)	(hem)

(Fred)	mean	(well)	(them)	(sped)	beat
eat	(hedge)	Pete	free	(yell)	mate

 Directions: Read the words in the four boxes. Circle two words that rhyme. Rhyming words have the same ending sound, such as <u>set</u> and <u>wet</u>.

路线：读四个框中的词。圈出押韵的两个词。押韵词有同样的尾 音，如，英语单词 set 和 wet。

bean	(neck)	(gem)	(stem)	(bell)	each
wise	(deck)	deal	pie	true	(spell)

shoe	meat	toe	(bed)	(edge)	zeal
(men)	(ten)	red	heal	(pledge)	they

Unit E
Lesson 5.2

Answer Key

Name: _____ Date: ___/___/_____ Score: _____

Lesson 5.2

Reading & Writing Words with the Short Vowel "e" Sound

✓ **Lesson Check Point**

Directions: Read each sentence and underline three words with the short vowel /ĕ/ sound. Then, write the underlined words on the lines below. The anchor word for the short vowel /ĕ/ sound is egg.

路线：读每个句子，划出含短元音/ĕ/ 的三个词。 然后，在下面的划线处写上带下划线的词。锚点词为短元音/ĕ/ 的英语单 词，egg。

Model

She placed her legs on the wet deck.

    legs   wet   deck

1. She will not let us get a pet.

    let   get   pet

2. We smell the three wet hens.

    smell   wet   hens

3. Andre bent his leg and fell.

    bent   leg   fell

4. Eve went to Ed's summer wedding.

    went   Ed's   wedding

5. We have to go to bed by ten o'clock for a restful night's sleep.

    bed   ten   restful

Learn To Read English With Directions In Chinese   Copyrighted Material

Classwork

 Name: _____ Date: ___/___/_____ Score: _____

Lesson 5.3

Reading Words with the Long Vowel "e" Sound

✓ **Lesson Check Point**

 Directions: Read the words in the four boxes. Circle two words with the long vowel /ē/ sound. The anchor word for the long vowel /ē/ sound is me.

路线：读四个框中的词。圈出带长元音 /ē/ 的两个词。 锚点词为含长元音 /ē/ 的英语单词 me。

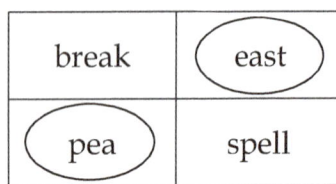

| break | (east) | | (cease) | (scene) | | chest | (these) |
| pea | spell | | clever | here | | cakes | (zebra) |

| (zero) | scent | | (east) | next | | (heal) | trend |
| (believe) | come | | (eating) | beard | | where | (react) |

 Directions: Read the words in the four boxes. Circle two words that rhyme. Rhyming words have the same ending sound, such as <u>beep</u> and <u>reap</u>.

路线：读四个框中的词。圈出押韵的两个词。押韵的词含同样的 尾音。如，英语单词 beep 和 reap。

| (speed) | (read) | | lead | (eat) | | (see) | were |
| bread | felt | | when | (heat) | | held | (tea) |

| (tease) | fence | | head | (theme) | | realm | temp |
| (lease) | there | | (scheme) | deck | | (leave) | (weave) |

Answer Key

Name: _____ Date: ___/___/_____ Score: _____

Lesson 5.3

Reading & Writing Words with the Long Vowel "e" Sound

✓ **Lesson Check Point**

Directions: Read each sentence and underline three words with the long vowel /ē/ sound. Then, write the underlined words on the lines below. The anchor word for the long vowel /ē/ sound is <u>me</u>.

路线：读每个句子，给带长元音/ē/的三个词加下划线。然后，在 下面的划线处写上带下划线的词。锚点词为长元音/ē/ 的英语单词，me。

Model

<u>We</u> are <u>reading</u> an article entitled, "<u>Eagles</u> Bird of Prey."

    We   reading   Eagles
  _____   _____   _____

1. <u>Irene</u> and <u>Lee</u> are relaxing under the <u>tree</u> with their pets.

    Irene   Lee   tree
  _____   _____   _____

2. The ten <u>Guyanese</u> <u>teams</u> are <u>extremely</u> talented.

   Guyanese   teams   extremely
  _____   _____   _____

3. This <u>evening</u>, Esther <u>received</u> a <u>speeding</u> ticket.

    evening   received   speeding
  _____   _____   _____

4. The <u>speaker</u> said, "<u>Lean</u> <u>meats</u> have relatively low-fat content."

    speaker   Lean   meats
  _____   _____   _____

5. The students will <u>speak</u> to the <u>dean</u> about the new <u>teachers</u>.

    speak   dean   teachers
  _____   _____   _____

Unit E Lesson 5.3

Classwork

 Name: _____ Date: ___/___/_____ Score: _____

Review Lessons 5.2 & 5.3

Reading Short Vowel and Long Vowel Words

✓ **Lesson Check Point**

 Directions: Read the target words in the word box. In the first column, write the words that have the short vowel /ĕ/ sound, as in the word egg. In the second column, write the words that have the long vowel /ē/ sound, as in the word me.

路线：读框中的目标词。在第一栏写上含短元音/ĕ/的词。如，英语单词 egg。在第二栏写上含长元音/ē/的单词。如，英语单词 me。

Target Word Box				
fled	theme	left	temp	went
these	step	scene	seeing	speed
held	athlete	complete	then	increase
extreme	self	west	free	test

Letter "e" has the /ĕ/ sound as in the word **egg**

- fled
- left
- test
- step
- held
- then
- self
- west
- went
- temp

Letter "e" has the /ē/ sound as in the word **me**

- free
- these
- theme
- scene
- seeing
- speed
- athlete
- complete
- increase
- extreme

 Name: _____ Date: ___/___/_____ Score: _____

Answer Key

Lesson 5.4

Reading Words with Letter "e" Vowel Pairs

 Lesson Check Point

Directions: Read each target word. Circle the word in the column that has the same vowel "ea," "ee," "ei," "eo" or "eu" sound as the target word.
路线：读每个目标词。圈出栏中单词含与目标词一样元音"ea," "ee," "ei," "eo" 或 "eu" 的词。

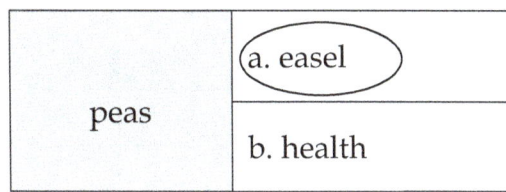
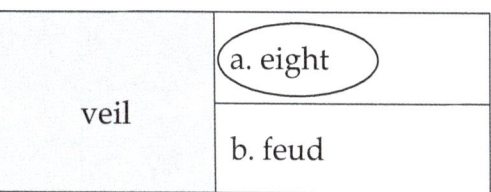

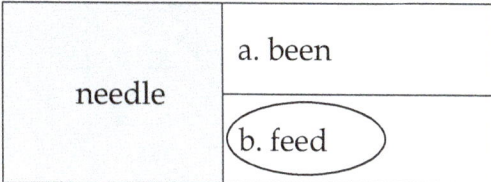

| peas | (a. easel) |
| | b. health |

| veil | (a. eight) |
| | b. feud |

| seize | a. video |
| | (b. people) |

| needle | a. been |
| | (b. feed) |

 Directions: Read each target word. Put a check (✓) under the correct column heading.
路线：读每个目标词。在符合要求的栏下打勾 (✓)。

Target Words	Words have the long "e" sound as in the word **tea**	Words do not have the long "e" sound
1. peas	✓	
2. veil		✓
3. seize	✓	
4. needle	✓	

Classwork

 Name: _____ Date:___/___/_____ Score:_____

Lesson 5.5

Reading Words with the Final Letter "e"

✓ **Lesson Check Point**

 Directions: Read each target word. Find the letter "e" and put a check (✓) in the column that identifies its position within the syllable.
路线：读每个目标词。找到字母 e 并在栏中打勾(✓)，标示其在 音节中的位置。

Target Words	"e" is at the end of a one syllable word	"e" is at the end of the first syllable	"e" is at the end of a multi-syllable word
1. becoming		✓	
2. he	✓		
3. recording		✓	
4. multiple			✓
5. we	✓		

 Directions: Read each target word. Put a check (✓) under the correct column heading.
路线：读每个目标词。在符合要求的栏下打勾 (✓)。

Target Words	"e" has the /ĕ/ sound as in the word <u>egg</u>	"e" has the /ē/ sound as in the word <u>me</u>	"e" has the /ə/ sound as in the word <u>item</u>	"e" is silent as in the word <u>great</u>
6. prefix		✓		
7. made				✓
8. marvel			✓	
9. season		✓		
10. travel			✓	

Answer Key

 Name: _____ Date:__/__/_____ Score:_____

Lesson 5.6

Reading Letter "e" Words with the Schwa Vowel Sound

✓ **Lesson Check Point**

 Directions: Read each target word. Circle the word in the column that has the same "e" sound as the target word.

路线：读每个目标词。圈出栏中与目标词含相同 e 音的单词。

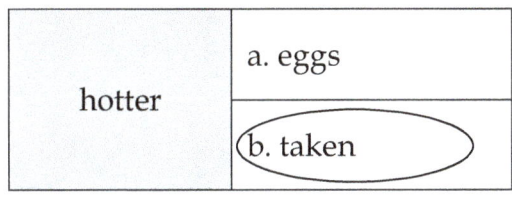

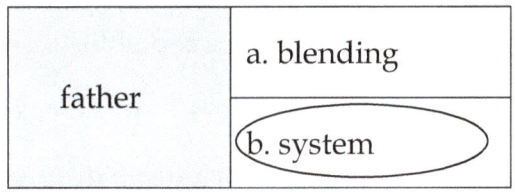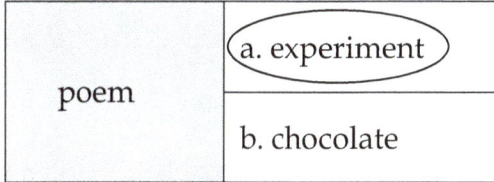

 Directions: Read each sentence and underline the letter "e" word that has the schwa vowel /ə/ sound. The anchor word for the letter "e" schwa vowel sound is <u>item</u>.

路线：读每个句子，给含 e 音且发施瓦 /ə/ 的单词加下划线。发 e 施瓦音的锚点词是 item。

1. At <u>dinner</u>, I ate a slice of roast beef.

2. Five <u>movers</u> organized my bedroom set.

3. Every year, we <u>celebrated</u> Andrew's birthday.

4. Three large <u>barrels</u> are located next to cabinets.

5. Our <u>fishermen</u> sailed their ships twenty miles from shore.

6. Large animal populations are <u>scattered</u> throughout Africa.

Classwork

 Name: _____ Date:___/___/_____ Score:_____

Lesson 5.7

Reading Words with the "er" Letter Combination

Dictionary Skills/ Vocabulary

✓ **Lesson Check Point**

 Directions: Read each target word and its definition. Write the letter of the definition on the line of each target word. Use a dictionary or the Internet to check your answers.

路线：读每个目标词及其定义。在目标词前线上写上正确定义的 字母编号。用词典或通过互联网检查你的答案。

Target Words	Definitions
1. _b_ river	a. something very bad or unacceptable
2. _e_ sister	b. a body of water that is larger than a creek
3. _a_ terrible	c. a small fruit that has red or purple drupelets
4. _c_ raspberry	d. a verbal or written response to a question
5. _d_ answer	e. a female who has the same parent(s) as another

 Directions: Read each sentence and write the target word that correctly completes the sentence.
路线：读每个句子和并在划线处填上合适的词。

6. My younger ____sister____ eats berries and cherries.

7. Jerry did not ____answer____ Sherry's difficult questions.

8. Have you ever eaten a sweet, juicy ____raspberry____?

9. Sherry's baked herring tasted ____terrible____.

10. We are going to take a ferry ride along the ____river____.

Answer Key

 Name: _____ Date: ___/___/_____ Score: _____

Lesson 5.8

Reading Words with the "eu" and "ew" Letter Combinations

✓ Lesson Check Point

 Directions: Read each sentence and underline the word that has a silent letter "e."
路线：读每个句子，给含不发音 e 的词加下划线。

Model
My father said, "The apricot <u>streusel</u> is very tasty."

1. In Germany, I bought many elegant gifts with <u>euros</u>.

2. Jennifer and Cathy painted the ceiling a <u>neutral</u> color.

3. The <u>European</u> bound flight will depart at eleven o'clock.

4. The bridal party was <u>euphoric</u> during the wonderful wedding.

 Directions: Read each sentence and underline the word with an "eu" or "ew" letter combination that has the long vowel /y$\overline{oo}$/ or /$\overline{oo}$/ sound, as in the words <u>feud</u> and <u>flew</u>.
路线：读每个句子，给含 "eu" 或 "ew" 字母组合且发长元音 /y$\overline{oo}$/ 或 /$\overline{oo}$/ 的词加下划线，如英语单词 feud 和 flew。

5. Mom's apple <u>streusel</u> is delicious.

6. <u>Lieutenant</u> Edwards is a strong leader.

7. The engineering students ate grapes and <u>cashews</u>.

8. Eddie learned a lot of interesting information about <u>Zeus</u>.

9. The Elton family is <u>feuding</u> over Grandmother's possessions.

10. The shower was extremely clean after Jane used <u>mildew</u> remover.

Classwork

 Name: _____ Date: ___/ ___/ _____ Score: _____

Lesson 5.9

Reading Words with the "ey" Letter Combination

✓ Lesson Check Point

 Directions: Read each target word. Put a check (✓) under the correct column heading.

路线：读每个目标词。在符合要求的栏下打勾 (✓)。

Target Words	"ey" has the long /ē/ sound as in the word honey	"ey" has the long /ā/ sound as in the word hey
1. monkey	✓	
2. survey		✓
3. convey		✓
4. kidney	✓	

 Directions: Read each sentence and underline the word with the "ey" letter combination. Put a check (✓) under the correct column heading.

路线：读每个句子，给含字母组合 "ey" 的词加下划线。在正确的 标题栏中打勾(✓)。

	"ey" has the long /ē/ sound as in the word honey	"ey" has the long /ā/ sound as in the word hey
5. The survey has ten questions.		✓
6. Lee received a new team jersey.	✓	
7. Today, they will have a yard sale.		✓
8. I did not obey my teachers' rules.		✓
9. Ethan enjoys playing volleyball.	✓	
10. The jockey's horse is on the track.	✓	

Answer Key

 Name: _____ Date: ___/___/_____ Score: _____

Lesson 5.10

Reading Words with a Silent Letter "e"

✓ **Lesson Check Point**

 Directions: Read the target words in the word box. Write the words that have a silent letter "e" in the first column. Write the words that do not have a silent letter "e" in the second column.

路线：读单词框中的目标词。在第一栏中写上含不发音 e 的词。 在第二栏中写上不带不发音 e 的词。

Target Word Box				
eating	cells	friends	game	vote
seat	base	depend	effect	fresh
tone	size	tube	beds	came
face	zebras	clue	drive	meal

Letter "e" is silent	Letter "e" has a letter "e" sound
clue	beds
vote	cells
base	seat
tone	meal
size	effect
tube	fresh
came	eating
face	zebras
drive	friends
game	depend

Unit E Lesson 5.10

Learn To Read English With Directions In Chinese

Classwork

 Name: _____ Date: ___/___/_____ Score: _____

Unit Review – E/e

Reading Words with Vowel "e" Sounds: /ĕ/, /ē/, /ə/ & Silent

✓ **Lesson Check Point**

 Directions: Read each target word. Circle the word in the column that has the same "e" sound as the target word.
路线：读每个目标词。圈出栏中单词的 e 发音与目标词一样的 词。

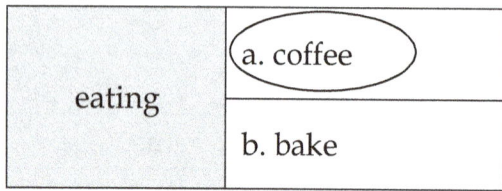

 Directions: Read each target word. Put a check (✓) under the correct column heading.
路线：读每个目标词。在符合要求的栏下打勾 (✓)。

Target Words	"e" has the /ĕ/ sound as in the word <u>egg</u>	"e" has the /ē/ sound as in the word <u>me</u>	"e" has the /ə/ sound as in the word <u>item</u>	"e" is silent as in the word <u>great</u>
1. eating		✓		
2. barrel			✓	
3. pollen			✓	
4. check	✓			

Answer Key

 Name: _____ Date: ___/___/_____ Score: _____

The Reading Challenge

Lesson 5.11

Reading Multisyllable Words

✓ **Lesson Check Point**

 Directions: Read and divide each target word into syllables. Write each word and place a hyphen (-) between the syllables in the second column. Write the number of syllables in the third column. Use a dictionary or the Internet to check your answers.

路线：读目标词后，划分音节。写下每个词，在第二栏中写上音 节，用 (-) 连接。在第三栏写上音节数。用词典或通过互联网检 查你的答案。

Target Words	Words Divided into Syllables	Number of Syllables
1. decreasing	de-creas-ing	3
2. between	be-tween	2
3. peanut	pea-nut	2
4. shipwreck	ship-wreck	2
5. nutmeg	nut-meg	2
6. leghorn	leg-horn	2
7. farewell	fare-well	2
8. anthem	an-them	2
9. modem	mo-dem	2
10. itemize	i-tem-ize	3

Unit E Lesson 5.11

Classwork

Name: _____ Date: ___/___/_____ Score: _____

The Reading Challenge

Lesson 5.11

Reading Multisyllable Words

✓ Lesson Check Point

Directions: Read each target word. Circle the word in the row that is divided correctly into syllables. Use a dictionary or the Internet to check your answers.

路线：读每个目标词。圈出行中音节划分正确的词。用词典或通过互联网检查你的答案。

Model

| megabyte | a. me-ga-byte | b. meg-a-byte ⭕ | c. me-gaby-te |

1. awaken	a. aw-a-ken	b. a-wak-en ⭕	c. a-wa-ken
2. legacy	a. le-ga-cy	b. leg-a-cy ⭕	c. leg-ac-y
3. forgiven	a. for-giv-en ⭕	b. for-gi-ven	c. fo-rgi-ven
4. acknowledge	a. ack-now-ledge	b. ac-know-ledge	c. ac-knowl-edge ⭕
5. turtleneck	a. tur-tle-neck ⭕	b. turt-len-eck	c. turt-le-neck
6. celebrate	a. cel-eb-rate	b. cel-e-brate ⭕	c. ce-le-brate
7. federal	a. fe-de-ral	b. fed-e-ral	c. fed-er-al ⭕
8. ascending	a. as-cend-ing ⭕	b. asc-end-ing	c. as-cen-ding

Name: _____ Date: ___/___/_____ Score: _____

Lesson 5.12

Reading and Writing

Proper and Common Nouns and Adjectives

✓ **Lesson Check Point**

 Directions: Read the words in the word box. Put an (X) on the line next to each word that is written incorrectly. Remember that all proper nouns and proper adjectives are capitalized. Use a dictionary or the Internet to check your answers.

路线：读单词框中的词。在书写错误的单词旁边的线上打叉(X)。记得合适的名词和形容词需要大写。用词典或通过互联网检查你 的答案。

Word Box		
_X_ eiffel Tower	_X_ Educator	_X_ east Asia
___ England	_X_ egyptian	_X_ el Dorado
___ egocentric	___ Estonia	___ editor
_X_ Envelope	___ European	___ environment

 Directions: Read each unedited sentence and underline the word that is written incorrectly. Write each sentence correctly on the line.

路线：读每个未经编辑的句子，并给书写错误的词加下划线。在线 上写上正确的句子。

Model
All my friends are <u>Excited</u> about the class trip to Europe.
<u>All my friends are excited about the class trip to Europe.</u>

1. I will meet my friend, <u>eileen</u>, at five o'clock EST.
<u>I will meet my friend, Eileen, at five o'clock EST.</u>

2. <u>evan</u> said, "Many of the citizens of Ethiopia speak English."
<u>Evan said, "Many of the citizens of Ethiopia speak English."</u>

3. The address on the envelope indicates that the letter is from <u>egypt</u>.
<u>The address on the envelope indicates that the letter is from Egypt.</u>

4. On Earth Day, Mr. <u>eglon's</u> class will discuss environmental issues.
<u>On Earth Day, Mr. Eglon's class will discuss environmental issues.</u>

Classwork

Name: _____ Date: ___/___/_____ Score: _____

Lesson 6.1

Reading Words with the Letter F/f

✓ **Lesson Check Point**

Directions: Read each target word. Find the letter "f" and put a check (✓) in the column that identifies its position: beginning, within or end.
路线：读每个目标词。找出字母 f 在栏中打勾 (✓) 示意： 开 始，中间 或末尾。

Target Words	Beginning (First Letter)	Within	End (Last Letter)
1. flip	✓		
2. fresh	✓		
3. leaf			✓
4. defrost		✓	
5. comfort		✓	

Directions: Read each sentence and underline the words that begin with the letter "f." Write all the underlined words in alphabetical order on the lines below.
路线：读每个句子，并给首字母为 f 的词加下划线。在下面的 线上按照字母顺序写出所有下划线标记的单词。

6. Ashley and <u>Fred</u> are citizens of <u>France</u>.

7. Brad and Alex are <u>fabulous</u> <u>flute</u> players.

8. The <u>fence</u> in <u>front</u> of the house is dark blue.

9. The <u>flowers</u> in the <u>field</u> are extremely beautiful.

10. The <u>flag</u> of Belgium is <u>flying</u> high over the building.

fabulous _____   fence _____   field _____
flag _____   flowers _____   flute _____
flying _____   France _____   Fred _____
                     front _____

Unit F Lesson 6.1

Learn To Read English With Directions In Chinese

Answer Key

Name: _____ Date:___/___/_____ Score: _____

Lesson 6.2

Reading Words with the "fr" Letter Combination

Dictionary Skills/ Vocabulary

✓ Lesson Check Point

Directions: Read each target word and its definition. Write the letter of the definition on the line of each target word. Use a dictionary or the Internet to check your answers.

路线：读每个目标词及其定义。在目标词前线上写上正确定义的 字母编号。用词典或通过互联网检查你的答案。

Target Words		Definitions
1. _d_	frog	a. to have broken or cracked something
2. _e_	framed	b. a branch of a business chain
3. _b_	franchise	c. to be ahead of someone or something
4. _a_	fractured	d. a small, smooth, tailless and wet-skinned animal
5. _c_	front	e. evidence or testimony presented to falsely incriminate

Directions: Read each sentence. Underline the word in the parentheses that correctly completes each sentence. Then, write the underlined word on the line.

路线：阅读每个句子。在括号中选择符合句子的词，并添加下划 线。然后，在线上写出下划线单词。

6. The ____frog____ is croaking by the water. (<u>frog</u>, framed)

7. On the bus, Freda sat in ____front____ of Frankie. (<u>front</u>, franchise)

8. At the game, Flo fell and ____fractured____ her ankle. (frog, <u>fractured</u>)

9. Frank was ____framed____ for a crime he didn't commit. (front, <u>framed</u>)

10. Flossy purchased a fast food ____franchise____. (<u>franchise</u>, framed)

Learn To Read English With Directions In Chinese

Classwork

Name: _____ Date: ___/___/_____ Score: _____

Lesson 6.3

Reading Words with the "fl" Letter Combination

Dictionary Skills/ Vocabulary

✓ Lesson Check Point

Directions: Read each target word and its definition. Write the target word on the line in front of its meaning. Use a dictionary or the Internet to check your answers.

路线：读每个目标词及其定义。在目标词前线上写上正确定义的 字母编号。用词典或通过互联网检查你的答案。

Target Word Box				
fleet	flash	flower	fluently	fly

1. <u>fly</u>   to travel through the air with wings
2. <u>flower</u>   the colorful part of a plant that contains seeds
3. <u>fleet</u>   a number of vehicles owned as a unit
4. <u>flash</u>   a device that provides light to brighten a picture
5. <u>fluently</u>   the ability to speak a language correctly

Directions: Read each sentence. Underline the word in the parentheses that correctly completes each sentence. Then, write the underlined word on the line.

路线：阅读每个句子。在括号中选择符合句子的词，并添加下划线。然后，在线上写出下划线单词。

6. Fred's camera has a built-in <u>flash</u>. (<u>flash</u>, flower)

7. Flamingos can <u>fly</u> up to 40 mph in the air. (flash, <u>fly</u>)

8. My friend speaks French and Finnish <u>fluently</u>. (<u>fluently</u>, flash)

9. The florist made a beautiful <u>flower</u> arrangement. (fluently, <u>flower</u>)

10. After the funeral, a <u>fleet</u> of cars drove down the avenue. (fly, <u>fleet</u>)

Answer Key

 Name: _____ Date: ___/___/_____ Score: _____

Lesson 6.3

Reading Words with the "fle" Letter Combination

✓ **Lesson Check Point**

 Directions: Read each target word. Find the "fle" letter combination and put a check (✓) in the column that identifies its position: beginning, within or end.

路线：读每个目标词。找到"fle"字母组合，并在栏中打勾(✓)示意： 开始，中间，结尾。

Target Words	Beginning (First 3 Letters)	Within	End (Last 3 Letters)
1. waffle			✓
2. flesh	✓		
3. fleet	✓		
4. reflect		✓	
5. duffle			✓

 Directions: Read each target word. Put a check (✓) in the "yes" column if the "fle" letter combination has the /f/ + /ə/ + /l/ sounds. Put a check (✓) in the "no" column if the "fle" letter combination does not have the /f/ + /ə/ + /l/ sounds.

路线：读每个目标词。如果"fle"字母组合发/f/ + /ə/ + /l/的音，在"是"栏中打勾 (✓)。如果"fle"字母组合不发/f/ + /ə/ + /l/的音，在"没有"栏中打勾(✓)。

Target Words	Yes	No
6. waffle	✓	
7. flesh		✓
8. fleet		✓
9. reflect		✓
10. duffle	✓	

Classwork

Name: _____ Date: ___/___/_____ Score: _____

Lesson 6.4

Reading Words with the "ft," "lf" and "ff" Letter Combinations

Dictionary Skills/ Vocabulary

✓ **Lesson Check Point**

Directions: Read each target word and its definition. Write the letter of the definition on the line of each target word. Use a dictionary or the Internet to check your answers.

路线：读每个目标词及其定义。在目标词前线上写上正确定义的　字母编号。用词典或通过互联网检查你的答案。

Target Words	Definitions
1. _d_ giraffe	a. a piece of writing that is not finalized
2. _e_ Gulf	b. to move along by wind or water
3. _a_ draft	c. a vehicle that can fly in the air
4. _c_ aircraft	d. the tallest land animal with dark spots
5. _b_ drift	e. a large body of water partially enclosed by land

Directions: Read each sentence and write the target word that correctly completes the sentence.
路线：读每个句子和并在划线处填上合适的词。

6. I will write the first _____draft_____ of the report in class.

7. The _____aircraft_____ flew from New York City to Atlantic City.

8. At sunset, the boats and rafts will _____drift_____ along the lake.

9. The hurricane damaged the houses along the _____Gulf_____ Coast.

10. The guide said, "The _____giraffe_____ is the tallest African animal."

Name: _____ Date: ___/___/_____ Score: _____

Answer Key

Lesson 6.5

Reading Words with a Silent Letter "f"

✓ **Lesson Check Point**

 Directions: Read the target words in the word box. Write the words that have a silent letter "f" in the first column. Write the words that do not have a silent letter "f" in the second column.

路线：读单词框中的目标词。在第一栏中写上含不发音 f 的词。 在第二栏中写上不带不发音 f 的词。

Target Word Box				
muffin	buffalo	infancy	faces	suffocate
wife	after	afresh	afford	flying
defect	effect	cliff	caffeine	officially
fitness	coffee	bullfrog	fast	taffy

Letter "f" is silent

- cliff
- taffy
- effect
- afford
- muffin
- coffee
- caffeine
- buffalo
- suffocate
- officially

Letter "f" has the /f/ sound

- wife
- fast
- defect
- after
- afresh
- faces
- flying
- fitness
- infancy
- bullfrog

Classwork

Name: _____ Date: ___/___/_____ Score: _____

Lesson 6.6

Reading Singular and Plural forms of Words Ending in "-f" & "-fe"

✓ **Lesson Check Point**

Directions: Read each target word. Put a check (✓) in the second column if the plural form of the target word ends with "-ves." Put a check (✓) in the third column if the plural form of the target word ends with "-s" or "-es."

路线：读每个目标词。如果目标词复数形式以"-ves"结尾，在第二栏中打勾(✓)。如果目标词的复数形式以"-s"或"-es"结尾，在第三栏中打勾(✓)。

Target Words	The plural form of the target word ends with "-ves"	The plural form of the target word ends with "-s" or "-es"
1. roof		✓
2. half	✓	
3. life	✓	
4. thief	✓	
5. chef		✓

Directions: Read each sentence. Complete each sentence by writing the plural form of the word on the line.

路线：读每个句子。在句子划线处填上单词正确的复数形式。

6. Doctors save _____lives_____ every day. (life)

7. The men gave flowers to their _____wives_____. (wife)

8. Frank built five _____shelves_____ by himself. (shelf)

9. The girls filmed the events by _____themselves_____. (herself)

10. Many _____wolves_____ attacked the farmer's chicken. (wolf)

Answer Key

 Name: _____ Date: ___/___/_____ Score: _____

The Reading Challenge

Lesson 6.7

Reading Multisyllable Words

✓ Lesson Check Point

 Directions: Read and divide each target word into syllables. Write each word and place a hyphen (-) between the syllables in the second column. Write the number of syllables in the third column. Use a dictionary or the Internet to check your answers.

路线：读目标词后，划分音节。写下每个词，在第二栏中写上音节，用 (-) 连接。在第三栏写上音节数。用词典或通过互联网检查你的答案。

Target Words	Words Divided into Syllables	Number of Syllables
1. fencing	fenc-ing	2
2. fabulous	fab-u-lous	3
3. friendship	friend-ship	2
4. facial	fa-cial	2
5. flawless	flaw-less	2
6. franchising	fran-chis-ing	3
7. falcon	fal-con	2
8. finalist	fi-nal-ist	3
9. florist	flo-rist	2
10. football	foot-ball	2

Classwork

Name: _____ Date:___/___/_____ Score:_____

The Reading Challenge

Lesson 6.7

Reading Multisyllable Words

✓ Lesson Check Point

Directions: Read each target word. Circle the word in the row that is divided correctly into syllables. Use a dictionary or the Internet to check your answers.

路线：读每个目标词。圈出行中音节划分正确的词。用词典或通过互联网检查你的答案。

Model

| factory | a. fac-tor-y | b. fac-to-ry ⭕ | c. fa-cto-ry |

| 1. flexible | b. fle-x-ible | b. fle-xi-ble | c. flex-i-ble ⭕ |

| 2. festival | a. fest-i-val | b. fe-stiv-al | c. fes-ti-val ⭕ |

| 3. fabricate | a. fab-ri-cate ⭕ | b. fa-bri-cate | c. fabr-ic-ate |

| 4. finale | a. fin-al-e | b. fi-nal-e ⭕ | c. fina-le |

| 5. forensic | a. for-e-nsic | b. for-en-sic | c. fo-ren-sic ⭕ |

| 6. fortify | a. fort-i-fy | b. for-ti-fy ⭕ | c. for-tif-y |

| 7. familiar | a. fa-mil-iar ⭕ | b. fam-i-liar | c. fam-il-iar |

| 8. flavoring | a. fla-vor-ing ⭕ | b. flav-or-ing | c. flav-o-ring |

Answer Key

 Name: _____ Date: ___/___/_____ Score: _____

Lesson 6.8

Reading and Writing

Proper and Common Nouns and Adjectives

✓ Lesson Check Point

 Directions: Read the words in the word box. Put an (X) on the line next to each word that is written incorrectly. Remember that all proper nouns and proper adjectives are capitalized. Use a dictionary or the Internet to check your answers.

路线：读单词框中的词。在书写错误的单词旁边的线上打叉(X)。记得合适的名词和形容词需要大写。用词典或通过互联网检查你 的答案。

Word Box					
__	flower	__	Florida	X	far East
X	franklin	__	flock	X	france
X	french	X	Finalist	__	fashion
__	flamingo	X	frankfort	__	florist

 Directions: Read each unedited sentence and underline the word that is written incorrectly. Write each sentence correctly on the line.

路线：读每个未经编辑的句子，并给书写错误的词加下划线。在线 上写上正确的句子。

Model

Fiji is my <u>Florist's</u> favorite holiday destination.
<u>Fiji is my florist's favorite holiday destination.</u>

1. Flossy and Frank were born in <u>france</u>.
<u>Flossy and Frank were born in France.</u>

2. <u>francis</u> speaks English and French fluently.
<u>Francis speaks English and French fluently.</u>

3. Freda works by <u>fort</u> Hamilton Parkway.
<u>Freda works by Fort Hamilton Parkway.</u>

4. Fred's baseball game is at <u>frankfurt</u> Field.
<u>Fred's baseball game is at Frankfurt Field.</u>

Classwork

Name: _____ Date: ___/___/_____ Score: _____

Lesson 7.1

Reading Words with the Letter G/g

✓ Lesson Check Point

Directions: Read each target word. Find the letter "g" and put a check (✓) in the column that identifies its position: beginning, within or end.
路线：读每个目标词。找出字母 g 在栏中打勾 (✓) 示意： 开始， 中间或末尾。

Target Words	Beginning (First Letter)	Within	End (Last Letter)
1. glossary	✓		
2. hexagon		✓	
3. landing			✓
4. oblong			✓
5. government	✓		

Directions: Read each sentence and underline the words that begin with the letter "g." Write all the underlined words in alphabetical order on the lines below.
路线：读每个句子，并给首字母为 g 的词加下划线。在下面的线上按照字母顺序写出所有下划线标记的单词。

6. Billy and Fran ate <u>green</u> <u>grapes</u>.

7. All the boys earned <u>good</u> <u>grades</u>.

8. My <u>guests</u> are <u>going</u> to the airport.

9. The <u>girls</u> forgot to put <u>gas</u> in the car.

10. The <u>golfers</u> play a challenging <u>game</u>.

game _____   gas _____   girls _____
going _____   golfers _____   good _____
grades _____   grapes _____   green _____
                    guests _____

Answer Key

 Name: _____ Date: ___/___/_____ Score: _____

Lesson 7.1

Reading Words with the Hard Letter "g"

✓ Lesson Check Point

 Directions: Read each target word. Put a check (✓) under the correct column heading.

路线：读每个目标词。在符合要求的栏下打勾 (✓)。

Target Words	Hard "g" has the /g/ sound as in the word <u>gum</u>	Soft "g" has the /j/ sound as in the word <u>gem</u>
1. gills	✓	
2. golden	✓	
3. gentle		✓
4. geese	✓	
5. gallops	✓	

 Directions: Read each sentence and underline the words that have the hard "g" sound. The anchor word for the hard "g" sound is <u>gum</u>. Write all the underlined words in alphabetical order on the lines below.

路线：读每个句子，给含硬 g 音的词加下划线。含硬 g 音的锚点词是 gum。在下面线上按字母顺序写上所有加了下划线的词。

6. <u>Gloria</u> and Gina have beautiful blue <u>glasses</u>.

7. Today, Georgette saw a cow, a <u>goat</u> and a <u>gazelle</u>.

8. Jennifer is <u>growing</u> geraniums in her <u>greenhouse</u>.

9. The children in Ms. George's class have <u>good</u> <u>grades</u>.

10. My <u>grandfather</u> has ginger chicken and corn on the <u>grill</u>.

gazelle   glasses   Gloria
goat   good   grades
grandfather   greenhouse   grill
                 growing

Unit G Lesson 7.1

Learn To Read English With Directions In Chinese

Classwork

 Name: _____ Date:___/___/_____ Score:_____

Lesson 7.2

Reading Words with the Soft Letter "g"

✓ Lesson Check Point

 Directions: Read each target word. Put a check (✓) under the correct column heading.
路线：读每个目标词。在符合要求的栏下打勾 (✓)。

Target Words	Soft "g" has the /j/ or /zh/ sound as in the words gem & massage	Hard "g" has the /g/ sound as in the word gum	Both soft "g" and hard "g" sounds as in the word gauge
1. garage			✓
2. gear		✓	
3. intelligent	✓		
4. progress		✓	
5. grammar		✓	

 Directions: Read each sentence and underline the words that have the soft "g" sound. The anchor word for the soft "g" sound is gem. Write all the underlined words in alphabetical order on the lines below.
路线：读每个句子，给含软 g 音的词加下划线。含软 g 音的 描点词是 gem。在下面的线上按照字母顺序写出所有加了下划线 的词。

6. Gloria's giant gem glistens in the sun.

7. Gianna is chewing gum in the gymnasium.

8. Ginny got a great grade in her biology class.

9. For graduation, I received a gigantic package.

10. The teenagers felt guilty because they did not go to the gym.

biology	gem	Gianna
giant	gigantic	Ginny
gym	gymnasium	package
	teenagers	

Answer Key

Name: _____ Date: ___/___/_____ Score: _____

Review Lessons 7.1 & 7.2

Reading Hard Letter "g" and Soft Letter "g" Words

✓ **Lesson Check Point**

Directions: Read each target word. Put a check (✓) under the correct column heading.

路线：读每个目标词。在符合要求的栏下打勾 (✓)。

Target Words	Soft "g" has the /j/ or /zh/ sound as in the words gem & massage	Hard "g" has the /g/ sound as in the word gum	Both soft "g" and hard "g" sounds as in the word gauge
1. get		✓	
2. biology	✓		
3. ground		✓	
4. ingested	✓		
5. fragrant		✓	

Directions: Read each sentence and underline the words that have the hard "g" sound. The anchor word for the hard "g" sound is gum. Write all the underlined words in alphabetical order on the lines below.

路线：读每个句子，给含硬 g 音的词加下划线。含硬 g 音的锚点词是 gum。在下面线上按字母顺序写上所有加了下划线的词。

6. Georgette has <u>good</u> <u>grades</u>.

7. <u>Greg</u> enjoys <u>going</u> to the gym.

8. Gina's <u>eyeglasses</u> are <u>glamorous</u>.

9. Ben <u>gave</u> me a bronze chain as a <u>gift</u>.

10. My friend, Gio, <u>graduated</u> and traveled to <u>Guyana</u>.

eyeglasses   gave   gift
glamorous   going   good
grades   graduated   Greg
                    Guyana

Classwork

 Name: _____ Date: ___/___/_____ Score: _____

Review Lessons 7.1 & 7.2

Reading Hard Letter "g" and Soft Letter "g" Words

✓ Lesson Check Point

 Directions: Read the target words in the word box. In the first column, write the words with the letter "g" that have the /g/ sound, as in the word <u>gum</u>. In the second column, write the words with the letter "g" that have the /j/ sound, as in the word <u>gem</u>.

路线：读框中的目标词。在第一栏中，写上 g 发/g/音的单词。 如，英语单词 gum。在第二栏中，写上字母 g 发/j/音的词。 如，英语单词 gem。

Target Word Box				
digital	green	geese	ginger	page
germs	greet	gems	organ	gulf
grandson	glasses	large	sugar	engine
gate	gifts	gym	stage	orange

Hard letter "g" has
the /g/ sound
as in the word
<u>gum</u>

- gifts
- gate
- green
- greet
- sugar
- gulf
- geese
- organ
- glasses
- grandson

Soft letter "g" has
the /j/ sound
as in the word
<u>gem</u>

- gym
- page
- gems
- stage
- large
- germs
- orange
- digital
- engine
- ginger

Name: _____ Date: ___/___/_____ Score: _____

Lesson 7.3

Reading Words with the "gr" Letter Combination

Dictionary Skills/ Vocabulary

 Lesson Check Point

 Directions: Read each target word and its definition. Write the letter of the definition on the line of each target word. Use a dictionary or the Internet to check your answers.

路线：读每个目标词及其定义。在目标词前线上写上正确定义的 字母编号。用词典或通过互联网检查你的答案。

Target Words	Definitions
1. _b_ grabs	a. to make a big, positive impression
2. _a_ grand	b. to take something quickly with one's hand(s)
3. _e_ gravel	c. something that contains or is covered with oil
4. _c_ greasy	d. to hold something firmly with one's hand(s)
5. _d_ grip	e. a mixture of very small rocks and pebbles

 Directions: Read each sentence. Underline the word in the parentheses that correctly completes each sentence. Then, write the underlined word on the line.

路线：阅读每个句子。在括号中选择符合句子的词，并添加下划线。然后，在线上写出下划线单词。

6. Grandpa's driveway is made of _____gravel_____. (greasy, <u>gravel</u>)

7. I can't eat the burger because it is too _____greasy_____. (grabs, <u>greasy</u>)

8. The gloves give me a better _____grip_____ on the bars. (<u>grip</u>, grabbed)

9. Greg _____grabs_____ the books with both hands. (<u>grabs</u>, gravel)

10. At the dance, the girls made a _____grand_____ entrance. (<u>grand</u>, greasy)

Classwork

Name: _____ Date: ___/___/_____ Score: _____

Lesson 7.4

Reading Words with the "gl" Letter Combination

Dictionary Skills/ Vocabulary

✓ Lesson Check Point

Directions: Read each target word and its definition. Write the target word on the line in front of its meaning. Use a dictionary or the Internet to check your answers.

路线：读每个目标词及其定义。在目标词前线上写上正确定义的　字母编号。用词典或通过互联网检查你的答案。

Target Word Box				
glaze	globe	gloom	glossary	glowing

1. __glowing__   to shine brightly like a light or the sun
2. __gloom__   a state of sadness, hopelessness and/or depression
3. __glaze__   to spread a thin layer of something on a surface
4. __globe__   a three-dimensional, sphere shaped model of the earth
5. __glossary__ an alphabetical list of text-related words with definitions

Directions: Read each sentence. Underline the word in the parentheses that correctly completes each sentence. Then, write the underlined word on the line.

路线：阅读每个句子。在括号中选择符合句子的词，并添加下划 线。然后，在线上写出下划线单词。

6. The beautiful, blushing bride is __glowing__. (gloom, <u>glowing</u>)

7. Gerald plans to travel around the __globe__. (<u>globe</u>, glowing)

8. Gloria __glazed__ the chicken with barbecue sauce. (<u>glazed</u>, globe)

9. The bad report brought deep __gloom__ to the family. (glossary, <u>gloom</u>)

10. The book's __glossary__ helps me define difficult words. (<u>glossary</u>, glowing)

Answer Key

 Name: _____ Date: ___/___/_____ Score: _____

Lesson 7.4

Reading Words with the "gle" Letter Combination

✓ Lesson Check Point

 Directions: Read each target word. Find the "gle" letter combination and put a check (✓) in the column that identifies its position: beginning, within or end.

路线：读每个目标词。找到"gle"字母组合，并在栏中打勾(✓) 示意：开始，中间，结尾。

Target Words	Beginning (First 3 Letters)	Within	End (Last 3 Letters)
1. glee	✓		
2. angle			✓
3. mangled		✓	
4. gleaming	✓		
5. triangle			✓

 Directions: Read each target word. Put a check (✓) in the "yes" column if the "gle" letter combination has the /g/ + /ə/ + /l/ sounds. Put a check (✓) in the "no" column if the "gle" letter combination does not have the /g/ + /ə/ + /l/ sounds.

路线：读每个目标词。如果"gle"字母组合发/g/ + /ə/ + /l/的音，在"是"栏中打 勾(✓)。如果"gle"字母组合不发/g/ + /ə/ + /l/的音，在"没有"栏中打勾(✓)。

Target Words	Yes	No
6. glee		✓
7. angle	✓	
8. mangled	✓	
9. gleaming		✓
10. triangle	✓	

Classwork

 Name: _____ Date: ___/___/_____ Score: _____

Lesson 7.5

Reading Words with the "gh" Letter Combination

✓ Lesson Check Point

 Directions: Read each target word. Circle the word in the column that has the same "gh" sound as the target word.
路线：读每个目标词。圈出栏中与目标词含相同"gh"音的单词。

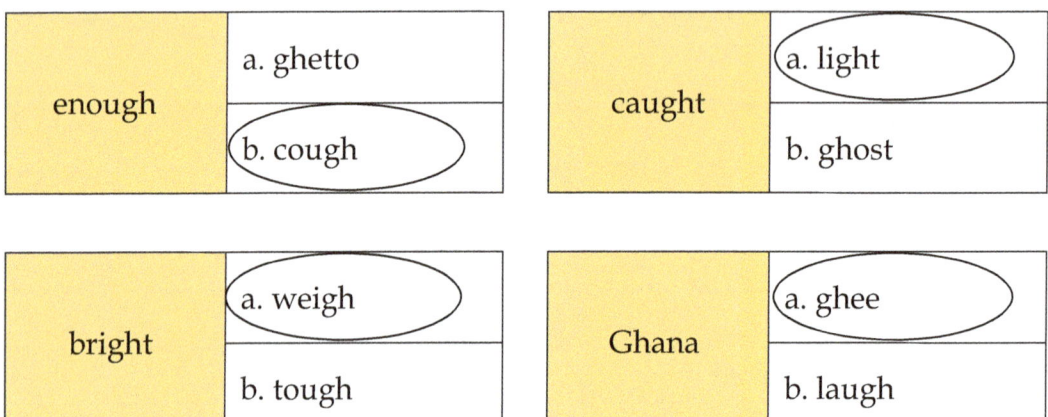

 Directions: Read each target word. Put a check (✓) under the correct column heading.
路线：读每个目标词。在符合要求的栏下打勾 (✓)。

Target Words	"gh" has the /g/ sound as in the word <u>ghetto</u>	"gh" has the /f/ sound as in the word <u>laugh</u>	"gh" is silent as in the word <u>light</u>
1. enough		✓	
2. caught			✓
3. bright			✓
4. Ghana	✓		

Name: _____   Date: ___/___/_____   Score: _____

Lesson 7.6
Reading Words with the "gn" Letter Combination

✓ **Lesson Check Point**

 Directions: Read each target word. Circle the word in the column that has the same "gn" sound(s) as the target word.
路线：读每个目标词。圈出栏中与目标词含相同"gn"音的单词。

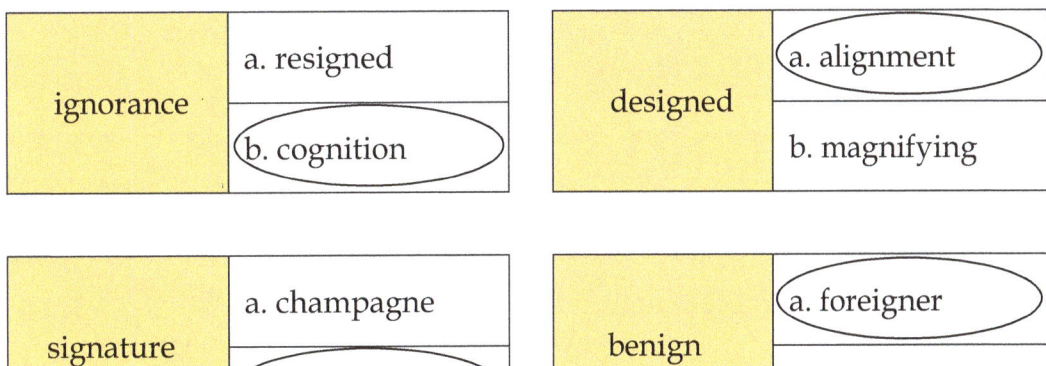

 Directions: Read each target word. Put a check (✓) under the correct column heading.
路线：读每个目标词。在符合要求的栏下打勾 (✓)。

Target Words	"gn" has the /g/ + /n/ sounds as in the word <u>ignite</u>	"gn" has the silent "g" + /n/ sound as in the word <u>sign</u>
1. ignorance	✓	
2. designed		✓
3. signature	✓	
4. benign		✓

Classwork

 Name: _____ Date: ___/___/_____ Score: _____

Lesson 7.7

Reading Words with a Silent Letter "g"

✓ **Lesson Check Point**

 Directions: Read the target words in the word box. Write the words that have a silent letter "g" in the first column. Write the words that do not have a silent letter "g" in the second column.

路线：读单词框中的目标词。在第一栏中写上含不发音 g 的词。 在第二栏中写上不带不发音 g 的词。

Target Word Box				
daughter	sleigh	image	hunger	signal
glance	fight	thought	campaign	dough
frog	dignify	sign	magnify	regent
elegant	neighbor	assign	grand	weigh

Letter "g" is silent

- sign
- fight
- dough
- assign
- weigh
- sleigh
- thought
- neighbor
- daughter
- campaign

Letter "g" has the /g/ or /j/ sound

- frog
- image
- glance
- dignify
- grand
- elegant
- signal
- regent
- hunger
- magnify

Unit G Lesson 7.7

Learn To Read English With Directions In Chinese

Answer Key

 Name: _____ Date:___/___/_____ Score:_____

The Reading Challenge

Lesson 7.8

Reading Multisyllable Words

✓ **Lesson Check Point**

 Directions: Read and divide each target word into syllables. Write each word and place a hyphen (-) between the syllables in the second column. Write the number of syllables in the third column. Use a dictionary or the Internet to check your answers.

路线：读目标词后，划分音节。写下每个词，在第二栏中写上音 节，用 (-) 连接。在第三栏写上音节数。用词典或通过互联网检 查你的答案。

Target Words	Words Divided into Syllables	Number of Syllables
1. grocery	gro-cer-y	3
2. Guyana	Guy-a-na	3
3. gardening	gar-den-ing	3
4. general	gen-er-al	3
5. glamorize	glam-or-ize	3
6. grandfather	grand-fa-ther	3
7. girlfriend	girl-friend	2
8. generous	gen-er-ous	3
9. guardian	guard-i-an	3
10. genetic	ge-net-ic	3

Classwork

Name: _____ Date: ___/___/_____ Score: _____

The Reading Challenge

Lesson 7.8

Reading Multisyllable Words

✓ Lesson Check Point

Directions: Read each target word. Circle the word in the row that is divided correctly into syllables. Use a dictionary or the Internet to check your answers.

路线：读每个目标词。圈出行中音节划分正确的词。用词典或通过互联网检查你的答案。

Model

galaxy	a. ga-lax-y	b. gal-ax-y ✓	c. gal-a-xy
1. glycerol	a. glyc-er-ol ✓	b. gly-cer-ol	c. glyc-e-rol
2. governess	a. go-ver-ness	b. gov-ern-ess	c. gov-er-ness ✓
3. general	a. gen-er-al ✓	b. ge-ner-al	c. gene-r-al
4. graduate	a. gra-du-ate	b. grad-u-ate ✓	c. grad-uat-e
5. granola	a. gra-nol-a	b. gra-no-la ✓	c. gran-ol-a
6. gestation	a. gest-a-tion	b. ge-sta-tion	c. ges-ta-tion ✓
7. germinate	a. ger-mi-nate ✓	b. germ-i-nate	c. ge-rmi-nate
8. gratify	a. grat-i-fy ✓	b. gra-tif-y	c. gr-ati-fy

Name: _____ Date: ___/___/_____ Score: _____

Answer Key

Lesson 7.9
Reading and Writing
Proper and Common Nouns and Adjectives

✓ **Lesson Check Point**

 Directions: Read the words in the word box. Put an (X) on the line next to each word that is written incorrectly. Remember that all proper nouns and proper adjectives are capitalized. Use a dictionary or the Internet to check your answers.

路线：读单词框中的词。在书写错误的单词旁边的线上打叉(X)。记得合适的名词和形容词需要大写。用词典或通过互联网检查你的答案。

Word Box					
X	Geology	X	gandhi	__	groom
X	Gym	X	Group	__	grammar
__	Greece	__	globe	X	georgetown
__	Guyana	X	germany	__	Ghana

 Directions: Read each unedited sentence and underline the word that is written incorrectly. Write each sentence correctly on the line.

路线：读每个未经编辑的句子，并给书写错误的词加下划线。在线上写上正确的句子。

Model
Ginger and <u>gene</u> are going to Georgetown, Guyana.
<u>Ginger and Gene are going to Georgetown, Guyana.</u>

1. The Gambia and <u>ghana</u> are amazing African countries.
<u>The Gambia and Ghana are amazing African countries.</u>

2. The bride and the <u>Groom</u> are getting married in Grenada.
<u>The bride and the groom are getting married in Grenada.</u>

3. Everyone says that Mr. Grant will be Georgia's <u>Governor</u>.
<u>Everyone says that Mr. Grant will be Georgia's governor.</u>

4. George and <u>gem</u> said, "Grandma has beautiful new glasses."
<u>George and Gem said, "Grandma has beautiful new glasses."</u>

Classwork

Name: _____ Date: ___/___/_____ Score: _____

Lesson 8.1

Reading Words with the Letter H/h

✓ Lesson Check Point

Directions: Read each target word. Find the letter "h" and put a check (✓) in the column that identifies its position: beginning, within or end.
路线：读每个目标词。找出字母 h 在栏中打勾 (✓) 示意： 开始，中间或末尾。

Target Words	Beginning (First Letter)	Within	End (Last Letter)
1. inch			✓
2. cheetah			✓
3. hallway	✓		
4. Fahrenheit		✓	
5. Savannah			✓

Directions: Read each sentence and underline the words that begin with the letter "h." Write all the underlined words in alphabetical order on the lines below.
路线：读每个句子，并给首字母为 h 的词加下划线。在下面的 线上按照字母顺序写出所有下划线标记的单词。

6. Barry's home is on top of the hill.

7. Henry lives in the center of Houston.

8. The hummingbirds' eggs are hatching.

9. The cats and hamsters are very hungry.

10. Heather Carrington is an honest person.

hamster   hatching   Heather
Henry   hill   home
honest   Houston   hummingbirds'
                 hungry

Unit H Lesson 8.1

Answer Key

 Name: _____ Date: ___/___/_____ Score: _____

Lesson 8.2

Reading Words with the Letter "h" Combinations:
"sh," "wh," "ch," "th," "rh," "ph" and "gh"

✓ **Lesson Check Point**

 Directions: Read the target words in the word box. Identify the words with the following letter combinations: "sh," "wh," "ch," "th," "rh," "ph" and "gh." Write the word on the line that shows the position of the letter combination: beginning, within or end.

路线：读框中的目标词。认识含下述字母组合的词："sh," "wh," "ch," "th," "rh," "ph" 和 "gh"。 在线上写出这些词，标示这些字母组 合的位置：开始，中间或末尾。

Target Word Box				
wheel	thanks	rhino	kitchen	sheep
dishes	paragraph	anywhere	phone	laugh
overheard	ghost	myrrh	nephew	brother
chocolate	south	goldfish	reach	caught

	Beginning	Within	End
sh	1. sheep	2. dishes	3. goldfish
wh	4. wheel	5. anywhere	
ch	6. chocolate	7. kitchen	8. reach
th	9. thanks	10. brother	11. south
rh	12. rhino	13. overheard	14. myrrh
ph	15. phone	16. nephew	17. paragraph
gh	18. ghost	19. caught	20. laugh

Classwork

Name: _____ Date: ___/___/_____ Score: _____

Lesson 8.2

Reading Words with the Letter "h" Combinations: "sh," "wh," "ch," "th," "rh," "ph," "gh" and "sch"

✓ **Lesson Check Point**

Directions: Read the target words in the word box. Identify the words with the following letter combinations: "sh," "wh," "ch," "th," "rh," "ph," "gh" and "sch." Write the target word that correctly completes each sentence on the line.

路线：读框中的目标词。认识带下述字母组合的词："sh," "wh," "ch," "th," "rh," "ph," "gh" 和 "sch"。 在线上写上正确目标词，完成 整个句子。

Target Word Box		
shower	Ghana	Children
Whales	theater	through
phones		Chemicals
school		rhombus

1. I am learning to read and write in _____school_____.

2. We are not allowed to have cellular ___phones___ in school.

3. The sun was shining brightly ___through___ the window.

4. Yesterday, Trevor used liquid soap during his ___shower___.

5. Brenda used her ruler to draw the shape of a ___rhombus___.

6. _Children_____ should obey their parents and teachers.

7. _Whales_____ are the largest mammals that live in the ocean.

8. The people from ____Ghana_____ speak many languages.

9. Thelma is hosting her birthday party at the movie ___theater___.

10. _Chemicals___ found in processed foods may harm your health.

Answer Key

 Name: _____ Date:___/___/_____ Score:_____

Lesson 8.3

Reading Words with a Silent Letter "h"

✓ **Lesson Check Point**

 Directions: Read the target words in the word box. Write the words that have a silent letter "h" in the first column. Write the words that do not have a silent letter "h" in the second column.

路线：读单词框中的目标词。在第一栏中写上含不发音 h 的词。在第二栏中写上不带不发音 h 的词。

Target Word Box				
inherent	beehive	unhappy	myrrh	dehydrate
exhibit	white	fright	hundred	holding
silhouette	behind	exhaust	honor	Fahrenheit
heirloom	house	comprehend	perhaps	whales

Letter "h" is silent

fright
white
exhaust
whales
myrrh
exhibit
honor
heirloom
silhouette
Fahrenheit

Letter "h" has the /h/ sound

house
behind
holding
hundred
beehive
inherent
unhappy
perhaps
dehydrate
comprehend

Classwork

Name: _____ Date: ___/___/_____ Score: _____

The Reading Challenge

Lesson 8.4

Reading Multisyllable Words

✓ Lesson Check Point

Directions: Read and divide each target word into syllables. Write each word and place a hyphen (-) between the syllables in the second column. Write the number of syllables in the third column. Use a dictionary or the Internet to check your answers.

路线：读目标词后，划分音节。写下每个词，在第二栏中写上音 节，用 (-) 连接。在第三栏写上音节数。用词典或通过互联网检 查你的答案。

Target Words	Words Divided into Syllables	Number of Syllables
1. hallway	hall-way	2
2. heartache	heart-ache	2
3. honeycomb	hon-ey-comb	3
4. hyperlink	hy-per-link	3
5. headlights	head-lights	2
6. harmonize	har-mo-nize	3
7. homonym	hom-o-nym	3
8. hardware	hard-ware	2
9. hesitant	hes-i-tant	3
10. hazelnut	ha-zel-nut	3

Unit H
Lesson 8.4

Learn To Read English With Directions In Chinese

Answer Key

Name: _____ Date: ___/___/_____ Score: _____

The Reading Challenge

Lesson 8.4

Reading Multisyllable Words

✓ **Lesson Check Point**

Directions: Read each target word. Circle the word in the row that is divided correctly into syllables. Use a dictionary or the Internet to check your answers.

路线：读每个目标词。圈出行中音节划分正确的词。用词典或通过互联网检查你的答案。

Model

heroic	a. he-roi-c	b. her-o-ic	**c. he-ro-ic** (circled)
1. hatchet	**a. hatch-et** (circled)	b. ha-tch-et	c. hatc-het
2. hazelnut	a. haz-e-lnut	b. haz-el-nut	**c. ha-zel-nut** (circled)
3. hexagon	a. he-xa-gon	**b. hex-a-gon** (circled)	c. hex-ag-on
4. historic	a. hi-stor-ic	**b. his-tor-ic** (circled)	c. hist-or-ic
5. halogen	a. hal-og-en	**b. hal-o-gen** (circled)	c. ha-lo-gen
6. hairdresser	**a. hair-dress-er** (circled)	b. ha-ir-dresser	c. hair-dresse-r
7. harvesting	a. harv-est-ing	b. har-ves-ting	**c. har-vest-ing** (circled)
8. handicap	**a. hand-i-cap** (circled)	b. han-dic-ap	c. hand-ic-ap

Classwork

Name: _____ Date: ___/___/_____ Score: _____

Lesson 8.5
Reading and Writing
Proper and Common Nouns and Adjectives

✓ Lesson Check Point

Directions: Read the words in the word box. Put an (X) on the line next to each word that is written incorrectly. Remember that all proper nouns and proper adjectives are capitalized. Use a dictionary or the Internet to check your answers.

路线：读单词框中的词。在书写错误的单词旁边的线上打叉(X)。记得合适的名词和形容词需要大写。用词典或通过互联网检查你 的答案。

Word Box					
__	Haiti	X	House	X	halifax
X	hebrew	X	Hexagon	__	Hawaii
__	horses	X	Haiku	__	hiccup
__	home	__	Hindu	X	hispanic

Directions: Read each unedited sentence and underline the word that is written incorrectly. Write each sentence correctly on the line.

路线：读每个未经编辑的句子，并给书写错误的词加下划线。在线 上写上正确的句子。

Model
Mr. Hitt has a big house on <u>hope</u> Avenue.
<u>Mr. Hitt has a big house on Hope Avenue.</u>

1. Henry is studying <u>haitian</u> history at Hunter College.
<u>Henry is studying Haitian history at Hunter College.</u>

2. The local historian lives in <u>hartford's</u> Historic District.
<u>The local historian lives in Hartford's Historic District.</u>

3. The thoroughbred <u>Horses</u> are galloping along Houston Harbor.
<u>The thoroughbred horses are galloping along Houston Harbor.</u>

4. <u>heather</u> is a hard working housekeeper at the Hilton Garden Hotel.
<u>Heather is a hard working housekeeper at the Hilton Garden Hotel.</u>

Answer Key

 Name: _____ Date: ___/___/_____ Score: _____

Lesson 9.1

Reading Words with the Letter I/i

✓ Lesson Check Point

 Directions: Read each target word. Find the letter "i" and put a check (✓) in the column that identifies its position: beginning, within or end.
路线：读每个目标词。找出字母 i 在栏中打勾 (✓) 示意： 开 始，中间或末尾。

Target Words	Beginning (First Letter)	Within	End (Last Letter)
1. incapable	✓		
2. Fuji			✓
3. alive		✓	
4. broccoli			✓
5. Ireland	✓		

 Directions: Read each target word. Read the words in the row and circle the word that has a different vowel "i" sound.
路线：读每个目标词。阅读这一行的词，圈出元音 i 发不同的词。

Target Words				
6. blimp	(child)	this	grim	lid
7. spin	fix	pin	dip	(bike)
8. trip	hip	(nine)	fin	pit
9. crib	big	dim	(mild)	six
10. king	hill	(kite)	grin	ship

Classwork

 Name: _____ Date: ___/___/_____ Score: _____

Lesson 9.2

Reading Words with the Short Vowel "i" Sound

✓ **Lesson Check Point**

 Directions: Read the words in the four boxes. Circle two words with the short vowel /ĭ/ sound. The anchor word for the short vowel /ĭ/ sound is <u>insect</u>.

路线：读四个框中的词。圈出含短元音 /ĭ/ 的两个词。锚点词词含短元音 /ĭ/ 为英语单词，insect。

(bin)	(sip)
child	mile

bike	(big)
(hid)	fine

dig	slim
bite	pike

line	kite
(crib)	(blip)

(tint)	(will)
like	nine

(twin)	pint
taxi	(list)

 Directions: Read the words in the four boxes. Circle two words that rhyme. Rhyming words have the same ending sound, such as <u>hip</u> and <u>dip</u>.

路线：读四个框中的词。圈出押韵的两个词。押韵词有同样的尾音，如，英语单词 hip 和 dip。

pine	(bib)
hike	(rib)

(clip)	wife
rice	(slip)

(fit)	(sit)
life	nice

mile	lime
(six)	(mix)

hide	(him)
(dim)	mice

(win)	pipe
(tin)	side

Answer Key

Name: _____ Date: ___/___/_____ Score: _____

Lesson 9.2

Reading & Writing Words with the Short Vowel "i" Sound

✓ **Lesson Check Point**

Directions: Read each sentence and underline three words with the short vowel /ĭ/ sound. Then, write the underlined words on the lines below. The anchor word for the short vowel /ĭ/ sound is <u>insect</u>.

路线：读每个句子，划出含短元音/ĭ/的三个词。 然后， 在下面的划线处 写上带下划线的词。锚点词为短元音/ĭ/的英语单 词，insect。

Model

<u>Jim</u> placed a <u>big</u> cup of ice on the <u>windowsill</u>.

    Jim   big   windowsill

1. Irene gave <u>Jill</u> a <u>big</u> <u>wig</u>.

    Jill   big   wig

2. The <u>kids</u> <u>did</u> not <u>kick</u> the ball on the field.

    kids   did   kick

3. <u>Billy</u> said, "<u>Tim</u> <u>licked</u> the ice pop."

    Billy   Tim   licked

4. <u>Milly</u> <u>sipped</u> the medium-sized <u>drink</u>.

    Milly   sipped   drink

5. The <u>big</u> <u>dishes</u> used to serve the pizza are by the <u>sink</u>.

    big   dishes   sink

Classwork

 Name: _____ Date: ___/___/_____ Score: _____

Lesson 9.3

Reading Words with the Long Vowel "i" Sound

✓ **Lesson Check Point**

 Directions: Read the words in the four boxes. Circle two words with the long vowel /ī/ sound. The anchor word for the long vowel /ī/ sound is ice.

路线：读四个框中的词。圈出带长元音/ī/的两个词。 锚点词为 含长元音 /ī/ 的英语单词 ice。

brain	(wild)		bill	(bike)		(hike)	taxi
kick	(fine)		(lime)	mini		sick	(dice)

(mine)	pink		chili	sing		pain	(vile)
train	(tile)		(mime)	(tide)		miss	(side)

 Directions: Read the words in the four boxes. Circle two words that rhyme. Rhyming words have the same ending sound, such as rice and nice.

路线：读四个框中的词。圈出押韵的两个词。押韵的词含同样的 尾音。如, 英语单词 rice 和 nice。

lift	(dime)		(nine)	link		bite	fill
pick	(time)		kids	(pine)		(kite)	crib

(line)	skill		like	(pike)		(life)	rib
(vine)	Mali		drill	dim		lick	(wife)

Name: _____ Date: ___/___/_____ Score: _____

Lesson 9.3

Reading & Writing Words with the Long Vowel "i" Sound

✓ **Lesson Check Point**

Directions: Read each sentence and underline three words with the long vowel /ī/ sound. Then, write the underlined words on the lines below. The anchor word for the long vowel /ī/ sound is ice.

路线：读每个句子，给带长元音/ī/的三个词加下划线。然后，在下面的划线处写上带下划线的词。锚点词为长元音 /ī/ 的英 语 单词, ice。

Model

David and I flew our big, white kite along the riverbank.

      I   white   kite

1. Brian has to fix his mountain bike's tire.

    Brian   bike's   tire

2. Mike went outside to climb the steep hill.

    Mike   outside   climb

3. Jill said, "The bride has a nice, white dress."

    bride   nice   white

4. Irene's husband retired from working as a firefighter.

    Irene's   retired   firefighter

5. The principal invited the entire class to his tiny office.

    invited   entire   tiny

Unit I Lesson 9.3

Classwork

Name: _____ Date:___/___/_____ Score:_____

Review Lessons 9.2 & 9.3

Reading Short Vowel and Long Vowel Words

✓ **Lesson Check Point**

Directions: Read the target words in the word box. In the first column, write the words that have the short vowel /ĭ/ sound, as in the word <u>insect</u>. In the second column, write the words that have the long vowel /ī/ sound, as in the word <u>ice</u>.

路线：读框中的目标词。在第一栏写上含短元音/ĭ/的词。如，英语单词 insect。在第二栏写上含长元音/ī/的单词。如，英语单词 ice。

Target Word Box				
child	dinner	trip	bill	gift
tie	hint	I	pink	diner
hi	bike	diet	skim	client
inward	pie	lint	ripe	disk

Letter "i" has the /ĭ/ sound as in the word <u>insect</u>

- lint
- trip
- bill
- gift
- disk
- hint
- pink
- skim
- inward
- dinner

Letter "i" has the /ī/ sound as in the word <u>ice</u>

- I
- hi
- pie
- tie
- bike
- diet
- ripe
- child
- client
- diner

Answer Key

 Name: _____ Date: ___/___/_____ Score: _____

Lesson 9.4

Reading Words with Letter "i" Vowel Pairs

 Lesson Check Point

Directions: Read each target word. Circle the word in the column that has the same vowel "ia," "ie," "io" or "iu" sound(s) as the target word.
路线：读每个目标词。圈出栏中含和目标词一样元音"ia,""ie,""io"或"iu"的词。

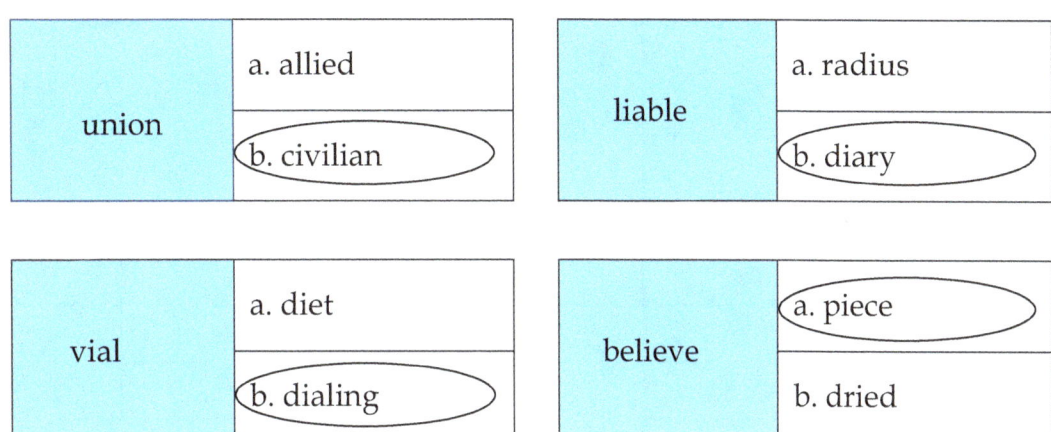

 Directions: Read each target word. Put a check (✓) under the correct column heading.
路线：读每个目标词。在符合要求的栏下打勾 (✓)。

Target Words	Words have the long "i" sound as in the word <u>dial</u>	Words do not have the long "i" sound
1. union		✓
2. liable	✓	
3. vial	✓	
4. believe		✓

Classwork

Name: _____ Date:___/___/_____ Score:_____

Lesson 9.5

Reading Words with the Final Letter "i"

✓ **Lesson Check Point**

Directions: Read each target word. Find the letter "i" and put a check (✓) in the column that identifies its position within the syllable.
路线：读每个目标词。找到字母 i，在栏中打勾(✓)标示其在 音节中的 位置。

Target Words	"i" is at the end of a one syllable word	"i" is at the end of the first syllable	"i" is at the end of a multi-syllable word
1. hi	✓		
2. final		✓	
3. alibi			✓
4. iron		✓	
5. dinosaur		✓	

Directions: Read each target word. Put a check (✓) under the correct column heading.
路线：读每个目标词。在符合要求的栏下打勾 (✓)。

Target Words	"i" has the /ĭ/ sound as in the word insect	"i" has the /ī/ sound as in the word bike	"i" has the /ə/ sound as in the word pencil	"i" is silent as in the word maid
6. kite		✓		
7. pilgrim			✓	
8. himself	✓			
9. business				✓
10. utensil			✓	

Answer Key

 Name: _____ Date: ___/___/_____ Score: _____

Lesson 9.6

Reading Letter "i" Words with the Schwa Vowel Sound

✓ Lesson Check Point

 Directions: Read each target word. Circle the word in the column that has the same "i" sound as the target word.

路线：读每个目标词。圈出栏中与目标词含相同 i 音的单词。

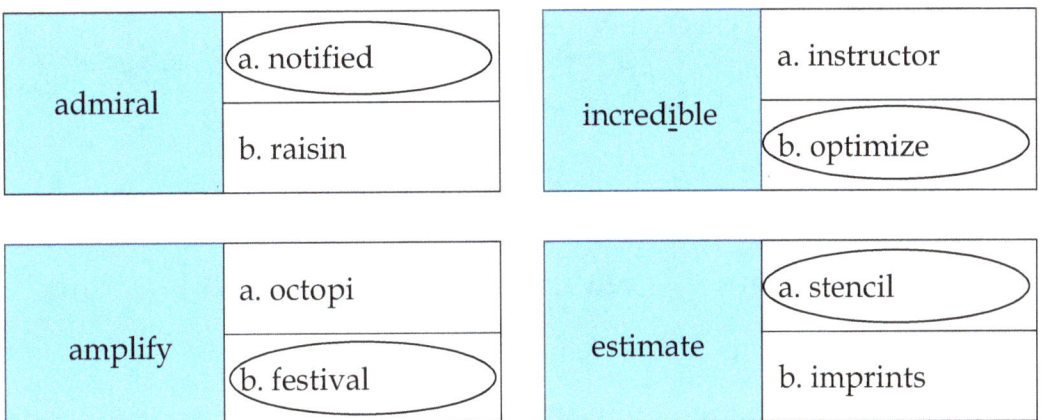

 Directions: Read each sentence and underline the letter "i" word that has the schwa vowel /ə/ sound. The anchor word for the letter "i" schwa vowel sound is <u>pencil</u>.

路线：读每个句子。给含字母 i 且发施瓦/ə/音的单词加下划线。锚点词为含字母 i 且发施瓦音的英语单词，pencil。

1. I will <u>notify</u> the girls about the field trip.

2. The child is experiencing pain in his <u>nostrils</u>.

3. Trinidad's <u>carnival</u> is a major cultural event.

4. The <u>binoculars</u> are inside my white briefcase.

5. I bought vanilla ice cream at the <u>convenience</u> store.

6. The president encouraged every <u>individual</u> to vote.

Classwork

Name: _____ Date: ___/___/_____ Score: _____

Lesson 9.7

Reading Words with the "ir" Letter Combination

Dictionary Skills/ Vocabulary

✓ Lesson Check Point

Directions: Read each target word and its definition. Write the letter of the definition on the line of each target word. Use a dictionary or the Internet to check your answers.
路线：读每个目标词及其定义。在目标词前线上写上正确定义的 字母编号。用词典或通过互联网检查你的答案。

Target Words	Definitions
1. _c_ shirt	a. a bushy-tailed rodent that lives in a tree or a burrow
2. _e_ birds	b. females
3. _a_ squirrel	c. clothing worn on the upper part of the body
4. _d_ twirl	d. to spin or turn something around with one's fingers
5. _b_ girls	e. egg-laying animals that have wings

Directions: Read each sentence and write the target word that completes the sentence.
路线：读每个句子，写上正确的单词，完成整个句子。

6. My white ____shirt____ has a clean collar.

7. The cheerleaders ____twirl____ their batons.

8. The ____girls____ like to eat ice cream cones.

9. Millions of ____birds____ migrate along the flyway.

10. The ____squirrel____ climbed up the tree quickly.

Learn To Read English With Directions In Chinese   108   Copyrighted Material

Name: _____ Date: ___/___/_____ Score: _____

Lesson 9.8

Reading Letter "i" Words with the Long Vowel "e" Sound

✓ **Lesson Check Point**

 Directions: Read each target word. Circle the word in the column that has the same "i" sound as the target word.

路线：读每个目标词。圈出栏中含有和目标词一样 i 音的单词。

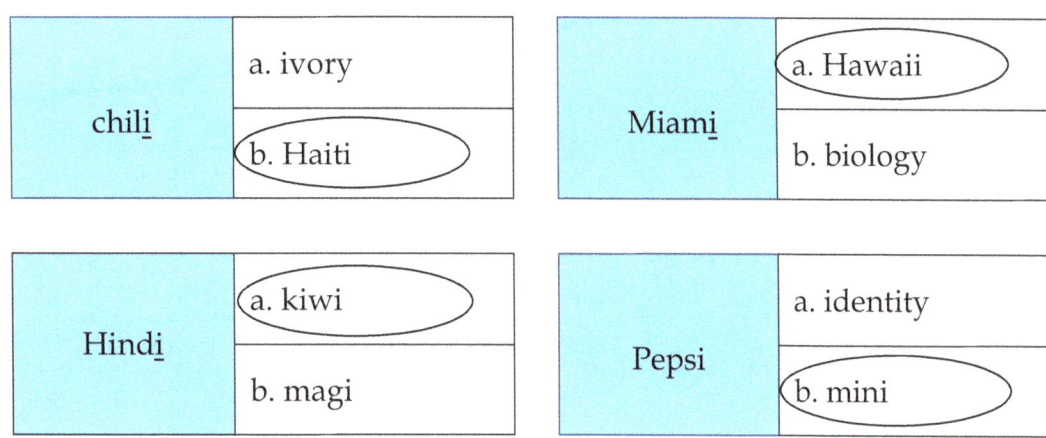

 Directions: Read each sentence and underline the letter "i" word that has the long vowel /ē/ sound. Then, write the word on the line. The anchor word, taxi has a letter "i" that represents the long vowel /ē/ sound.

路线：读每个句子，给单词含 i 且发长元音/ē/音的单词加下划 线。然后，在线上写出这个单词。描点词 taxi 有一个字母 i，发 长元音/ē/。

1. It is not wise to go <u>skiing</u> at night.   ___skiing___

2. Jim and Mike enjoy eating <u>pita</u> bread.   ___pita___

3. The children admire the <u>police</u> officers.   ___police___

4. My family likes to eat dinner on the <u>patio</u>.   ___patio___

5. I will use the sewing <u>machine</u> to sew a pillow.   ___machine___

6. Baked <u>ziti</u> is a classic Italian-American dish.   ___ziti___

Classwork

Name: _____ Date: ___/___/_____ Score: _____

Lesson 9.9

Reading Words with a Silent Letter "i"

✓ Lesson Check Point

Directions: Read the target words in the word box. Write the words that have a silent letter "i" in the first column. Write the words that do not have a silent letter "i" in the second column.

路线：读单词框中的目标词。在第一栏中写上含不发音 i 的词。 在第二栏中写上不带不发音i的词。

Target Word Box				
aside	camping	Jamaica	sailboat	stained
waist	afraid	giggles	bail	fifteen
bigger	city	hiking	railroad	distinct
attaining	finish	suit	helping	again

Letter "i" is silent

suit
bail
again
waist
afraid
stained
railroad
Jamaica
sailboat
attaining

Letter "i" has a letter "i" sound

city
aside
finish
hiking
bigger
giggles
helping
distinct
fifteen
camping

Answer Key

 Name: _____ Date: ___/___/_____   Score: _____

Unit Review - I/i

Reading Words with Vowel "i" Sounds: /ĭ/, /ī/, /ə/ & Silent

✓ Lesson Check Point

 Directions: Read each target word. Circle the word in the column that has the same "i" sound as the target word.
路线：读每个目标词。圈出栏中含有和目标词一样 i 音的单词。

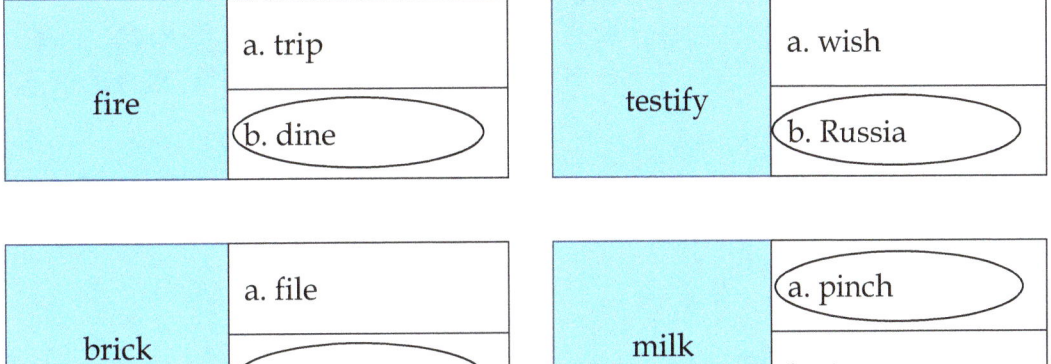

 Directions: Read each target word. Put a check (✓) under the correct column heading.
路线：读每个目标词。在符合要求的栏下打勾 (✓)。

Target Words	"i" has the /ĭ/ sound as in the word <u>insect</u>	"i" has the /ī/ sound as in the word <u>bike</u>	"i" has the /ə/ sound as in the word <u>pencil</u>	"i" is silent as in the word <u>maid</u>
1. fire		✓		
2. testify			✓	
3. brick	✓			
4. milk	✓			

Classwork

 Name: _____ Date:___/___/_____ Score: _____

The Reading Challenge

Lesson 9.10

Reading Multisyllable Words

✓ Lesson Check Point

 Directions: Read and divide each target word into syllables. Write each word and place a hyphen (-) between the syllables in the second column. Write the number of syllables in the third column. Use a dictionary or the Internet to check your answers.

路线：读目标词后，划分音节。写下每个词，在第二栏中写上音 节，用 (-) 连接。在第三栏写上音节数。用词典或通过互联网检 查你的答案。

Target Words	Words Divided into Syllables	Number of Syllables
1. drinking	drink-ing	2
2. mentoring	men-tor-ing	3
3. spider	spi-der	2
4. Haiti	Hai-ti	2
5. kiwi	ki-wi	2
6. providing	pro-vid-ing	3
7. diner	din-er	2
8. beside	be-side	2
9. mineral	min-er-al	3
10. fictional	fic-tion-al	3

Answer Key

 Name: _____ Date:___/___/_____ Score:_____

The Reading Challenge

Lesson 9.10

Reading Multisyllable Words

✓ **Lesson Check Point**

 Directions: Read each target word. Circle the word in the row that is divided correctly into syllables. Use a dictionary or the Internet to check your answers.

路线：读每个目标词。圈出行中音节划分正确的词。用词典或通过互联网检查你的答案。

Model

| interesting | a. (in-ter-est-ing) | b. int-er-est-ing | c. inte-rest-ing |

| 1. bifocal | a. bif-o-cal | b. (bi-fo-cal) | c. bi-foc-al |

| 2. hibernate | a. (hi-ber-nate) | b. hib-er-nate | c. hi-bern-ate |

| 3. Malawi | a. (Ma-la-wi) | b. Ma-law-i | c. Mal-a-wi |

| 4. tribunal | a. trib-un-al | b. trib-u-nal | c. (tri-bu-nal) |

| 5. safari | a. (sa-fa-ri) | b. saf-a-ri | c. sa-far-i |

| 6. unicorn | a. (u-ni-corn) | b. un-i-corn | c. u-nic-orn |

| 7. imagine | a. im-a-gine | b. i-ma-gine | c. (i-mag-ine) |

| 8. dialect | a. di-ale-ct | b. (di-a-lect) | c. dial-e-ct |

Classwork

Name: _____ Date: ___/___/_____ Score: _____

Lesson 9.11

Reading and Writing

Proper and Common Nouns and Adjectives

✓ **Lesson Check Point**

Directions: Read the words in the word box. Put an (X) on the line next to each word that is written incorrectly. Remember that all proper nouns and proper adjectives are capitalized. Use a dictionary or the Internet to check your answers.

路线：读单词框中的词。在书写错误的单词旁边的线上打叉(X)。记得合适的名词和形容词需要大写。用词典或通过互联网检查你 的答案。

Word Box					
__	identify	X	illinois	X	Invincible
__	Iroquois	X	Insanity	__	illusion
__	Indo-European	__	itching	__	Ivory Coast
X	italy	X	irish	X	ida Mount

Directions: Read each unedited sentence and underline the word that is written incorrectly. Write each sentence correctly on the line.

路线：读每个未经编辑的句子，并给书写错误的词加下划线。在线 上写上正确的句子。

Model
New Delhi and Indore are beautiful cities in <u>india</u>.
<u>New Delhi and Indore are beautiful cities in India.</u>

1. My teacher said, "The <u>incas</u> inhabited the Americas."
<u>My teacher said, "The Incas inhabited the Americas."</u>

2. In April, Isabella will attend <u>iowa</u> Community College.
<u>In April, Isabella will attend Iowa Community College.</u>

3. Ida looked up information about <u>indonesia</u> on the Internet.
<u>Ida looked up information about Indonesia on the Internet.</u>

4. On <u>independence</u> Day, Ian ignited a massive display of fireworks.
<u>On Independence Day, Ian ignited a massive display of fireworks.</u>

Answer Key

Name: _____ Date: ___/___/_____   Score: _____

Lesson 10.1

Reading Words with the Letter J/j

✓ **Lesson Check Point**

Directions: Read each target word. Find the letter "j" and put a check (✓) in the column that identifies its position: beginning, within or end.
路线：读每个目标词。找出字母j在栏中打勾(✓)示意： 开始，中间 或末尾。

Target Words	Beginning (First Letter)	Within	End (Last Letter)
1. conjunct		✓	
2. jacket	✓		
3. jersey	✓		
4. reject		✓	
5. jumbo	✓		

Directions: Read each sentence and underline the words that begin with the letter "j." Write all the underlined words in alphabetical order on the lines below.
路线：读每个句子，并给首字母为 j 的词加下划线。在下面的 线上按照字母顺序写出所有下划线标记的单词。

6. Henry has a <u>jug</u> of apple <u>juice</u>.

7. The <u>jockey's</u> horse is named <u>Jupiter</u>.

8. We flew in a <u>jet</u> from New York to <u>Japan</u>.

9. Hadia took a long <u>journey</u> through the <u>jungle</u>.

10. In <u>January</u>, Mrs. Adams is going to <u>Jacksonville</u>, Florida.

Jacksonville   January   Japan
jet   jockey's   journey
juice   jug   jungle
                   Jupiter

Classwork

 Name: _____ Date: ___/___/_____ Score: _____

The Reading Challenge

Lesson 10.2

Reading Multisyllable Words

✓ **Lesson Check Point**

 Directions: Read and divide each target word into syllables. Write each word and place a hyphen (-) between the syllables in the second column. Write the number of syllables in the third column. Use a dictionary or the Internet to check your answers.

路线：读目标词后，划分音节。写下每个词，在第二栏中写上音 节，用 (-) 连接。在第三栏写上音节数。用词典或通过互联网检 查你的答案。

Target Words	Words Divided into Syllables	Number of Syllables
1. jackpot	jack-pot	2
2. joey	jo-ey	2
3. jealous	jeal-ous	2
4. judgmental	judg-men-tal	3
5. journal	jour-nal	2
6. judo	ju-do	2
7. Japanese	Jap-a-nese	3
8. joyously	joy-ous-ly	3
9. justify	jus-ti-fy	3
10. juicy	juic-y	2

Answer Key

 Name: _____ Date: ___/___/_____ Score: _____

The Reading Challenge

Lesson 10.2

Reading Multisyllable Words

✓ **Lesson Check Point**

 Directions: Read each target word. Circle the word in the row that is divided correctly into syllables. Use a dictionary or the Internet to check your answers.

路线：读每个目标词。圈出行中音节划分正确的词。用词典或通过互联网检查你的答案。

Model

| janitor | a. ja-ni-tor | b. jan-it-or | (c. jan-i-tor) |

| 1. January | (a. Jan-u-ar-y) | b. Jan-u-ary | c. Jan-uar-y |

| 2. jeopardize | (a. jeop-ard-ize) | b. jeop-ar-dize | c. jeo-pard-ize |

| 3. jubilant | a. ju-bila-nt | (b. ju-bi-lant) | c. ju-bil-ant |

| 4. javelin | a. javel-in | (b. jave-lin) | c. ja-vel-in |

| 5. judgmental | (a. judg-men-tal) | b. jud-gmen-tal | c. judg-ment-al |

| 6. jubilance | (a. ju-bi-lance) | b. ju-bil-ance | c. jub-i-lance |

| 7. justify | a. ju-sti-fy | b. jus-tif-y | (c. jus-ti-fy) |

| 8. jalopy | a. jal-o-py | (b. ja-lop-y) | c. jal-op-y |

Learn To Read English With Directions In Chinese Copyrighted Material

Classwork

Name: _____ Date:___/___/_____ Score: _____

Lesson 10.3

Reading and Writing

Proper and Common Nouns and Adjectives

 Lesson Check Point

 Directions: Read the words in the word box. Put an (X) on the line next to each word that is written incorrectly. Remember that all proper nouns and proper adjectives are capitalized. Use a dictionary or the Internet to check your answers.
路线：读单词框中的词。在书写错误的单词旁边的线上打叉(X)。记得合适的名词和形容词需要大写。用词典或通过互联网检查你 的答案。

Word Box					
__	Jasmine	X	jupiter	__	jigsaw
X	june	__	jelly	X	january
__	jersey	__	jockey	X	Juice
X	japan	X	Jewelry	__	Jackson

 Directions: Read each unedited sentence and underline the word that is written incorrectly. Write each sentence correctly on the line.
路线：读每个未经编辑的句子，并给书写错误的词加下划线。在线 上写上正确的句子。

Model
Joey and his family live in New <u>jersey</u>.
<u>Joey and his family live in New Jersey.</u>

1. In <u>january</u>, Jack will wear a warm jacket.
<u>In January, Jack will wear a warm jacket.</u>

2. In <u>june</u>, Jordan had five jars of jalapenos.
<u>In June, Jordan had five jars of jalapenos.</u>

3. The kids are playing with a <u>Jigsaw</u> puzzle and a jet.
<u>The kids are playing with a jigsaw puzzle and a jet.</u>

4. <u>jillian</u> has a new job at Johnson and Johnson Incorporated.
<u>Jillian has a new job at Johnson and Johnson Incorporated.</u>

Answer Key

 Name: _____ Date: ___/___/_____ Score: _____

Lesson 11.1

Reading Words with the Letter K/k

✓ Lesson Check Point

 Directions: Read each target word. Find the letter "k" and put a check (✓) in the column that identifies its position: beginning, within or end.
路线：读每个目标词。找出字母 k 在栏中打勾 (✓) 示意： 开 始，中间 或末尾。

Target Words	Beginning (First Letter)	Within	End (Last Letter)
1. shock			✓
2. king	✓		
3. choke		✓	
4. homework			✓
5. keycard	✓		

 Directions: Read each sentence and underline the words that begin with the letter "k." Write all the underlined words in alphabetical order on the lines below.
路线：读每个句子，并给首字母为 k 的词加下划线。在下面的 线上按照字母顺序写出所有下划线标记的单词。

6. <u>Kangaroos</u> and <u>koalas</u> live in Australia.

7. Alex is learning to <u>kick</u> in his <u>karate</u> class.

8. <u>King</u> George III had a very powerful <u>kingdom</u>.

9. My friend, <u>Karen</u>, was born in <u>Kingston</u>, Jamaica.

10. Some <u>keys</u> on the computer <u>keyboard</u> are not working.

Kangaroos   karate   Karen
keyboard   keys   kick
King   kingdom   Kingston
    koalas

Classwork

Name: _____ Date: ___/___/_____ Score: _____

Lesson 11.2

Reading Words with the Letter "k" and "ck" Letter Combination

✓ **Lesson Check Point**

Directions: Read each target word. Put a check (✓) in the second column if the target word has one vowel. Put a check (✓) in the third column if the target word has two vowels.

路线：读每个目标词。如果目标词有一个元音，在第二栏中打勾 (✓)。如果目标词有两个元音，在第三栏中打勾(✓)。

Target Words	Words with 1 Vowel	Words with 2 Vowels
1. pike		✓
2. smack	✓	
3. sneak		✓
4. lock	✓	
5. broke		✓

Directions: Read each target word in the first column and write the number of vowels within the word in the second column. Read each target word in the third column and write the number of vowels within the word in the fourth column.

路线：读第一栏中的目标词，在第二栏中写出单词含有的元音数。读第三栏 的目标词，在第四栏中写上单词含有的元音数。

Target Words	Number of Vowels	Target Words	Number of Vowels
6. stoke	2	stock	1
7. smock	1	smoke	2
8. Blake	2	black	1
9. tack	1	take	2
10. pick	1	pike	2

Answer Key

 Name: _____ Date:___/___/_____ Score:_____

Lesson 11.3

Reading Words with the "kle" Letter Combination

✓ Lesson Check Point

 Directions: Read each target word. Find the "kle" letter combination and put a check (✓) in the column that identifies its position: beginning, within or end.

路线：读每个目标词。找到"kle"字母组合，并在栏中打勾(✓)示意：开始，中间，或末尾。

Target Words	Beginning (First 3 Letters)	Within	End (Last 3 Letters)
1. knuckle			✓
2. Kleenex	✓		
3. anklets		✓	
4. sparkles		✓	
5. wrinkle			✓

 Directions: Read each target word. Put a check (✓) in the "yes" column if the "kle" letter combination has the /k/ + /ə/ + /l/ sounds. Put a check (✓) in the "no" column if the "kle" letter combination does not have the /k/ + /ə/ + /l/ sounds.

路线：读每个目标词。如果"kle"字母组合发/k/ + /ə/ + /l/的音，在"是"栏中打 勾(✓)。如果"kle"字母组合不发/k/ + /ə/ + /l/的音，在"没有"栏中打勾(✓)。

Target Words	Yes	No
6. knuckle	✓	
7. Kleenex		✓
8. anklets		✓
9. sparkles	✓	
10. wrinkle	✓	

Classwork

 Name: _____ Date: ___/___/_____ Score: _____

Lesson 11.4

Reading Words with a Silent Letter "k"

✓ Lesson Check Point

 Directions: Read the target words in the word box. Write the words that have a silent letter "k" in the first column. Write the words that do not have a silent letter "k" in the second column.

路线：读单词框中的目标词。在第一栏中写上含不发音 k 的词。 在第二栏中写上不带不发音 k 的词。

Target Word Box				
knee	known	doorknob	seeking	knead
shaking	parking	knocking	keyboard	knew
keeping	karate	kennel	knap	sharks
knish	knives	knuckle	milky	kneed

Letter "k" is silent	Letter "k" has the /k/ sound
knee	milky
knew	knish
knap	sharks
knead	karate
kneed	kennel
known	parking
knives	seeking
knuckle	shaking
doorknob	keeping
knocking	keyboard

Answer Key

Name: _____ Date: ___/___/_____ Score: _____

The Reading Challenge

Lesson 11.5

Reading Multisyllable Words

 Lesson Check Point

 Directions: Read and divide each target word into syllables. Write each word and place a hyphen (-) between the syllables in the second column. Write the number of syllables in the third column. Use a dictionary or the Internet to check your answers.

路线：读目标词后，划分音节。写下每个词，在第二栏中写上音 节，用 (-) 连接。在第三栏写上音节数。用词典或通过互联网检 查你的答案。

Target Words	Words Divided into Syllables	Number of Syllables
1. kayak	kay-ak	2
2. Kenya	Ken-ya	2
3. Korean	Ko-re-an	3
4. kindly	kind-ly	2
5. ketchup	ketch-up	2
6. keyboard	key-board	2
7. Kuwaiti	Ku-wait-i	3
8. kidnap	kid-nap	2
9. knowledge	knowl-edge	2
10. kudos	ku-dos	2

Classwork

Name: _____ Date: ___/___/_____ Score: _____

The Reading Challenge

Lesson 11.5

Reading Multisyllable Words

✓ **Lesson Check Point**

Directions: Read each target word. Circle the word in the row that is divided correctly into syllables. Use a dictionary or the Internet to check your answers.

路线：读每个目标词。圈出行中音节划分正确的词。用词典或通过互联网检查你的答案。

Model

| kangaroo | a. kang-a-roo | **b. kan-ga-roo** (circled) | c. kan-gar-oo |

1. karate	**a. ka-ra-te** (circled)	b. ka-rate	c. kar-ate
2. kilobyte	a. ki-lo-byte	**b. kil-o-byte** (circled)	c. kil-ob-yte
3. Kentucky	a. Ken-tuc-ky	b. Kent-uck-y	**c. Ken-tuck-y** (circled)
4. kilowatt	a. ki-lo-watt	**b. kil-o-watt** (circled)	c. ki-low-att
5. keratin	a. ke-ra-tin	b. ker-at-in	**c. ker-a-tin** (circled)
6. Korea	a. Ko-r-ea	**b. Ko-re-a** (circled)	c. Kor-e-a
7. koala	**a. ko-a-la** (circled)	b. koa-la	c. ko-ala
8. kilogram	a. ki-log-ram	b. ki-lo-gram	**c. kil-o-gram** (circled)

Unit K Lesson 11.5

Answer Key

 Name: _____ Date: ___/___/_____ Score: _____

Lesson 11.6

Reading and Writing

Proper and Common Nouns and Adjectives

✓ Lesson Check Point

 Directions: Read the words in the word box. Put an (X) on the line next to each word that is written incorrectly. Remember that all proper nouns and proper adjectives are capitalized. Use a dictionary or the Internet to check your answers.

路线：读单词框中的词。在书写错误的单词旁边的线上打叉(X)。记得合适的名词和形容词需要大写。用词典或通过互联网检查你 的答案。

Word Box		
__ Kenya	X key Largo	__ Korea
X Kept	__ Kensington	X Know
X Kid	__ knock	__ knight
X kansas	X kentucky	__ kind

 Directions: Read each unedited sentence and underline the word that is written incorrectly. Write each sentence correctly on the line.

路线：读每个未经编辑的句子，并给书写错误的词加下划线。在线 上写上正确的句子。

Model
Helen <u>keller</u> was a kind person.
<u>Helen Keller was a kind person.</u>

1. <u>karen</u> and Kim speak Korean fluently.
<u>Karen and Kim speak Korean fluently.</u>

2. Kimberly is going to <u>kingston</u>, Jamaica.
<u>Kimberly is going to Kingston, Jamaica.</u>

3. My best friend, Kara, is from <u>kuwait</u>.
<u>My best friend, Kara, is from Kuwait.</u>

4. Kennedy and I are reading about <u>king</u> George III.
<u>Kennedy and I are reading about King George III.</u>

Classwork

Name: _____ Date: ___/___/_____ Score: _____

Lesson 12.1

Reading Words with the Letter L/l

✓ **Lesson Check Point**

Directions: Read each target word. Find the letter "l" and put a check (✓) in the column that identifies its position: beginning, within or end.
路线：读每个目标词。找出字母 l 在栏中打勾 (✓) 示意：开始，中间或末尾。

Target Words	Beginning (First Letter)	Within	End (Last Letter)
1. kneel			✓
2. imply		✓	
3. leave	✓		
4. juvenile		✓	
5. lasting	✓		

Directions: Read each sentence and underline the words that begin with the letter "l." Write all the underlined words in alphabetical order on the lines below.
路线：读每个句子，并给首字母为 l 的词加下划线。在下面的线上按照字母顺序写出所有下划线标记的单词。

6. The <u>little</u> <u>light</u> bulb is very bright.

7. We are <u>learning</u> about <u>Lewis</u> and Clark.

8. Abraham <u>Lincoln</u> was a brilliant <u>lawyer</u>.

9. My friend, Tim, enjoys <u>licking</u> cherry <u>lollipops</u>.

10. Everyone in my <u>Latin</u> class speaks another <u>language</u>.

language   Latin   lawyer
learning   Lewis   licking
light   Lincoln   little
                lollipops

Answer Key

 Name: _____ Date: ___/___/_____ Score: _____

Lesson 12.2

Reading Words with the Letter "l" Combinations:
"cl," "fl," "pl" & "sl"

Dictionary Skills/ Vocabulary

✓ Lesson Check Point

 Directions: Read each target word and its definition. Write the target word on the line in front of its meaning. Use a dictionary or the Internet to check your answers.

路线：读每个目标词及其定义。在目标词前线上写上正确定义的 字母编号。用词典或通过互联网检查你的答案。

Target Word Box				
class	flowers	placed	play	sleet

1. __play__   the act of doing something fun
2. __sleet__   small icy pieces that fall from the sky
3. __flowers__   the colorful part of a plant that contains seeds
4. __placed__   to put something in a particular position or location
5. __class__   group of students who is taught by the same teacher

 Directions: Read each sentence. Underline the word in the parentheses that correctly completes each sentence. Then, write the underlined word on the line.

路线：阅读每个句子。在括号中选择符合句子的词，并添加下划线。然后，在线上写出下划线单词。

6. I _____placed_____ two plants in large pots. (class, <u>placed</u>)

7. The kids like to _____play_____ at the playground. (placed, <u>play</u>)

8. The _____sleet_____ caused the skiers to stop skiing. (<u>sleet</u>, flowers)

9. The garden in your backyard has beautiful _____flowers_____ . (<u>flowers</u>, play)

10. Ms. Brown's _____class_____ is going on an exciting trip. (<u>class</u>, sleet)

Learn To Read English With Directions In Chinese

Classwork

 Name: _____ Date:___/___/_____ Score:_____

Lesson 12.3

Reading Words with a Silent Letter "l"

✓ Lesson Check Point

 Directions: Read the target words in the word box. Write the words that have a silent letter "l" in the first column. Write the words that do not have a silent letter "l" in the second column.

路线：读单词框中的目标词。在第一栏中写上含不发音 l 的词。 在第二栏中写上不带不发音l的词。

Target Word Box				
could	build	soul	cool	likes
yolk	halves	salmon	slam	behalf
calf	loves	talking	helpful	pencil
leaf	slime	chalk	should	almond

Letter "l" is silent

- calf
- yolk
- chalk
- behalf
- could
- halves
- almond
- should
- talking
- salmon

Letter "l" has the /l/ sound

- leaf
- likes
- slam
- loves
- soul
- cool
- build
- slime
- pencil
- helpful

Answer Key

Name: _____ Date: ___/___/_____ Score: _____

The Reading Challenge

Lesson 12.4

Reading Multisyllable Words

 Lesson Check Point

 Directions: Read and divide each target word into syllables. Write each word and place a hyphen (-) between the syllables in the second column. Write the number of syllables in the third column. Use a dictionary or the Internet to check your answers.

路线：读目标词后，划分音节。写下每个词，在第二栏中写上音 节，用 (-) 连接。在第三栏写上音节数。用词典或通过互联网检 查你的答案。

Target Words	Words Divided into Syllables	Number of Syllables
1. limber	lim-ber	2
2. lumber	lum-ber	2
3. leveling	lev-el-ing	3
4. licensing	li-cens-ing	3
5. liberty	lib-er-ty	3
6. loyalty	loy-al-ty	3
7. landlord	land-lord	2
8. liable	li-a-ble	3
9. lioness	li-on-ess	3
10. leotard	le-o-tard	3

Classwork

Name: _____ Date: ___/___/_____ Score: _____

The Reading Challenge

Lesson 12.4

Reading Multisyllable Words

✓ Lesson Check Point

Directions: Read each target word. Circle the word in the row that is divided correctly into syllables. Use a dictionary or the Internet to check your answers.

路线：读每个目标词。圈出行中音节划分正确的词。用词典或通过互联网检查你的答案。

Model

liberty	a. li-ber-ty	(b. lib-er-ty)	c. lib-ert-y
1. luxury	(a. lux-u-ry)	b. lu-xu-ry	c. lux-ur-y
2. lasagna	a. las-a-gna	(b. la-sa-gna)	c. la-sag-na
3. lemonade	a. lem-o-nade	(b. lem-on-ade)	c. le-mo-nade
4. limited	(a. lim-it-ed)	b. li-mit-ed	c. lim-i-ted
5. levitate	a. le-vi-tate	(b. lev-i-tate)	c. lev-it-ate
6. lavender	(a. lav-en-der)	b. lave-n-der	c. la-ven-der
7. legislate	a. leg-i-slate	b. le-gis-late	(c. leg-is-late)
8. levity	a. le-vit-y	b. le-vi-ty	(c. lev-i-ty)

Learn To Read English With Directions In Chinese   130   Copyrighted Material

Answer Key

 Name: _____ Date: ___/___/_____ Score: _____

Lesson 12.5

Reading and Writing

Proper and Common Nouns and Adjectives

✓ Lesson Check Point

 Directions: Read the words in the word box. Put an (X) on the line next to each word that is written incorrectly. Remember that all proper nouns and proper adjectives are capitalized. Use a dictionary or the Internet to check your answers.

路线：读单词框中的词。在书写错误的单词旁边的线上打叉(X)。记得合适的名词和形容词需要大写。用词典或通过互联网检查你 的答案。

Word Box		
__ ladder	__ leopard	X Ladybug
X lincoln	X lebanon	__ language
__ Laos	X Lobster	__ London
X latin	__ Labrador	X Lawyer

 Directions: Read each unedited sentence and underline the word that is written incorrectly. Write each sentence correctly on the line.

路线：读每个未经编辑的句子，并给书写错误的词加下划线。在线 上写上正确的句子。

Model
I am studying <u>latin</u> at Lutheran Life Academy.
<u>I am studying Latin at Lutheran Life Academy.</u>

1. My family and I had a <u>Lovely</u> time in Liberia.
<u>My family and I had a lovely time in Liberia.</u>

2. Abraham <u>lincoln</u> was a loyal American president.
<u>Abraham Lincoln was a loyal American president.</u>

3. Lucy said, "The <u>labrador</u> Current is a cold ocean current."
<u>Lucy said, "The Labrador Current is a cold ocean current."</u>

4. Larry learned that the capital of Arkansas is <u>little</u> Rock.
<u>Larry learned that the capital of Arkansas is Little Rock.</u>

Classwork

Name: _____ Date: ___/___/_____ Score: _____

Lesson 13.1

Reading Words with the Letter M/m

✓ Lesson Check Point

Directions: Read each target word. Find the letter "m" and put a check (✓) in the column that identifies its position: beginning, within or end.
路线：读每个目标词。找出字母 m 在栏中打勾 (✓) 示意： 开 始，中 间或末尾。

Target Words	Beginning (First Letter)	Within	End (Last Letter)
1. money	✓		
2. common		✓	
3. multiple	✓		
4. eardrum			✓
5. dilemma		✓	

Directions: Read each sentence and underline the words that begin with the letter "m." Write all the underlined words in alphabetical order on the lines below.
路线：读每个句子，并给首字母为 m 的词加下划线。在下面的 线上按照字母顺序写出所有下划线标记的单词。

6. Danny has <u>more</u> <u>mittens</u> than gloves.

7. Our aunt, <u>Mary</u>, is baking <u>macaroons</u>.

8. Dan and <u>Madison</u> are from <u>Morocco</u>.

9. Did <u>Miller</u> eat the <u>mozzarella</u> cheese?

10. His <u>mom</u> baked <u>mini</u> pies for our snack.

macaroons	Madison	Mary
Miller	mini	mittens
mom	more	Morocco
	mozzarella	

Unit M Lesson 13.1

Answer Key

 Name: _____ Date: ___/___/_____ Score: _____

Lesson 13.2

Reading Words with a Silent Letter "m"

✓ Lesson Check Point

 Directions: Read each target word. Find the letter "m" and put a check (✓) in the column that identifies its position: beginning, within or end.
路线：读每个目标词。找到字母 m 在栏中打勾(✓)标示其位 置：开始，中间或末尾。

Target Words	Beginning (First Letter)	Within	End (Last Letter)
1. program			✓
2. immediate		✓	
3. basement		✓	
4. submarine		✓	
5. moving	✓		

 Directions: Read each target word. Put a check (✓) in the "yes" column if the target word has a silent letter "m." Put a check (✓) in the "no" column if the target word does not have a silent letter "m."
路线：读每个目标词。如果目标词有一个不发音 m 在"是"栏中打勾(✓)。如果目标词没有不发音 m 则在"没有"栏中打勾 (✓)。

Target Words	Yes	No
6. mnemonic	✓	
7. immense	✓	
8. commit	✓	
9. compromise		✓
10. momentum		✓

Learn To Read English With Directions In Chinese

Classwork

 Name: _____ Date: ___/___/_____ Score: _____

The Reading Challenge

Lesson 13.3

Reading Multisyllable Words

✓ Lesson Check Point

 Directions: Read and divide each target word into syllables. Write each word and place a hyphen (-) between the syllables in the second column. Write the number of syllables in the third column. Use a dictionary or the Internet to check your answers.

路线：读目标词后，划分音节。写下每个词，在第二栏中写上音 节，用 (-) 连接。在第三栏写上音节数。用词典或通过互联网检 查你的答案。

Target Words	Words Divided into Syllables	Number of Syllables
1. menu	men-u	2
2. minuteman	min-ute-man	3
3. monsoon	mon-soon	2
4. meaningful	mean-ing-ful	3
5. migrant	mi-grant	2
6. monkey	mon-key	2
7. macaroni	mac-a-ro-ni	4
8. meadow	mead-ow	2
9. morsel	mor-sel	2
10. Mexico	Mex-i-co	3

Name: _____ Date:___/___/_____ Score:_____

The Reading Challenge

Lesson 13.3

Reading Multisyllable Words

✓ Lesson Check Point

Directions: Read each target word. Circle the word in the row that is divided correctly into syllables. Use a dictionary or the Internet to check your answers.

路线：读每个目标词。圈出行中音节划分正确的词。用词典或通过互联网检查你的答案。

Model

| magazine | **a. mag-a-zine** (circled) | b. ma-ga-zine | c. mag-az-ine |

1. mineral	a. mi-ner-al	**b. min-er-al** (circled)	c. min-e-ral
2. magnify	**a. mag-ni-fy** (circled)	b. mag-nif-y	c. ma-gni-fy
3. malpractice	**a. mal-prac-tice** (circled)	b. mal-pract-ice	c. ma-lprac-tice

4. mechanics	a. mech-an-ics	b. me-cha-nics	**c. me-chan-ics** (circled)
5. monopoly	a. mon-op-o-ly	b. mo-no-po-ly	**c. mo-nop-o-ly** (circled)
6. metaphor	a. me-ta-phor	b. met-aph-or	**c. met-a-phor** (circled)
7. monument	a. mon-um-ent	**b. mon-u-ment** (circled)	c. mo-nu-ment
8. memorize	**a. mem-o-rize** (circled)	b. mem-or-ize	c. me-mor-ize

Classwork

Name: _____ Date: ___/___/_____ Score: _____

Lesson 13.4

Reading and Writing

Proper and Common Nouns and Adjectives

✓ Lesson Check Point

Directions: Read the words in the word box. Put an (X) on the line next to each word that is written incorrectly. Remember that all proper nouns and proper adjectives are capitalized. Use a dictionary or the Internet to check your answers.

路线：读单词框中的词。在书写错误的单词旁边的线上打叉(X)。记得合适的名词和形容词需要大写。用词典或通过互联网检查你的答案。

Word Box					
X	Manager	X	Monkey	__	menu
__	Manchester	__	market	__	mentor
X	manhattan	__	Margaret	X	Mailbox
X	malawi	X	malta	__	Mother

Directions: Read each unedited sentence and underline the word that is written incorrectly. Write each sentence correctly on the line.

路线：读每个未经编辑的句子，并给书写错误的词加下划线。在线 上写上正确的句子。

Model
My son, Mark, is going to attend MIT in <u>massachusetts</u>.
<u>My son, Mark, is going to attend MIT in Massachusetts.</u>

1. My <u>Mom</u> is cooking macaroni and cheese for dinner.
<u>My mom is cooking macaroni and cheese for dinner.</u>

2. Mary and <u>max</u> read a book about the planet Mars.
<u>Mary and Max read a book about the planet Mars.</u>

3. Beth and Mom will meet in Midtown <u>manhattan</u>.
<u>Beth and Mom will meet in Midtown Manhattan.</u>

4. I received my master's degree from <u>mombasa</u> College.
<u>I received my master's degree from Mombasa College.</u>

 Name: _____ Date: ___/___/_____ Score: _____

Lesson 14.1

Reading Words with the Letter N/n

✓ **Lesson Check Point**

 Directions: Read each target word. Find the letter "n" and put a check (✓) in the column that identifies its position: beginning, within or end.
路线：读每个目标词。找出字母 n 在栏中打勾 (✓) 示意：开始，中间或末尾。

Target Words	Beginning (First Letter)	Within	End (Last Letter)
1. university		✓	
2. glutton			✓
3. twin			✓
4. nurse	✓		
5. newspaper	✓		

 Directions: Read each sentence and underline the words that begin with the letter "n." Write all the underlined words in alphabetical order on the lines below.
路线：读每个句子，并给首字母为 n 的词加下划线。在下面的 线上按照字母顺序写出所有下划线标记的单词。

6. Mommy <u>never</u> tasted chicken <u>noodle</u> soup.

7. <u>Napoleon</u> read ten books about the <u>Nile</u> River.

8. My <u>neighbors</u> enjoy celebrating <u>New</u> Year's Eve.

9. <u>Nick</u> wants to move from Kansas to <u>North</u> Dakota.

10. Everyone knows that many <u>nice</u> people live in <u>Norway</u>.

<u>Napoleon</u> _____ <u>neighbors</u> _____ <u>never</u> _____
<u>New</u> _____ <u>nice</u> _____ <u>Nick</u> _____
<u>Nile</u> _____ <u>noodle</u> _____ <u>North</u> _____
  <u>Norway</u> _____

Classwork

 Name: _____ Date: ___/___/_____ Score: _____

Lesson 14.2

Reading Words with the "ng" Letter Combination

✓ **Lesson Check Point**

 Directions: Read each target word. Circle the word in the column that has the same "ng" sound(s) as the target word.
路线：读每个目标词。圈出栏中与目标词含相同 "ng" 音的单词。

anger	a. exchange
	b. language (circled)

congratulate	a. congruence (circled)
	b. engineer

congeniality	a. jingle
	b. danger (circled)

singer	a. boxing (circled)
	b. triangle

 Directions: Read each target word. Put a check (✓) under the correct column heading.
路线：读每个目标词。在符合要求的栏下打勾 (✓)。

Target Words	"ng" has the /n/ + /g/ sounds as in the word <u>ingrain</u>	"ng" has the /n/ + /j/ sounds as in the word <u>ginger</u>	"ng" has the /ng/ sound as in the word <u>bang</u>	"ng" has the /ng/ + /g/ sounds as in the word <u>congress</u>
1. anger				✓
2. congratulate	✓			
3. congeniality		✓		
4. singer			✓	

Answer Key

 Name: _____ Date:___/___/_____ Score:_____

Lesson 14.3

Reading Words with a Silent Letter "n"

✓ **Lesson Check Point**

 Directions: Read the target words in the word box. Write the words that have a silent letter "n" in the first column. Write the words that do not have a silent letter "n" in the second column.

路线：读单词框中的目标词。在第一栏中写上含不发音 n 的词。 在第二栏中写上不带不发 n 的词。

Target Word Box				
animals	hymn	encounter	botanical	annex
comments	behind	hunter	nouns	penny
autumn	annual	cinnamon	monsieur	condemn
chimneys	tennis	handy	nominate	columns

Letter "n" is silent

- hymn
- annex
- tennis
- penny
- annual
- autumn
- monsieur
- condemn
- columns
- cinnamon

Letter "n" has the /n/ sound

- handy
- nouns
- hunter
- animals
- behind
- botanical
- comments
- encounter
- chimneys
- nominate

Learn To Read English With Directions In Chinese

Classwork

 Name: _____ Date: ___/___/_____ Score: _____

The Reading Challenge

Lesson 14.4

Reading Multisyllable Words

✓ Lesson Check Point

 Directions: Read and divide each target word into syllables. Write each word and place a hyphen (-) between the syllables in the second column. Write the number of syllables in the third column. Use a dictionary or the Internet to check your answers.

路线：读目标词后，划分音节。写下每个词，在第二栏中写上音 节，用 (-) 连接。在第三栏写上音节数。用词典或通过互联网检 查你的答案。

Target Words	Words Divided into Syllables	Number of Syllables
1. nighttime	night-time	2
2. nationwide	na-tion-wide	3
3. nuance	nu-ance	2
4. needlessly	need-less-ly	3
5. normalize	nor-mal-ize	3
6. ninety	nine-ty	2
7. nimbleness	nim-ble-ness	3
8. noble	no-ble	2
9. nectarine	nec-tar-ine	3
10. notion	no-tion	2

Name: _____ Date: ___/___/_____ Score: _____

Answer Key

The Reading Challenge

Lesson 14.4

Reading Multisyllable Words

✓ **Lesson Check Point**

 Directions: Read each target word. Circle the word in the row that is divided correctly into syllables. Use a dictionary or the Internet to check your answers.

路线：读每个目标词。圈出行中音节划分正确的词。用词典或通过互联网检查你的答案。

Model

| napkin | a. na-pkin | b. napk-in | **c. nap-kin** (circled) |

1. neighbor	a. neighb-or	**b. neigh-bor** (circled)	c. nei-gh-bor
2. notify	**a. no-ti-fy** (circled)	b. no-tif-y	c. not-i-fy
3. natural	**a. nat-u-ral** (circled)	b. na-tu-ral	c. na-tur-al
4. nevermore	a. ne-ver-more	b. nev-erm-ore	**c. nev-er-more** (circled)
5. nobody	**a. no-bod-y** (circled)	b. no-body	c. no-bo-dy
6. newcomer	a. ne-wcom-er	b. new-co-mer	**c. new-com-er** (circled)
7. nutrition	**a. nu-tri-tion** (circled)	b. nut-ri-tion	c. nu-trit-ion
8. nausea	a. na-us-ea	b. n-au-sea	**c. nau-se-a** (circled)

Unit N Lesson 14.4

Learn To Read English With Directions In Chinese   141   Copyrighted Material

Classwork

Name: _____ Date:___/___/_____ Score: _____

Lesson 14.5

Reading and Writing

Proper and Common Nouns and Adjectives

✓ Lesson Check Point

Directions: Read the words in the word box. Put an (X) on the line next to each word that is written incorrectly. Remember that all proper nouns and proper adjectives are capitalized. Use a dictionary or the Internet to check your answers.

路线：读单词框中的词。在书写错误的单词旁边的线上打叉(X)。记得合适的名词和形容词需要大写。用词典或通过互联网检查你 的答案。

Word Box					
X	Nugget	X	north Africa	X	nigeria
__	Nepal	X	nile	__	napkin
__	Napoleon	__	news	X	Noodle
__	New Delhi	X	Number	__	Nicaragua

Directions: Read each unedited sentence and underline the word that is written incorrectly. Write each sentence correctly on the line.

路线：读每个未经编辑的句子，并给书写错误的词加下划线。在线 上写上正确的句子。

Model
Nick and Nancy live in the <u>netherlands</u>.
<u>Nick and Nancy live in the Netherlands.</u>

1. I received a <u>Needle</u> from Nurse Nutley.
<u>I received a needle from Nurse Nutley.</u>

2. The <u>Newscasters</u> collaborate about national news stories.
<u>The newscasters collaborate about national news stories.</u>

3. Mrs. Newton taught a lesson about the <u>Nervous</u> system.
<u>Mrs. Newton taught a lesson about the nervous system.</u>

4. The <u>nile</u> River derives its name from the Greek word, Nelios.
<u>The Nile River derives its name from the Greek word, Nelios.</u>

Name: _____ Date: ___/___/_____ Score: _____

Lesson 15.1

Reading Words with the Letter O/o

✓ Lesson Check Point

 Directions: Read each target word. Find the letter "o" and put a check (✓) in the column that identifies its position: beginning, within or end.
路线：读每个目标词。找出字母 o 在栏中打勾 (✓) 示意： 开 始，中间或末尾。

Target Words	Beginning (First Letter)	Within	End (Last Letter)
1. combine		✓	
2. older	✓		
3. outreach	✓		
4. cargo			✓
5. embargo			✓

 Directions: Read each target word. Read the words in the row and circle the word that has a different vowel "o" sound.
路线：读每个目标词。阅读这一行的词，圈出元音 o 发不同的 词。

Target Words				
6. almost	go	code	(song)	dole
7. drop	(host)	prom	stop	clog
8. solo	(lock)	joke	tone	coat
9. gold	soap	(toss)	aloe	so
10. shopping	rock	clock	frost	(poll)

Classwork

 Name: _____ Date:___/___/_____ Score: _____

Lesson 15.2

Reading Words with the Short Vowel "o" Sound

✓ Lesson Check Point

 Directions: Read the words in the four boxes. Circle two words with the short vowel /ŏ/ or /ô/ sound. The anchor word for the short vowel /ŏ/ and /ô/ sounds is frog.

路线：读每个句子，给含短元音/ŏ/或/ô/的单词加下划线。然后，在下面划线处写上带下划线的词。含短元音/ŏ/和/ô/的描点词是英文单词 frog。

| (stop) | poll | | colt | (flog) | | post | both |
| old | (plot) | | host | (drop) | | (slot) | (chop) |

| (fond) | (prom) | | (blot) | mole | | (rock) | (clop) |
| told | go | | (knot) | don't | | hold | roll |

 Directions: Read the words in the four boxes. Circle two words that rhyme. Rhyming words have the same ending sound, such as hot and not.

路线：读四个框中的词。圈出押韵的两个词。押韵词有同样的尾音，如，英语单词 hot 和 not。

| (shot) | (spot) | | (shop) | roll | | hydro | phone |
| no | chosen | | solo | (crop) | | (bond) | (pond) |

| ago | (lock) | | (boss) | (toss) | | (long) | joke |
| gold | (dock) | | ocean | hotel | | (song) | sold |

Answer Key

Name: _____ Date:___/___/_____ Score:_____

Lesson 15.2

Reading & Writing Words with the Short Vowel "o" Sound

✓ **Lesson Check Point**

Directions: Read each sentence and underline three words with the short vowel /ŏ/ or /ô/ sound. Then, write the underlined words on the lines below. The anchor word for the short vowel /ŏ/ and /ô/ sounds is frog.

路线：读每个句子，划出含短元音/ŏ/或/ô/的三个词。然后，在下面的划线处写上带下划线的词。锚点词为短元音/ŏ/和/ô/的 英语单 词，frog。

Model
Everyone saw the frog hop close to the rock.

    frog   hop   rock

1. The ropes on the mop are very soft.

    on   mop   soft

2. The policeman stopped the robber in the office.

    stopped   robber   office

3. Tom walked around the block in his socks.

    Tom   block   socks

4. Joan's job assignment is to mop the spotty tiles.

    job   mop   spotty

5. Moss develops from spores and grows in damp logs.

    Moss   from   logs

Classwork

 Name: _____ Date: ___/___/_____ Score: _____

Lesson 15.3

Reading Words with the Long Vowel "o" Sound

✓ **Lesson Check Point**

 Directions: Read the words in the four boxes. Circle two words with the long vowel /ō/ sound. The anchor word for the long vowel /ō/ sound is <u>open</u>.

路线：读四个框中的词。圈出含长元音/ō/的两个词。含长元音/ō/的描点词是 open。

cross	(yo-yo)		boss	(joke)		rock	took
(roll)	lock		lost	so		(pony)	(sold)

(both)	pond		drop	shop		prompt	(soap)
(boat)	sock		(poke)	(toad)		floss	(poll)

 Directions: Read the words in the four boxes. Circle two words that rhyme. Rhyming words have the same ending sound, such as <u>hope</u> and <u>soap</u>.

路线：读四个框中的词。圈出押韵的两个词。押韵的词含同样的尾音。如，英语单词 hope 和 soap。

go	(folk)		(boat)	(coat)		toss	home
(yolk)	clock		rose	song		(post)	(most)

frost	(pole)		so	(cold)		poet	(roast)
told	(role)		strong	(sold)		(toast)	spot

Name: _____ Date: ___/___/_____ Score: _____

Lesson 15.3
Reading & Writing Words with the Long Vowel "o" Sound

✓ **Lesson Check Point**

Directions: Read each sentence and underline three words with the long vowel /ō/ sound. Then, write the underlined words on the lines below. The anchor word for the long vowel /ō/ sound is <u>open</u>.

路线：读每个句子，给带长元音 /ō/ 的三个词加下划线。然后，在下面的划线处写上带下划线的词。锚点词为长元音 /ō/ 的英语 单词，open。

Model

We will <u>go</u> to the <u>rodeo</u> and <u>limbo</u> competitions for fun.

    go   rodeo   limbo

1. <u>Owen</u> said <u>hello</u> to the <u>ponies</u> in the zoo.

    Owen   hello   ponies

2. The <u>hotel's</u> <u>frozen</u> <u>donuts</u> do not taste good.

    hotel's   frozen   donuts

3. The <u>coeducational</u> golf team is <u>going</u> to <u>enroll</u> in the competition.

    coeducational   going   enroll

4. Tom, the <u>yodeler</u>, will change his <u>tempo</u> in a <u>moment</u>.

    yodeler   tempo   moment

5. My son said, "<u>Both</u> <u>hippos</u> and <u>dodo</u> birds are interesting animals."

    Both   hippos   dodo

Classwork

 Name: _____ Date: ___/___/_____ Score: _____

Review Lessons 15.2 & 15.3

Reading Short Vowel and Long Vowel Words

✓ **Lesson Check Point**

 Directions: Read the target words in the word box. In the first column, write the words that have the short vowel /ŏ/ or /ô/ sound, as in the word <u>frog</u>. In the second column, write the words that have the long vowel /ō/ sound, as in the word <u>open</u>.

路线：读框中的目标词。在第一栏中写上含 frog一样短元音/ŏ/或 /ô/的词。在第二栏写上含与英语单词 open一样长元音/ō/的词。

Target Word Box				
scaffold	cross	billfold	prompt	shopping
disposal	postal	bonding	going	rocking
stock	revolt	lost	enroll	grocery
plot	clock	mostly	strong	hippos

Letter "o" has the /ŏ/ or /ô/ sound as in the word <u>frog</u>

- plot
- lost
- clock
- cross
- stock
- strong
- prompt
- rocking
- bonding
- shopping

Letter "o" has the /ō/ sound as in the word <u>open</u>

- enroll
- revolt
- grocery
- mostly
- postal
- hippos
- going
- billfold
- scaffold
- disposal

Answer Key

 Name: _____ Date: ___/___/_____ Score: _____

Lesson 15.4

Reading Words with Letter "o" Vowel Pairs

✓ Lesson Check Point

 Directions: Read each target word. Circle the word in the column that has the same vowel "oa," "oe," "oo" or "ou" sound(s) as the target word.
路线：读每个目标词。圈出栏中含与目标词一样元音"oa,""oe,""oo"或"ou"的词。

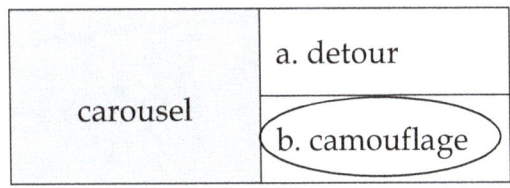

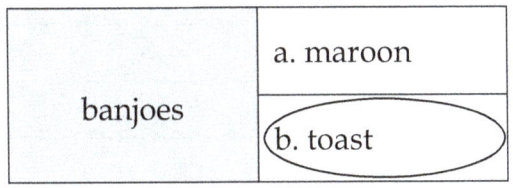 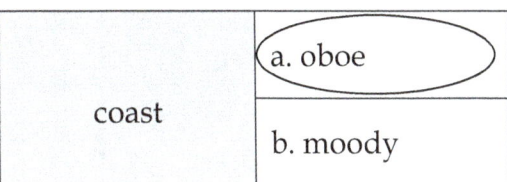

 Directions: Read each target word. Put a check (✓) under the correct column heading.
路线：读每个目标词。在符合要求的栏下打勾(✓)。

Target Words	Words have the long "o" sound as in the word <u>coat</u>	Words do not have the long "o" sound
1. carousel		✓
2. gloat	✓	
3. banjoes	✓	
4. coast	✓	

Classwork

 Name: _____ Date: ___/___/_____ Score: _____

Lesson 15.5

Reading Words with the Final Letter "o"

✓ Lesson Check Point

 Directions: Read each target word. Find the letter "o" and put a check (✓) in the column that identifies its position within the syllable.
路线：读每个目标词。找到字母 o 并在栏中打勾(✓), 标示其 在音节中的位置。

Target Words	"o" is at the end of a one syllable word	"o" is at the end of the first syllable	"o" is at the end of a multi-syllable word
1. m<u>o</u>tor		✓	
2. piano			✓
3. chosen		✓	
4. go	✓		
5. ago			✓

 Directions: Read each target word. Put a check (✓) under the correct column heading.
路线：读每个目标词。在符合要求的栏下打勾 (✓)。

Target Words	"o" has the /ŏ/ sound as in the word <u>frog</u>	"o" has the /ō/ sound as in the word <u>go</u>	"o" has the /ə/ sound as in the word <u>carrot</u>	"o" is silent as in the word <u>people</u>
6. roaches		✓		
7. turbo		✓		
8. contain			✓	
9. mopping	✓			
10. vaporize			✓	

Name: _____ Date: ___/___/_____ Score: _____

Lesson 15.6

Reading Letter "o" Words with the Schwa Vowel Sound

✓ **Lesson Check Point**

 Directions: Read each target word. Circle the word in the column that has the same "o" sound as the target word.

路线：读每个目标词。圈出栏中与目标词含相同 o 音的单词。

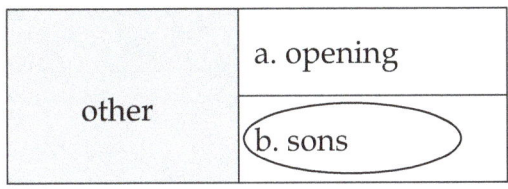
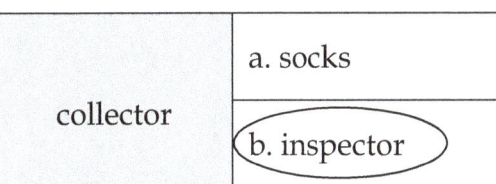
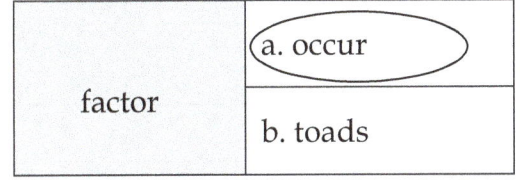
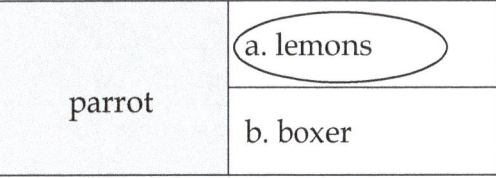

 Directions: Read each sentence and underline the letter "o" word that has the schwa vowel /ə/ sound or short vowel /ŭ/ sound. The anchor word for the letter "o" schwa vowel /ə/ sound is <u>carrot</u> and the letter "o" short vowel /ŭ/ sound is <u>dove</u>.

路线：读每个句子，给含字母 o 且发施瓦 /ə/或/ŭ/音的单词加下划线。含字母 o 且发施瓦 /ə/音的描点词是 carrot。含字母 o 且发/ŭ/ 短音的词是 dove。

1. The orange <u>sponge</u> is in the old pot.

2. The boys <u>won</u> the bowling tournament.

3. Mommy enjoys eating <u>onion</u> noodle soup.

4. This year, our school will start at eight <u>o'clock</u>.

5. On <u>Monday</u>, I closed the window before the storm.

6. In October, my <u>doctor</u> gave me an intensive examination.

Classwork

 Name: _____ Date: ___/___/_____ Score: _____

Lesson 15.7

Reading Words with Vowel "o" Sounds: /ŏ/, /ō/ & /o͞o/

✓ Lesson Check Point

 Directions: Read each target word. Put a check (✓) under the correct column heading.

路线：读每个目标词。在符合要求的栏下打勾 (✓)。

Target Words	"o" has the /ŏ/ sound as in the word frog	"o" has the /ō/ sound as in the word go	"o" has the /o͞o/ sound as in the word to
1. mopping	✓		
2. who			✓
3. moving			✓
4. October	✓		
5. soul		✓	

 Directions: Read each sentence and underline the word that has a letter "o" that has the vowel /o͞o/ sound, as in the word two.

路线：读每个句子，给含字母 o 且发 /o͞o/ 音的单词加下划线，如英语单词 two。

6. <u>Do</u> we have a box of colorful rocks?

7. On Monday, Ron and Tom will <u>move</u> out.

8. We may <u>lose</u> our money in the stock market.

9. <u>Who</u> read the book about the fox in the woods?

10. The outspoken lawyer <u>proved</u> that his client is not guilty.

 Name: _____ Date: ___/___/_____ Score: _____

Lesson 15.8

Reading Words with the "or" Letter Combination

 Lesson Check Point

Directions: Read each target word. Circle the word in the column that has the same "o" + "r" sounds as the target word.
路线：读每个目标词。圈出栏中与目标词含相同 o + r 音的 单 词。

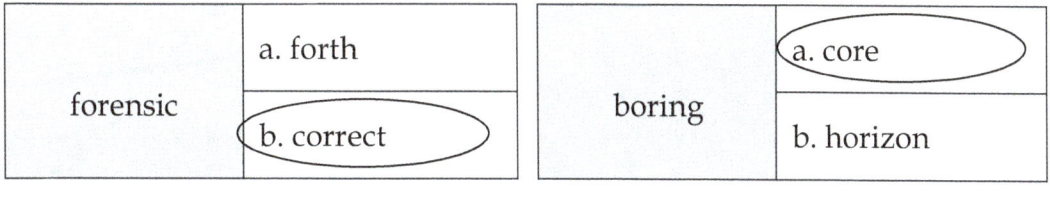

Directions: Read each target word. Put a check (✓) under the correct column heading.
路线：读每个目标词。在符合要求的栏下打勾 (✓)。

Target Words	"or" has the /ô/ + /r/ sounds as in the word <u>door</u>	"or" has the /ə/ + /r/ sounds as in the word <u>doctor</u>
1. forensic		✓
2. boring	✓	
3. portion	✓	
4. original		✓

 Learn To Read English With Directions In Chinese

Classwork

Name: _____ Date: ___/___/_____ Score: _____

Lesson 15.8

Reading Words with the "or" Letter Combination

Dictionary Skills/ Vocabulary

✓ **Lesson Check Point**

Directions: Read each target word and its definition. Write the target word on the line in front of its meaning. Use a dictionary or the Internet to check your answers.

路线：读每个目标词及其定义。在目标词前线上写上正确定义的 字母编号。用词典或通过互联网检查你的答案。

Target Word Box				
worn	orbits	important	story	forgot

1. <u>forgot</u>   inability to remember
2. <u>important</u>   something or someone of great value
3. <u>worn</u>   fabric that has become thinner or damaged
4. <u>orbits</u>   the act of moving around another object
5. <u>story</u>   a spoken or written description of characters and events

Directions: Read each sentence and write the target word that correctly completes the sentence.

路线：读每个句子和并在划线处填上合适的词。

6. My old blue jeans are ____<u>worn</u>____ out.

7. The science teacher said, "The Earth <u>orbits</u> the Sun."

8. It is _____<u>important</u>_____ to attend school every day.

9. Molly told the teacher she ____<u>forgot</u>____ to do her homework.

10. The _____<u>story</u>_____ "The Fox and the Wise Owl" has a great plot.

Answer Key

 Name: _____ Date: ___/___/_____ Score: _____

Lesson 15.9

Reading Words with a Silent Letter "o"

✓ **Lesson Check Point**

 Directions: Read the target words in the word box. Write the words that have a silent letter "o" in the first column. Write the words that do not have a silent letter "o" in the second column.

路线：读单词框中的目标词。在第一栏中写上含不发音 o 的词。 在第二栏中写上不带不发音 o 的词。

Target Word Box				
combat	leopards	horse	Phoenician	subpoena
body	jeopardy	subpoenas	know	hold
Leonard	assort	open	leopard	collect
expose	phoenix	people	octopus	jeopardize

Letter "o" is silent

- leopards
- jeopardy
- leopard
- people
- phoenix
- subpoena
- subpoenas
- Leonard
- jeopardize
- Phoenician

Letter "o" has a letter "o" sound

- open
- horse
- know
- body
- hold
- assort
- combat
- collect
- expose
- octopus

Unit O
Lesson 15.9

Classwork

 Name: _____ Date: ___/___/_____ Score: _____

Unit Review - O/o

Reading Words with Vowel "o" Sounds: /ŏ/, /ō/, /ə/ & Silent

✓ **Lesson Check Point**

 Directions: Read each target word. Circle the word in the column that has the same "o" sound as the target word.

路线：读每个目标词。圈出栏中与目标词含相同 o 音的单词。

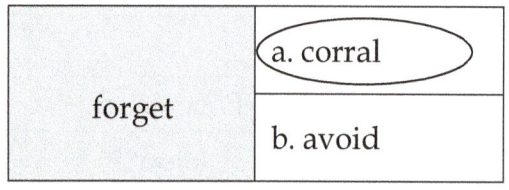
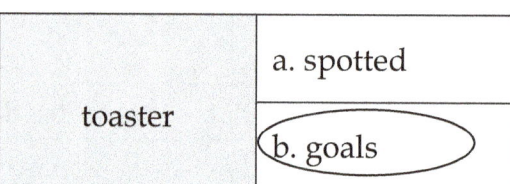
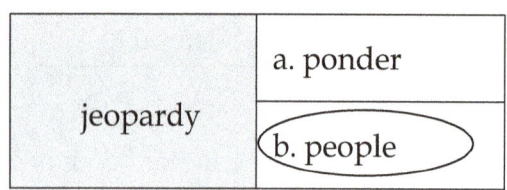
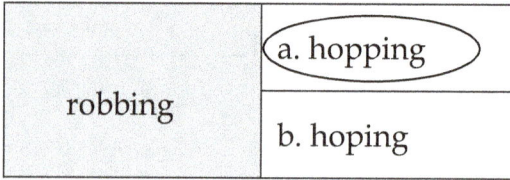

 Directions: Read each target word. Put a check (✓) under the correct column heading.

路线：读每个目标词。在符合要求的栏下打勾 (✓)。

Target Words	"o" has the /ŏ/ sound as in the word **frog**	"o" has the /ō/ sound as in the word **go**	"o" has the /ə/ sound as in the word **carrot**	"o" is silent as in the word **people**
1. forget			✓	
2. toaster		✓		
3. jeopardy				✓
4. robbing	✓			

Answer Key

Name: _____ Date: ___/___/_____ Score: _____

The Reading Challenge

Lesson 15.10

Reading Multisyllable Words

✓ **Lesson Check Point**

Directions: Read and divide each target word into syllables. Write each word and place a hyphen (-) between the syllables in the second column. Write the number of syllables in the third column. Use a dictionary or the Internet to check your answers.

路线：读目标词后，划分音节。写下每个词，在第二栏中写上音 节，用 (-) 连接。在第三栏写上音节数。用词典或通过互联网检 查你的答案。

Target Words	Words Divided into Syllables	Number of Syllables
1. solar	so-lar	2
2. motel	mo-tel	2
3. token	to-ken	2
4. composer	com-pos-er	3
5. Romania	Ro-ma-ni-a	4
6. lotion	lo-tion	2
7. orderly	or-der-ly	3
8. rodent	ro-dent	2
9. provoking	pro-vok-ing	3
10. Bohemian	Bo-he-mi-an	4

Unit O Lesson 15.10

Classwork

 Name: _____ Date: ___/___/_____ Score: _____

The Reading Challenge

Lesson 15.10

Reading Multisyllable Words

✓ **Lesson Check Point**

 Directions: Read each target word. Circle the word in the row that is divided correctly into syllables. Use a dictionary or the Internet to check your answers.

路线：读每个目标词。圈出行中音节划分正确的词。用词典或通过互联网检查你的答案。

Model

proposal	a. prop-o-sal	b. pro-po-sal	c. pro-pos-al ⭕

1. portable	a. por-table	b. por-ta-ble ⭕	c. port-a-ble
2. asteroid	a. as-te-roid	b. ast-e-roid	c. as-ter-oid ⭕
3. corporate	a. cor-po-rate ⭕	b. corpo-ra-te	c. corp-o-rate
4. potato	a. pot-at-o	b. po-ta-to ⭕	c. pot-a-to
5. repertoire	a. rep-er-toire ⭕	b. re-pert-oire	c. re-per-toire
6. investor	a. in-ves-tor ⭕	b. in-vest-or	c. i-nvest-or
7. cockatoo	a. cock-at-oo	b. co-cka-too	c. cock-a-too ⭕
8. October	a. Oct-o-ber	b. Oc-to-ber ⭕	c. Oct-ob-er

Answer Key

 Name: _____ Date: ___/___/_____ Score: _____

Lesson 15.11

Reading and Writing

Proper and Common Nouns and Adjectives

✓ Lesson Check Point

 Directions: Read the words in the word box. Put an (X) on the line next to each word that is written incorrectly. Remember that all proper nouns and proper adjectives are capitalized. Use a dictionary or the Internet to check your answers.

路线：读单词框中的词。在书写错误的单词旁边的线上打叉(X)。记得合适的名词和形容词需要大写。用词典或通过互联网检查你 的答案。

Word Box		
___ Oxbridge	___ octopus	_X_ orlando
_X_ ontario	___ Onega Bay	___ organizer
___ Old English	_X_ october	_X_ Atlantic ocean
_X_ Occasion	___ objective	_X_ Original

 Directions: Read each unedited sentence and underline the word that is written incorrectly. Write each sentence correctly on the line.

路线：读每个未经编辑的句子，并给书写错误的词加下划线。在线 上写上正确的句子。

Model
At One o'clock, the Owens family went to Onega Bay.
At one o'clock, the Owens family went to Onega Bay.

1. Mr. o'Connor is planning an outstanding trip to the Orient.
Mr. O'Connor is planning an outstanding trip to the Orient.

2. Marie, Octavia and I are Overjoyed about our trip to Oktoberfest.
Marie, Octavia and I are overjoyed about our trip to Oktoberfest.

3. Mr. O'Keeffe gave the class a fact sheet about the oregon Trail.
Mr. O'Keeffe gave the class a fact sheet about the Oregon Trail.

4. In October, the official olympic Games tryouts will begin.
In October, the official Olympic Games tryouts will begin.

Classwork

Name: _____ Date: ___/___/_____ Score: _____

Lesson 16.1

Reading Words with the Letter P/p

✓ **Lesson Check Point**

Directions: Read each target word. Find the letter "p" and put a check (✓) in the column that identifies its position: beginning, within or end.
路线：读每个目标词。找出字母 p 在栏中打勾 (✓) 示意： 开始，中间或末尾。

Target Words	Beginning (First Letter)	Within	End (Last Letter)
1. price	✓		
2. pest	✓		
3. plans	✓		
4. asleep			✓
5. concept		✓	

Directions: Read each sentence and underline the words that begin with the letter "p." Write all the underlined words in alphabetical order on the lines below.
路线：读每个句子，并给首字母为 p 的词加下划线。在下面的 线上按照字母顺序写出所有下划线标记的单词。

6. The <u>pitcher</u> threw <u>powerful</u> fastballs.

7. Lydia is sending a <u>package</u> to <u>Panama</u>.

8. Gabby's <u>pageant</u> gown is white and <u>purple</u>.

9. The <u>police</u> officer is <u>patrolling</u> our college campus.

10. <u>People</u> in the courtroom said the <u>plaintiff</u> has a strong case.

package	pageant	Panama
patrolling	People	pitcher
plaintiff	police	powerful
	purple	

Answer Key

Name: _____ Date: ___/___/_____ Score: _____

Lesson 16.2

Reading Words with the "ph" Letter Combination

✓ Lesson Check Point

Directions: Read each target word. Circle the word in the column that has the same "ph" sound(s) as the target word.
路线：读每个目标词。圈出栏中与目标词含相同"ph"音的单词。

orphan	(a. pamphlet)
	b. haphazard

upheaval	(a. haphazard)
	b. photograph

alphabet	a. uphold
	(b. biography)

amphibian	(a. esophagus)
	b. shepherd

Directions: Read each target word. Put a check (✓) under the correct column heading.
路线：读每个目标词。在符合要求的栏下打勾 (✓)。

Target Words	"ph" has the /f/ sound as in the word <u>phone</u>	"ph" has the /p/ + /h/ sounds as in the word <u>uphill</u>
1. orphan	✓	
2. upheaval		✓
3. alphabet	✓	
4. amphibian	✓	

Classwork

Name: _____ Date: ___/___/_____ Score: _____

Lesson 16.3

Reading Words with the "pr" Letter Combination

Dictionary Skills/ Vocabulary

✓ Lesson Check Point

Directions: Read each target word and its definition. Write the letter of the definition on the line of each target word. Use a dictionary or the Internet to check your answers.
路线：读每个目标词及其定义。在目标词前线上写上正确定义的 字母编号。用词典或通过互联网检查你的答案。

Target Words	Definitions
1. _b_ praised	a. an educator/instructor at a university or college
2. _c_ predators	b. to have expressed words of admiration or approval
3. _d_ president	c. animals that kill and eat other animals for survival
4. _a_ professor	d. an elected or appointed leader of a country
5. _e_ program	e. an organized business that provides activities

Directions: Read each sentence and write the target word that correctly completes the sentence.
路线：读每个句子和并在划线处填上合适的词。

6. The great white whales and lions are alpha ____predators____.

7. Dr. Pringle is a _____professor_____ at Pratt University.

8. The _____president_____ was elected for a four-year term.

9. The teacher _____praised_____ her hardworking students.

10. My sister and I attend an after-school _____program_____.

Answer Key

Name: _____ Date: ___/___/_____ Score: _____

Lesson 16.4

Reading Words with the "pl" Letter Combination

Dictionary Skills/ Vocabulary

 Lesson Check Point

 Directions: Read each target word and its definition. Write the target word on the line in front of its meaning. Use a dictionary or the Internet to check your answers.
路线：读每个目标词及其定义。在目标词前线上写上正确定义的 字母编号。用词典或通过互联网检查你的答案。

Target Word Box				
plaintiff	pleasure	plowing	plum	plush

1. _plowing_ the act of breaking up the land for farming
2. _plush_   a luxury item that is nice and expensive
3. _plaintiff_ a person or group of people who file a lawsuit
4. _pleasure_ an experience that is enjoyable or satisfying
5. _plum_   purple, smooth-skinned fruit that is very sweet

 Directions: Read each sentence. Underline the word in the parentheses that correctly completes each sentence. Then, write the underlined word on the line.
路线：阅读每个句子。在括号中选择符合句子的词，并添加下划 线。然后，在线上写出下划线单词。

6. The ___plaintiff___ filed a case at the courthouse. (pleasure, <u>plaintiff</u>)

7. The farmer is ___plowing___ the center of his field. (<u>plowing</u>, plush)

8. I spent a lot of money for my ___plush___ condo. (plum, <u>plush</u>)

9. I bought peaches and ___plums___ from the fruit store. (<u>plums</u>, pleasure)

10. I agree that it is a ___pleasure___ to work with children. (<u>pleasure</u>, plaintiff)

Learn To Read English With Directions In Chinese

Classwork

Name: _____ Date: ___/___/_____ Score: _____

Lesson 16.4

Reading Words with the "ple" Letter Combination

 Lesson Check Point

 Directions: Read each target word. Find the "ple" letter combination and put a check (✓) in the column that identifies its position: beginning, within or end.
路线：读每个目标词。找到"ple"字母组合，并在栏中打勾(✓)示意：开始，中间或末尾。

Target Words	Beginning (First 3 Letters)	Within	End (Last 3 Letters)
1. participle			✓
2. multiple			✓
3. displeased		✓	
4. simple			✓
5. plentiful	✓		

 Directions: Read each target word. Put a check (✓) in the "yes" column if the "ple" letter combination has the /p/ + /ə/ + /l/ sounds. Put a check (✓) in the "no" column if the "ple" letter combination does not have the /p/ + /ə/ + /l/ sounds.
路线：读每个目标词。如果"ple"字母组合发/p/ + /ə/ + /l/的音，在"是"栏中打 勾(✓)。如果"ple"字母组合不发/p/ + /ə/ + /l/的音，在"没有"栏中打勾(✓)。

Target Words	Yes	No
6. participle	✓	
7. multiple	✓	
8. displeased		✓
9. simple	✓	
10. plentiful		✓

Answer Key

Name: _____ Date: ___/___/_____ Score: _____

Lesson 16.5

Reading Words with a Silent Letter "p"

✓ **Lesson Check Point**

 Directions: Read the target words in the word box. Write the words that have a silent letter "p" in the first column. Write the words that do not have a silent letter "p" in the second column.

路线：读单词框中的目标词。在第一栏中写上含不发音 p 的词。 在第二栏中写上不带不发音 p 的词。

Target Word Box				
apple	receipt	sleep	compose	slippery
suppose	point	puppy	hopping	raspberry
tips	sample	corps	predict	play
plot	psychic	cupboard	stamps	surprise

Letter "p" is silent	Letter "p" has the /p/ sound
corps	plot
apple	tips
receipt	play
slippery	sleep
puppy	point
psychic	predict
raspberry	sample
cupboard	stamps
suppose	surprise
hopping	compose

Classwork

 Name: _____ Date:___/___/_____ Score: _____

The Reading Challenge

Lesson 16.6

Reading Multisyllable Words

✓ **Lesson Check Point**

 Directions: Read and divide each target word into syllables. Write each word and place a hyphen (-) between the syllables in the second column. Write the number of syllables in the third column. Use a dictionary or the Internet to check your answers.

路线：读目标词后，划分音节。写下每个词，在第二栏中写上音 节，用 (-) 连接。在第三栏写上音节数。用词典或通过互联网检 查你的答案。

Target Words	Words Divided into Syllables	Number of Syllables
1. people	peo-ple	2
2. plural	plu-ral	2
3. powder	pow-der	2
4. privatized	pri-va-tized	3
5. platform	plat-form	2
6. politeness	po-lite-ness	3
7. plastic	plas-tic	2
8. persistence	per-sis-tence	3
9. parsley	pars-ley	2
10. peanut	pea-nut	2

Answer Key

 Name: _____ Date: ___/___/_____ Score: _____

The Reading Challenge

Lesson 16.6

Reading Multisyllable Words

✓ **Lesson Check Point**

 Directions: Read each target word. Circle the word in the row that is divided correctly into syllables. Use a dictionary or the Internet to check your answers.

路线：读每个目标词。圈出行中音节划分正确的词。用词典或通过互联网检查你的答案。

Model

| paragraph | **a. par-a-graph** (circled) | b. pa-ra-graph | c. par-ag-raph |

1. period	a. per-i-od	**b. pe-ri-od** (circled)	c. pe-r-iod
2. pyramid	**a. pyr-a-mid** (circled)	b. py-ra-mid	c. pyr-am-id
3. personal	**a. per-son-al** (circled)	b. pers-on-al	c. per-so-nal
4. parakeet	a. pa-ra-keet	**b. par-a-keet** (circled)	c. pa-rak-eet
5. punctual	a. pun-ctu-al	b. punc-t-ual	**c. punc-tu-al** (circled)
6. Panama	a. Pan-am-a	**b. Pan-a-ma** (circled)	c. Pa-na-ma
7. perigee	a. pe-rig-ee	**b. per-i-gee** (circled)	c. per-ig-ee
8. peculiar	a. pec-u-liar	b. pe-cul-iar	**c. pe-cu-liar** (circled)

Classwork

 Name: _____ Date:___/___/_____ Score:_____

Lesson 16.7

Reading and Writing

Proper and Common Nouns and Adjectives

✓ Lesson Check Point

 Directions: Read the words in the word box. Put an (X) on the line next to each word that is written incorrectly. Remember that all proper nouns and proper adjectives are capitalized. Use a dictionary or the Internet to check your answers.

路线：读单词框中的词。在书写错误的单词旁边的线上打叉(X)。记得合适的名词和形容词需要大写。用词典或通过互联网检查你的答案。

Word Box					
__	Poland	X	philippine	__	place
__	passport	__	Peruvian	X	panama
X	Penguin	__	people	X	Passenger
__	pharmacist	X	pennsylvania	X	Poodle

 Directions: Read each unedited sentence and underline the word that is written incorrectly. Write each sentence correctly on the line.

路线：读每个未经编辑的句子，并给书写错误的词加下划线。在线 上写上正确的句子。

Model
The poem, "<u>puddles</u>," was written by Patrick Parker.
<u>The poem, "Puddles," was written by Patrick Parker.</u>

1. The <u>panama</u> Canal is a powerful structure.
<u>The Panama Canal is a powerful structure.</u>

2. The City of <u>philadelphia</u> is located in Pennsylvania.
<u>The City of Philadelphia is located in Pennsylvania.</u>

3. The <u>peruvian</u> coast bordering the Pacific Ocean is a desert strip.
<u>The Peruvian coast bordering the Pacific Ocean is a desert strip.</u>

4. <u>perry</u> the Platypus is the star of the hit show "Phineas and Ferb."
<u>Perry the Platypus is the star of the hit show "Phineas and Ferb."</u>

Answer Key

 Name: _____ Date: ___/___/_____ Score: _____

Lesson 17.1

Reading Words with the Letter Q/q

✓ **Lesson Check Point**

 Directions: Read each target word. Find the letter "q" and put a check (✓) in the column that identifies its position: beginning, within or end.
路线：读每个目标词。找出字母 q 在栏中打勾 (✓) 示意：开始，中间或末尾。

Target Words	Beginning (First Letter)	Within	End (Last Letter)
1. question	✓		
2. squabbled		✓	
3. quotation	✓		
4. Iraq			✓
5. consequent		✓	

 Directions: Read each sentence and underline the words that begin with the letter "q." Write all the underlined words in alphabetical order on the lines below.
路线：读每个句子，并给首字母为 q 的词加下划线。在下面的 线上按照字母顺序写出所有下划线标记的单词。

6. <u>Quincy</u> and his family are from <u>Quebec</u>, Canada.

7. The new <u>quilts</u> are made with high <u>quality</u> fabrics.

8. My sister, <u>Queenisha</u>, sleeps on a <u>queen-sized</u> bed.

9. All the children in the <u>Quinn</u> family have four <u>quarters</u>.

10. All the candidates are highly <u>qualified</u> for the job at <u>Quick</u> Inc.

qualified   quality   quarters
Quebec   Queenisha   queen-sized
Quick   quilts   Quincy
                  Quinn

Learn To Read English With Directions In Chinese   169   Copyrighted Material

Classwork

 Name: _____ Date: ___/___/_____ Score: _____

Lesson 17.2

Reading Words with the Letter "q" and "qu" Letter Combination

✓ Lesson Check Point

 Directions: Read each target word. Circle the word in the column that has the same "q" or "qu" sound(s) as the target word.
路线：读每个目标词。圈出栏中与目标词含相同"q"或"qu"音的单词。

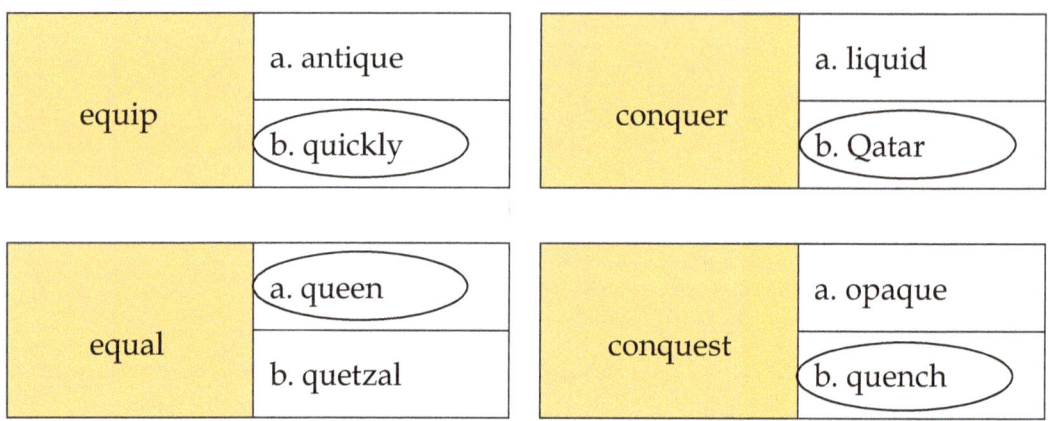

 Directions: Read each target word. Put a check (✓) under the correct column heading.
路线：读每个目标词。在符合要求的栏下打勾 (✓)。

Target Words	"qu" has the /k/ sound as in the word <u>plaque</u>	"qu" has the /k/ + /w/ sounds as in the word <u>queen</u>
1. equip		✓
2. conquer	✓	
3. equal		✓
4. conquest		✓

 Name: _____ Date: ___/___/_____ Score: _____

Answer Key

Lesson 17.2

Reading Words with the "qu" Letter Combination

✓ **Lesson Check Point**

 Directions: Read each target word. Circle the word in the column that has the same "qu" sound(s) as the target word.

路线：读每个目标词。圈出栏中与目标词含相同"qu"音的单词。

inquire	(a. queen)
	b. boutique

lacquer	a. quilt
	(b. racquet)

technique	(a. antique)
	b. conquest

questions	(a. quarterly)
	b. techniques

 Directions: Read each target word. Put a check (✓) under the correct column heading.

路线：读每个目标词。在符合要求的栏下打勾 (✓)。

Target Words	"qu" has the /k/ + /w/ sounds as in the word **queen**	"qu" has the /k/ sound as in the word **plaque**	"qu" is silent as in the word **racquet**
1. inquire	✓		
2. lacquer			✓
3. technique		✓	
4. questions	✓		

Classwork

Name: _____ Date: ___/___/_____ Score: _____

The Reading Challenge

Lesson 17.3

Reading Multisyllable Words

 Lesson Check Point

 Directions: Read and divide each target word into syllables. Write each word and place a hyphen (-) between the syllables in the second column. Write the number of syllables in the third column. Use a dictionary or the Internet to check your answers.

路线：读目标词后，划分音节。写下每个词，在第二栏中写上音 节，用 (-) 连接。在第三栏写上音节数。用词典或通过互联网检 查你的答案。

Target Words	Words Divided into Syllables	Number of Syllables
1. quarantine	quar-an-tine	3
2. quintet	quin-tet	2
3. quiver	quiv-er	2
4. quota	quo-ta	2
5. query	que-ry	2
6. quartet	quar-tet	2
7. quantities	quan-ti-ties	3
8. qualified	qual-i-fied	3
9. quadruple	quad-ru-ple	3
10. quietness	qui-et-ness	3

Name: _____ Date: ___/___/_____ Score: _____

The Reading Challenge

Lesson 17.3

Reading Multisyllable Words

✓ **Lesson Check Point**

Answer Key

 Directions: Read each target word. Circle the word in the row that is divided correctly into syllables. Use a dictionary or the Internet to check your answers.

路线：读每个目标词。圈出行中音节划分正确的词。用词典或通过互联网检查你的答案。

Model

| quarter | a. quart-er | (b. quar-ter) | c. qu-arter |

1. quantum	(a. quan-tum)	b. quant-um	c. qua-ntum
2. qualify	(a. qual-i-fy)	b. qua-li-fy	c. qua-lif-y
3. quiver	a. qui-ver	(b. quiv-er)	c. qu-iver
4. question	(a. ques-tion)	b. quest-ion	c. que-stion
5. quotient	a. quot-ient	b. qu-otient	(c. quo-tient)
6. quota	a. qu-ota	(b. quo-ta)	c. quot-a
7. Quebec	a. Qu-ebec	(b. Que-bec)	c. Queb-ec
8. quietude	(a. qui-e-tude)	b. quiet-ude	c. quie-tu-de

Learn To Read English With Directions In Chinese   Copyrighted Material

Classwork

 Name: _____ Date: ___/___/_____ Score: _____

Lesson 17.4

Reading and Writing

Proper and Common Nouns and Adjectives

✓ Lesson Check Point

 Directions: Read the words in the word box. Put an (X) on the line next to each word that is written incorrectly. Remember that all proper nouns and proper adjectives are capitalized. Use a dictionary or the Internet to check your answers.

路线：读单词框中的词。在书写错误的单词旁边的线上打叉(X)。记得合适的名词和形容词需要大写。用词典或通过互联网检查你 的答案。

Word Box					
__	quarrel	X	quebec	__	Quakers
X	Quotient	__	Qatar	__	questionable
X	Quotes	__	quickly	X	queen Anne
X	Quiver	X	Quiche	__	Quincy

 Directions: Read each unedited sentence and underline the word that is written incorrectly. Write each sentence correctly on the line.

路线：读每个未经编辑的句子，并给书写错误的词加下划线。在线 上写上正确的句子。

Model
The queen of England is very quiet.
The Queen of England is very quiet.

1. According to my Quartz watch, it is a Quarter after two.
According to my Quartz watch, it is a quarter after two.

2. My good friends, Mr. and Mrs. Quinn, are quakers.
My good friends, Mr. and Mrs. Quinn, are Quakers.

3. The queen is going to visit quezon City in the Philippines.
The queen is going to visit Quezon City in the Philippines.

4. After reading the article, I asked a Question about Queen Elizabeth.
After reading the article, I asked a question about Queen Elizabeth.

Answer Key

 Name: _____ Date: ___/___/_____ Score: _____

Lesson 18.1

Reading Words with the Letter R/r

✓ Lesson Check Point

 Directions: Read each target word. Find the letter "r" and put a check (✓) in the column that identifies its position: beginning, within or end.
路线：读每个目标词。找出字母 r 在栏中打勾 (✓) 示意： 开始，中间或末尾。

Target Words	Beginning (First Letter)	Within	End (Last Letter)
1. cashier			✓
2. recent	✓		
3. folder			✓
4. grape		✓	
5. runaway	✓		

 Directions: Read each sentence and underline the words that begin with the letter "r." Write all the underlined words in alphabetical order on the lines below.
路线：读每个句子，并给首字母为 r 的词加下划线。在下面的 线上按照字母顺序写出所有下划线标记的单词。

6. At <u>recess</u>, Brianna and I <u>ran</u> quickly on the track.

7. The green <u>rowboat</u> is floating along the Nile <u>River</u>.

8. Brian <u>rode</u> his bike along the base of the <u>Rocky</u> Mountains.

9. The <u>residents</u> have the new Long Island <u>Railroad</u> schedule.

10. We can preserve our planet by <u>recycling</u> and <u>reusing</u> items.

<u>Railroad</u>   <u>ran</u>   <u>recess</u>
<u>recycling</u>   <u>residents</u>   <u>reusing</u>
<u>River</u>   <u>Rocky</u>   <u>rode</u>
               <u>rowboat</u>

Classwork

Name: _____ Date:___/___/_____ Score:_____

Lesson 18.2

Reading Words with the Letter "r" Combinations:
"br," "cr," "dr," "fr," "gr," "pr" and "tr"

✓ Lesson Check Point

Directions: Read the target words in the word box. Identify the words with the following letter combinations: "br," "cr," "dr," "fr," "gr," "pr" and "tr." Write the target word on the line that correctly completes each sentence.

路线：读框中的目标词。认识带以下字母组合的单词："br," "cr," "dr," "fr," "gr," "pr" 和 "tr"。在线上写上正确目标词，完成整个句 子。

Target Word Box			
friends	traveling	bread	groom
principal	cruise		drifting
brochure	program		trucks

1. The _____cruise_____ brochure is on the brass table.

2. Francis and Brad are best _____friends_____.

3. The new _____principal_____ is our school's leader.

4. Yesterday, I saw logs _____drifting_____ along the riverbank.

5. The two loaves of ___bread___ are fresh out of the oven.

6. The train is ___traveling___ from New York to Chicago.

7. The college admission ___brochure___ is very informative.

8. My social service ___program___ distributes food to needy families.

9. Testa's electric ___trucks___ travel up to 100 miles without recharging.

10. The bride and ___groom___ received lots of expensive wedding presents.

Answer Key

Name: _____ Date: ___/___/_____ Score: _____

The Reading Challenge

Lesson 18.3

Reading Multisyllable Words

✓ Lesson Check Point

Directions: Read and divide each target word into syllables. Write each word and place a hyphen (-) between the syllables in the second column. Write the number of syllables in the third column. Use a dictionary or the Internet to check your answers.

路线：读目标词后，划分音节。写下每个词，在第二栏中写上音节，用 (-) 连接。在第三栏写上音节数。用词典或通过互联网检查你的答案。

Target Words	Words Divided into Syllables	Number of Syllables
1. reviewing	re-view-ing	3
2. rigorously	rig-or-ous-ly	4
3. rapidly	rap-id-ly	3
4. ready	read-y	2
5. rocky	rock-y	2
6. rather	rath-er	2
7. reading	read-ing	2
8. rapture	rap-ture	2
9. reflection	re-flec-tion	3
10. reporting	re-port-ing	3

Learn To Read English With Directions In Chinese

Classwork

Name: _____ Date: ___/___/_____ Score: _____

The Reading Challenge

Lesson 18.3

Reading Multisyllable Words

✓ Lesson Check Point

Directions: Read each target word. Circle the word in the row that is divided correctly into syllables. Use a dictionary or the Internet to check your answers.

路线：读每个目标词。圈出行中音节划分正确的词。用词典或通过互联网检查你的答案。

Model

| runaway | a. ru-na-way | (b. run-a-way) | c. run-aw-ay |

| 1. robotics | (a. ro-bot-ics) | b. rob-ot-ics | c. ro-bo-tics |

| 2. radius | (a. ra-di-us) | b. rad-i-us | c. ra-diu-s |

| 3. radical | (a. rad-i-cal) | b. ra-dic-al | c. ra-di-cal |

| 4. reception | a. re-cept-ion | b. rec-ep-tion | (c. re-cep-tion) |

| 5. royalist | a. ro-yal-ist | b. roy-a-list | (c. roy-al-ist) |

| 6. reconcile | a. re-con-cile | (b. rec-on-cile) | c. rec-onc-ile |

| 7. recliner | a. rec-lin-er | b. re-cli-ner | (c. re-clin-er) |

| 8. refresher | (a. re-fresh-er) | b. ref-res-her | c. ref-resh-er |

Name: _____ Date: ___/___/_____ Score: _____

Lesson 18.4
Reading and Writing
Proper and Common Nouns and Adjectives

✓ Lesson Check Point

 Directions: Read the words in the word box. Put an (X) on the line next to each word that is written incorrectly. Remember that all proper nouns and proper adjectives are capitalized. Use a dictionary or the Internet to check your answers.

路线：读单词框中的词。在书写错误的单词旁边的线上打叉(X)。记得合适的名词和形容词需要大写。用词典或通过互联网检查你的答案。

Word Box					
__	runner	_X_	Amazon river	_X_	Red CRoss
__	Richard	__	Ryan	__	rainforest
_X_	romanian	__	Richmond, VA	_X_	Railroad
_X_	The rockies	__	roaches	_X_	rome

 Directions: Read each unedited sentence and underline the word that is written incorrectly. Write each sentence correctly on the line.

路线：读每个未经编辑的句子，并给书写错误的词加下划线。在线上写上正确的句子。

Model
We saw two <u>Retired</u> racehorses at Richardson Ranch.
<u>We saw two retired racehorses at Richardson Ranch.</u>

1. Raphael said, "<u>russia</u> is the world's largest country."
<u>Raphael said, "Russia is the world's largest country."</u>

2. My friends, Rachel and Ricky, went to the Amazon <u>rainforest</u>.
<u>My friends, Rachel and Ricky, went to the Amazon Rainforest.</u>

3. Mr. Richards received the <u>rockefeller</u> Merit Award for Excellence.
<u>Mr. Richards received the Rockefeller Merit Award for Excellence.</u>

4. Do you know that Rose Robin <u>restaurant</u> serves the best ribs?
<u>Do you know that Rose Robin Restaurant serves the best ribs?</u>

Classwork

Name: _____ Date: ___/___/_____ Score: _____

Lesson 19.1

Reading Words with the Letter S/s

✓ Lesson Check Point

Directions: Read each target word. Find the letter "s" and put a check (✓) in the column that identifies its position: beginning, within or end.
路线：读每个目标词。找出字母 s 在栏中打勾 (✓) 示意： 开始，中间 或末尾。

Target Words	Beginning (First Letter)	Within	End (Last Letter)
1. safety	✓		
2. matches			✓
3. runners			✓
4. shower	✓		
5. construct		✓	

Directions: Read each sentence and underline the words that begin with the letter "s." Write all the underlined words in alphabetical order on the lines below.
路线：读每个句子，并给首字母为 s 的词加下划线。在下面的 线上按照字母顺序写出所有下划线标记的单词。

6. Dexter ate a tasty <u>salami</u> <u>sandwich</u> for lunch.

7. My brother received two <u>scholarships</u> for <u>school</u>.

8. Melanie <u>said</u>, "My grandmother is a great <u>singer</u>."

9. Melissa is using <u>scissors</u> to cut ten <u>sheets</u> of paper.

10. Both Josiah and <u>Simone</u> are <u>seventy-six</u> years old.

<u>said</u>　　　　　　　　<u>salami</u>　　　　　　　　<u>sandwich</u>
<u>scholarship</u>　　　　　<u>school</u>　　　　　　　　<u>scissors</u>
<u>singer</u>　　　　　　　　<u>seventy-six</u>　　　　　　<u>sheets</u>
　　　　　　　　　　　　<u>Simone</u>

Unit S Lesson 19.1

Learn To Read English With Directions In Chinese　　180　　Copyrighted Material

Answer Key

Name: _____ Date: ___/___/_____ Score: _____

Lesson 19.1

Reading Words with the Letter S/s

 Lesson Check Point

 Directions: Read each target word. Circle the word in the column that has the same "s" sound as the target word.
路线：读每个目标词。圈出栏中与目标词含相同 s 音的单词。

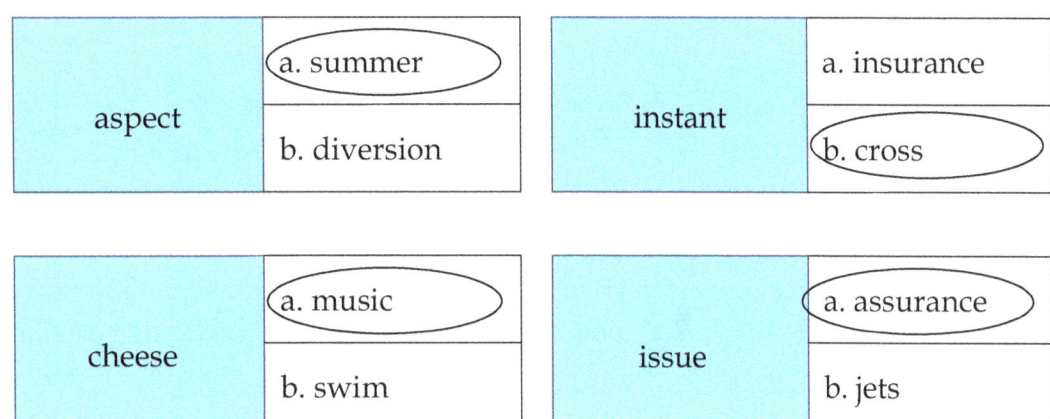

 Directions: Read each target word. Put a check (✓) under the correct column heading.
路线：读每个目标词。在符合要求的栏下打勾 (✓)。

Target Words	"s" has the /s/ sound as in the word sun	"s" has the /sh/ sound as in the word sugar	"s" has the /z/ sound as in the word his	"s" has the /zh/ sound as in the word vision
1. aspect	✓			
2. instant	✓			
3. cheese			✓	
4. issue		✓		

Learn To Read English With Directions In Chinese

Classwork

 Name: _____ Date: ___/___/_____ Score: _____

Lesson 19.2

Reading Words with the "sion," "sial" & "scious" Suffixes

✓ Lesson Check Point

 Directions: Read each target word. Circle the word in the column that has the same "sion," "sial" or "scious" sound as the target word.
路线：读每个目标词。圈出栏中与目标词发相同"sion,""sial"或"scious"音的词。

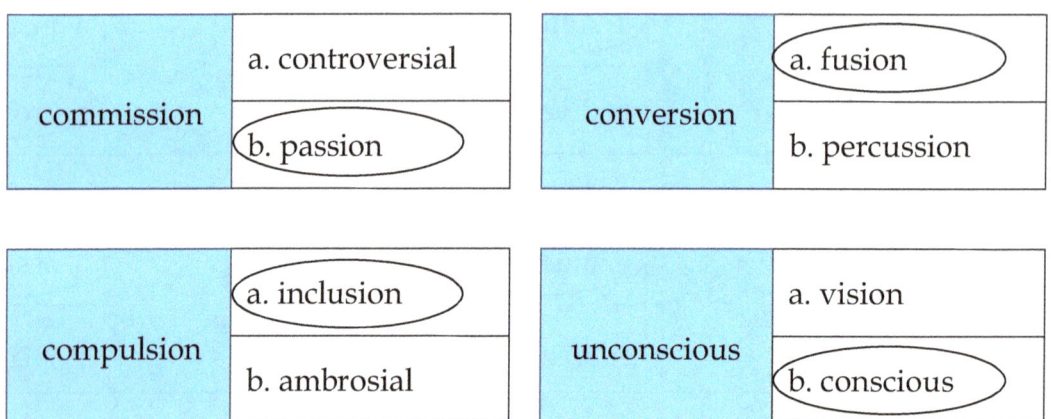

 Directions: Read each target word. Put a check (✓) under the correct column heading.
路线：读每个目标词。在符合要求的栏下打勾 (✓)。

Target Words	"sion" has the /sh/ +/ə/+/n/ sounds as in the word <u>passion</u>	"sion" has the /zh/ +/ə/+/n/ sounds as in the word <u>vision</u>	"scious" has the /sh/ +/ə/+/s/ sounds as in the word <u>conscious</u>
1. commission	✓		
2. conversion		✓	
3. compulsion	✓		
4. unconscious			✓

Answer Key

 Name: _____ Date:___/___/_____ Score: _____

Lesson 19.3

Reading Words with the "sch" Letter Combination

✓ **Lesson Check Point**

 Directions: Read each target word. Circle the word in the column that has the same "sch" sound(s) as the target word.
路线：读每个目标词。圈出栏中与目标词含相同"sch"音的单词。

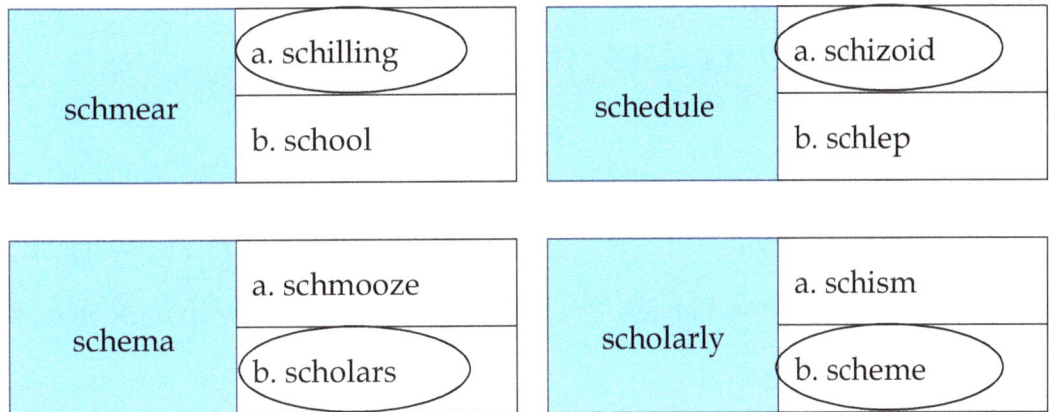

 Directions: Read each target word. Put a check (✓) under the correct column heading.
路线：读每个目标词。在符合要求的栏下打勾 (✓)。

Target Words	"sch" has the /s/ + /k/ sounds as in the word school	"sch" has the /sh/ sound as in the word schilling
1. schmear		✓
2. schedule	✓	
3. schema	✓	
4. scholarly	✓	

Classwork

 Name: _____ Date: ___/___/_____ Score: _____

Lesson 19.4

Reading Words with the "scr," "shr," "spr" & "str" Letter Combinations

Dictionary Skills/ Vocabulary

✓ Lesson Check Point

 Directions: Read each target word and its definition. Write the letter of the definition on the line of each target word. Use a dictionary or the Internet to check your answers.

路线：读每个目标词及其定义。在目标词前线上写上正确定义的 字母编号。用词典或通过互联网检查你的答案。

Target Words	Definitions
1. _c_ scrub	a. a device used to sprinkle water on a lawn
2. _b_ strawberries	b. sweet, red berries with a green leaf on top
3. _e_ shredder	c. to clean something by brushing
4. _d_ street	d. a paved road in a town or city
5. _a_ sprinkler	e. a machine that cuts paper into small pieces

 Directions: Read each sentence. Underline the word in the parentheses that correctly completes each sentence. Then, write the underlined word on the line.

路线：阅读每个句子。在括号中选择符合句子的词，并添加下划 线。然后，在线上写出下划线单词。

6. I will water my grass with a __sprinkler__ system. (street, sprinkler)

7. She will __scrub__ the dirty floor with a firm brush. (street, scrub)

8. Stan shreds documents with a __shredder__. (shredder, sprinkler)

9. The driver drove down the __street__ at a high speed. (street, scrub)

10. I enjoy __strawberries__ with my breakfast cereal. (shredder, strawberries)

Answer Key

 Name: _____ Date: ___/___/_____ Score: _____

Lesson 19.5

Reading Words with the "sl" & "sle" Letter Combinations

Dictionary Skills/ Vocabulary

✓ **Lesson Check Point**

 Directions: Read each target word and its definition. Write the target word on the line in front of its meaning. Use a dictionary or the Internet to check your answers.

路线：读每个目标词及其定义。在目标词前线上写上正确定义的 字母编号。用词典或通过互联网检查你的答案。

Target Word Box				
sleeves	slippery	slope	sloth	sly

1. slippery   causing to slip and/or slide
2. sly   a characteristic of a tricky person
3. sloth   a furry mammal that moves very slowly
4. slopes   a falling or rising land surface
5. sleeves   the parts of a garment that cover a person's arms

 Directions: Read each sentence. Underline the word in the parentheses that correctly completes each sentence. Then, write the underlined word on the line.

路线：阅读每个句子。在括号中选择符合句子的词，并添加下划 线。然后，在线上写出下划线单词。

6. In the woods, the tricky fox has a _____sly_____ smile. (sloth, <u>sly</u>)

7. I could not hold the _____slippery_____ starfish. (<u>slippery</u>, slopes)

8. The _____sloth_____ is hanging on the tropical tree. (<u>sloth</u>, slippery)

9. Sam is wearing a shirt with short _____sleeves_____. (sly, <u>sleeves</u>)

10. The ski _____slopes_____ are covered with snow and ice. (<u>slopes</u>, sleeves)

Classwork

 Name: _____ Date: ___/___/_____ Score: _____

Lesson 19.5

Reading Words with the "sle" Letter Combination

✓ Lesson Check Point

 Directions: Read each target word. Find the "sle" letter combination and put a check (✓) in the column that identifies its position: beginning, within or end.
路线：读每个目标词。找到"sle"字母组合，并在栏中打勾(✓)示 意：开始，中间或末尾。

Target Words	Beginning (First 3 Letters)	Within	End (Last 3 Letters)
1. sleet	✓		
2. sleeves	✓		
3. sleigh	✓		
4. tussle			✓
5. measles		✓	

 Directions: Read each target word. Put a check (✓) in the "yes" column if the "sle" letter combination has the /s/ + /ə/ + /l/ or /z/ + /ə/ + /l/ sounds. Put a check (✓) in the "no" column if the "sle" letter combination does not have the /s/ + /ə/ + /l/ or /z/ + /ə/ + /l/ sounds.
路线：读每个目标词。如果"sle"字母组合发/s/ + /ə/ + /l/ 或/z/ + /ə/ + /l/ 的音，在"是"栏 中 打勾 (✓)。如果"sle"字母组合不发/s/ + /ə/ + /l/ 或/z/ + /ə/ + /l/的音，在"没有"栏中 打勾(✓)。

Target Words	Yes	No
6. sleet		✓
7. sleeves		✓
8. sleigh		✓
9. tussle	✓	
10. measles	✓	

 Name: _____ Date: __/__/____ Score: _____

Answer Key

Lesson 19.6

Reading Words with the "sm" Letter Combination

✓ **Lesson Check Point**

 Directions: Read each target word. Circle the word in the column that has the same "sm" sounds as the target word.

路线：读每个目标词。圈出栏中与目标词含相同"sm"音的单词。

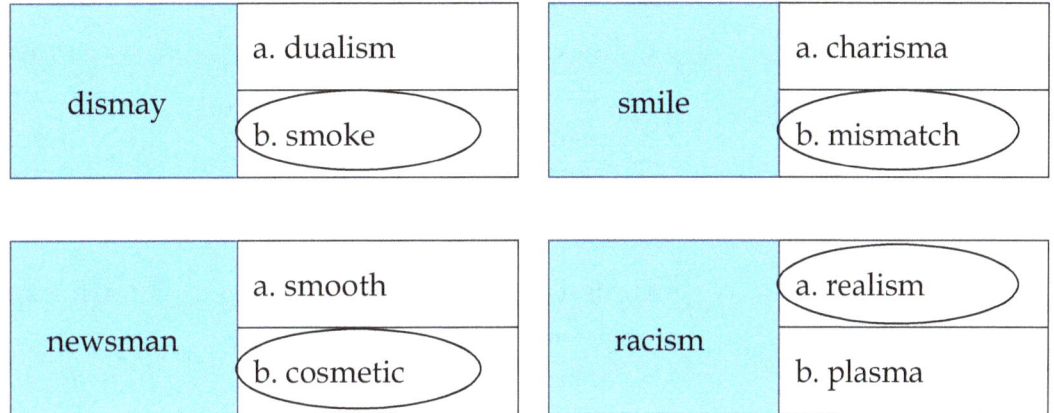

 Directions: Read each target word. Put a check (✓) under the correct column heading.

路线：读每个目标词。在符合要求的栏下打勾 (✓)。

Target Words	"sm" has the /s/ + /m/ sounds as in the word smell	"sm" has the /z/ + /m/ sounds as in the word cosmic	"sm" has the /z/ + /ə/ + /m/ sounds as in the word autism
1. dismay	✓		
2. smile	✓		
3. newsman		✓	
4. racism			✓

Classwork

Name: _____ Date: ___/___/_____ Score: _____

Lesson 19.7

Reading Words with the "ss" Letter Combination

✓ **Lesson Check Point**

Directions: Read each target word. Circle the word in the column that has the same "ss" sound(s) as the target word.
路线：读每个目标词。圈出栏中与目标词含相同"ss"音的单词。

misshaped	a. dissolving
	(b. dissatisfy)

Missouri	a. compassion
	(b. dissolve)

expression	a. misstated
	(b. concussion)

mission	a. misspell
	(b. aggression)

Directions: Read each target word. Put a check (✓) under the correct column heading.
路线：读每个目标词。在符合要求的栏下打勾 (✓)。

Target Words	"ss" has the /sh/ sound as in the word <u>tissue</u>	"ss" has the /s/ + /s/ sounds as in the word <u>misspell</u>	"ss" has the /z/ sound as in the word <u>dissolve</u>
1. misshaped		✓	
2. Missouri			✓
3. expression	✓		
4. mission	✓		

Answer Key

 Name: _____ Date:___/___/_____ Score:_____

Lesson 19.8

Reading Words with a Silent Letter "s"

✓ **Lesson Check Point**

 Directions: Read the target words in the word box. Write the words that have a silent letter "s" in the first column. Write the words that do not have a silent letter "s" in the second column.

路线：读单词框中的目标词。在第一栏中写上含不发音 s 的词。 在第二栏中写上不带不发音 s 的词。

Target Word Box				
class	horses	handsome	island	debris
aisle	passage	estate	assess	becomes
request	hotels	Arkansas	consider	aside
optimist	address	discover	embassy	isle

Letter "s" is silent	Letter "s" has the /s/, /z/ or /sh/ sound
isle	aside
aisle	estate
assess	hotels
class	becomes
debris	request
island	horses
address	consider
embassy	optimist
passage	discover
Arkansas	handsome

Unit S Lesson 19.8

Learn To Read English With Directions In Chinese

Classwork

Name: _____ Date: ___/___/_____ Score: _____

The Reading Challenge

Lesson 19.9

Reading Multisyllable Words

✓ Lesson Check Point

Directions: Read and divide each target word into syllables. Write each word and place a hyphen (-) between the syllables in the second column. Write the number of syllables in the third column. Use a dictionary or the Internet to check your answers.

路线：读目标词后，划分音节。写下每个词，在第二栏中写上音 节，用 (-) 连接。在第三栏写上音节数。用词典或通过互联网检 查你的答案。

Target Words	Words Divided into Syllables	Number of Syllables
1. safety	safe-ty	2
2. senior	sen-ior	2
3. sampling	sam-pling	2
4. shampoo	sham-poo	2
5. seaport	sea-port	2
6. soldiers	sol-diers	2
7. satisfaction	sat-is-fac-tion	4
8. sequential	se-quen-tial	3
9. shadowing	shad-ow-ing	3
10. sisterhood	sis-ter-hood	3

Learn To Read English With Directions In Chinese   190   Copyrighted Material

Answer Key

 Name: _____ Date: ___/___/_____ Score: _____

The Reading Challenge

Lesson 19.9

Reading Multisyllable Words

✓ **Lesson Check Point**

 Directions: Read each target word. Circle the word in the row that is divided correctly into syllables. Use a dictionary or the Internet to check your answers.

路线：读每个目标词。圈出行中音节划分正确的词。用词典或通过互联网检查你的答案。

Model

| Saturday | a. Sa-tur-day | b. Sat-ur-day ⭕ | c. Sa-turd-ay |

| 1. seminar | a. sem-i-nar ⭕ | b. se-mi-nar | c. se-min-ar |

| 2. satisfy | a. sa-tis-fy | b. sa-tisf-y | c. sat-is-fy ⭕ |

| 3. seasonal | a. seas-on-al | b. sea-so-nal | c. sea-son-al ⭕ |

| 4. several | a. se-ver-al | b. sev-er-al ⭕ | c. sev-e-ral |

| 5. singular | a. sing-u-lar | b. sin-gu-lar ⭕ | c. sin-gul-ar |

| 6. semester | a. se-mest-er | b. sem-est-er | c. se-mes-ter ⭕ |

| 7. skeleton | a. skel-e-ton ⭕ | b. ske-le-ton | c. ske-let-on |

| 8. salary | a. sa-lar-y | b. sal-ar-y | c. sal-a-ry ⭕ |

Learn To Read English With Directions In Chinese

Classwork

Name: _____ Date: ___/___/_____ Score: _____

Lesson 19.10

Reading and Writing

Proper and Common Nouns and Adjectives

✓ **Lesson Check Point**

 Directions: Read the words in the word box. Put an (X) on the line next to each word that is written incorrectly. Remember that all proper nouns and proper adjectives are capitalized. Use a dictionary or the Internet to check your answers.

路线：读单词框中的词。在书写错误的单词旁边的线上打叉(X)。记得合适的名词和形容词需要大写。用词典或通过互联网检查你的答案。

Word Box					
_X_	Sandbox	_X_	siberia	___	Samoa
_X_	Salon	___	shrimp	_X_	Dr. samuel
___	San Juan	___	sample	_X_	Sailor
___	seagull	_X_	senator Sam	___	seahorse

 Directions: Read each unedited sentence and underline the word that is written incorrectly. Write each sentence correctly on the line.

路线：读每个未经编辑的句子，并给书写错误的词加下划线。在线上写上正确的句子。

Model
<u>sandy</u> is going to Salt Lake City on Sunday.
<u>Sandy is going to Salt Lake City on Sunday.</u>

1. On <u>saturday</u>, we are going sailing around South Bay.
<u>On Saturday, we are going sailing around South Bay.</u>

2. My <u>Siblings</u> received scholarships to Sidney School.
<u>My siblings received scholarships to Sidney School.</u>

3. On Sunday, I am going to have lunch with <u>sergeant</u> Smith.
<u>On Sunday, I am going to have lunch with Sergeant Smith.</u>

4. My grandparents, Samuel and Samantha, are <u>Senior</u> citizens.
<u>My grandparents, Samuel and Samantha, are senior citizens.</u>

Name: _____ Date: ___/___/_____ Score: _____

Lesson 20.1

Reading Words with the Letter T/t

✓ Lesson Check Point

 Directions: Read each target word. Find the letter "t" and put a check (✓) in the column that identifies its position: beginning, within or end.
路线：读每个目标词。找出字母 t 在栏中打勾 (✓) 示意： 开始，中间或末尾。

Target Words	Beginning (First Letter)	Within	End (Last Letter)
1. reporter		✓	
2. teenager	✓		
3. merchant			✓
4. Tuesday	✓		
5. section		✓	

 Directions: Read each sentence and underline the words that begin with the letter "t." Write all the underlined words in alphabetical order on the lines below.
路线：读每个句子，给以字母 t 开头的单词加下划线。在下面 的线上按照字母顺序写出所有加了下划线的单词。

6. My <u>teacher</u>, Ms. Peters, does not like <u>tarantulas</u>.

7. My sister <u>tossed</u> her interactive <u>toys</u> everywhere.

8. At <u>Thanksgiving</u> dinner, Danny ate rice and <u>turkey</u>.

9. <u>Terrence</u> likes putting <u>tartar</u> sauce on his fish sandwiches.

10. An intense <u>thunderstorm</u> caused damage <u>throughout</u> our county.

tarantulas	tartar	teacher
Terrence	Thanksgiving	throughout
thunderstorm	tossed	toys
	turkey	

Classwork

 Name: _____ Date: ___/___/_____ Score: _____

Lesson 20.2

Reading Words with the "thm" Letter Combination

✓ **Lesson Check Point**

 Directions: Read each target word. Circle the word in the column that has the same "thm" sound(s) as the target word.
路线：读每个目标词。圈出栏中与目标词含相同"thm"音的单词。

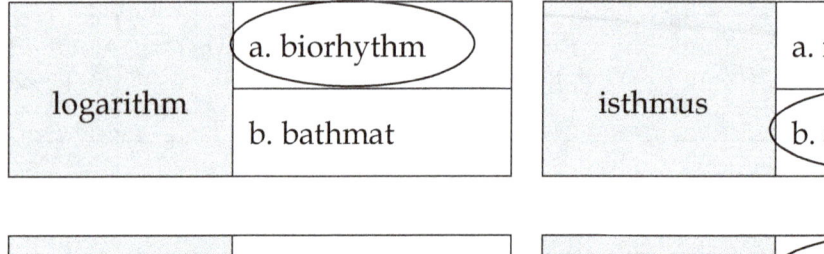

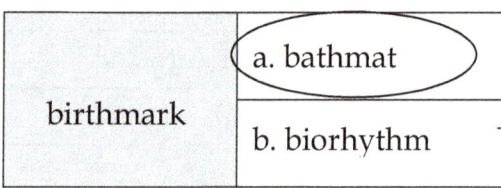

 Directions: Read each target word. Put a check (✓) under the correct column heading.
路线：读每个目标词。在符合要求的栏下打勾 (✓)。

Target Words	"thm" has the /th/ + /ə/ + /m/ sounds as in the word **rhythm**	"thm" has the /th/ + /m/ sounds as in the word **bathmat**	"thm" silent "th" + /m/ sound as in the word **asthma**
1. logarithm	✓		
2. isthmus			✓
3. algorithm	✓		
4. birthmark		✓	

Name: _____ Date: ___/___/_____ Score: _____

Lesson 20.3

Reading Words with the "tion," "tial" & "tious" Suffixes

✓ **Lesson Check Point**

 Directions: Read each target word. Circle the word in the column that has the same "tion," "tial" or "tious" sound as the target word.
路线：读每个目标词。圈出栏中含与目标词一样"tion"，"tial"或"tious"的词。

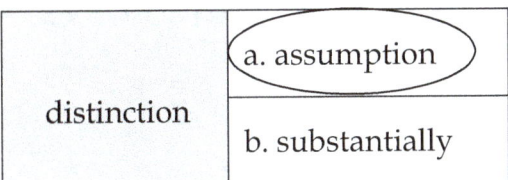

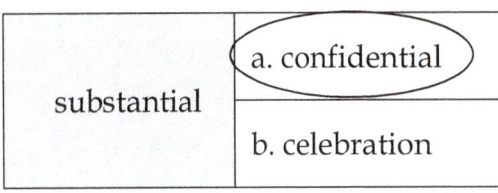

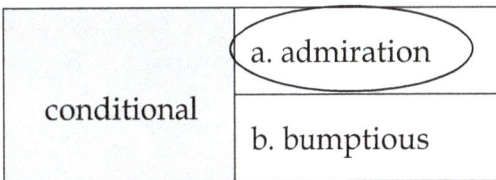

 Directions: Read each target word. Put a check (✓) under the correct column heading.
路线：读每个目标词。在符合要求的栏下打勾 (✓)。

Target Words	"tion" has the /sh/ +/ə/+/n/ sounds as in the word <u>education</u>	"tial" has the /sh/ +/ə/+/l/ sounds as in the word <u>partial</u>	"tious" has the /sh/ +/ə/+/s/ sounds as in the word <u>ambitious</u>
1. distinction	✓		
2. substantial		✓	
3. infectious			✓
4. conditional	✓		

Classwork

Name: _____ Date:___/___/_____ Score:_____

Lesson 20.4

Reading Words with the "tr" Letter Combination

Dictionary Skills/ Vocabulary

✓ Lesson Check Point

Directions: Read each target word and its definition. Write the letter of the definition on the line of each target word. Use a dictionary or the Internet to check your answers.

路线：读每个目标词及其定义。在目标词前线上写上正确定义的 字母编号。用词典或通过互联网检查你的答案。

Target Words	Definitions
1. _d_ tragic	a. a problematic situation, a conflict
2. _e_ trampled	b. to write words from one language to another
3. _c_ transfer	c. to move from one place to another
4. _b_ translate	d. a disastrous occurrence or event
5. _a_ trouble	e. the act of beating a surface down with one's feet

Directions: Read each sentence. Underline the word in the parentheses that correctly completes each sentence. Then, write the underlined word on the line.

路线：阅读每个句子。在括号中选择符合句子的词，并添加下划 线。然后，在线上写出下划线单词。

6. I ____translated____ the report from English to Arabic. (translated, tragic)

7. He got in ____trouble____ for breaking the class rules. (trouble, transfer)

8. Tress cried when she read the story's ____tragic____ ending. (tragic, trample)

9. Terrance will ____transfer____ to his connecting flight. (transfer, translate)

10. The horse ____trampled____ the crops in the field. (trouble, trampled)

Name: _____ Date: ___/___/_____ Score: _____

Answer Key

Lesson 20.5

Reading Words with the "tle" Letter Combination

✓ Lesson Check Point

 Directions: Read each target word. Find the "tle" letter combination and put a check (✓) in the column that identifies its position: beginning, within or end.

路线：读每个目标词。找到"tle"字母组合，并在栏中打勾(✓) 示意：开始，中间，结尾。

Target Words	Beginning (First 3 Letters)	Within	End (Last 3 Letters)
1. hurtle			✓
2. cutlet		✓	
3. outlet		✓	
4. settle			✓
5. countless		✓	

 Directions: Read each target word. Put a check (✓) in the "yes" column if the "tle" letter combination has the /t/ + /ə/ + /l/ sounds. Put a check (✓) in the "no" column if the "tle" letter combination does not have the /t/ + /ə/ + /l/ sounds.

路线：读每个目标词。如果"tle"字母组合发/t/ + /ə/ + /l/的音，在"是"栏中打勾 (✓)。如果"tle"字母组合不发/t/ + /ə/ + /l/的音，在"没有"栏中打勾(✓)。

Target Words	Yes	No
6. hurtle	✓	
7. cutlet		✓
8. outlet		✓
9. settle	✓	
10. countless		✓

Learn To Read English With Directions In Chinese

Classwork

Name: _____ Date: ___/ ___/ _____ Score: _____

Lesson 20.6

Reading Words with the Letter "t" Sounds

✓ Lesson Check Point

Directions: Read each target word. Circle the word in the column that has the same "t" sound as the target word.
路线：读每个目标词。圈出栏中与目标词含相同 t 音的单词。

| mention | (a. ambition) |
| | b. righteous |

| culture | (a. picture) |
| | b. contact |

| electric | (a. connect) |
| | b. action |

| actual | (a. denture) |
| | b. expect |

Directions: Read each target word. Put a check (✓) under the correct column heading.
路线：读每个目标词。在符合要求的栏下打勾 (✓)。

Target Words	"t" has the /t/ sound as in the word <u>multiply</u>	"t" has the /ch/ sound as in the word <u>picture</u>	"t" has the /sh/ sound as in the word <u>position</u>
1. mention			✓
2. culture		✓	
3. electric	✓		
4. actual		✓	

Name: _____ Date: ___/___/_____ Score: _____

Lesson 20.7

Reading Words with a Silent Letter "t"

✓ Lesson Check Point

 Directions: Read the target words in the word box. Write the words that have a silent letter "t" in the first column. Write the words that do not have a silent letter "t" in the second column.

路线：读单词框中的目标词。在第一栏中写上含不发音 t 的词。在第二栏中写上不带不发音 t 的词。

Target Word Box				
continue	itch	crochet	entrance	totally
pottery	curtain	kitchen	heart	factory
clothes	defeat	denote	listening	dieting
castle	postman	sitting	mortgage	snitch

Letter "t" is silent	Letter "t" has the /t/ sound
itch	heart
kitchen	denote
castle	defeat
clothes	curtain
snitch	totally
sitting	factory
pottery	entrance
crochet	dieting
listening	continue
mortgage	postman

Classwork

 Name: _____ Date:___/___/_____ Score:_____

The Reading Challenge

Lesson 20.8

Reading Multisyllable Words

✓ **Lesson Check Point**

 Directions: Read and divide each target word into syllables. Write each word and place a hyphen (-) between the syllables in the second column. Write the number of syllables in the third column. Use a dictionary or the Internet to check your answers.

路线：读目标词后，划分音节。写下每个词，在第二栏中写上音 节，用 (-) 连接。在第三栏写上音节数。用词典或通过互联网检 查你的答案。

Target Words	Words Divided into Syllables	Number of Syllables
1. traveling	trav-el-ing	3
2. tiny	ti-ny	2
3. treasure	treas-ure	2
4. textbooks	text-books	2
5. tonight	to-night	2
6. timbering	tim-ber-ing	3
7. tweezers	tweez-ers	2
8. turquoise	tur-quoise	2
9. transplanting	trans-plant-ing	3
10. title	ti-tle	2

Learn To Read English With Directions In Chinese

Name: _____ Date: ___/___/_____ Score: _____

The Reading Challenge

Lesson 20.8

Reading Multisyllable Words

✓ **Lesson Check Point**

 Directions: Read each target word. Circle the word in the row that is divided correctly into syllables. Use a dictionary or the Internet to check your answers.

路线：读每个目标词。圈出行中音节划分正确的词。用词典或通过互联网检查你的答案。

Model

| telephone | a. te-lep-hone | (b. tel-e-phone) | c. te-le-phone |

| 1. teenager | (a. teen-ag-er) | b. teen-a-ger | c. teena-g-er |

| 2. taxicab | a. ta-xic-ab | b. tax-ic-ab | (c. tax-i-cab) |

| 3. technical | a. te-chnic-al | b. tech-nic-al | (c. tech-ni-cal) |

| 4. triangle | a. tri-ang-le | (b. tri-an-gle) | c. tria-n-gle |

| 5. testify | (a. tes-ti-fy) | b. te-stif-y | c. tes-tif-y |

| 6. temperate | a. temp-er-ate | b. tem-pe-rate | (c. tem-per-ate) |

| 7. typical | a. ty-pi-cal | b. ty-pic-al | (c. typ-i-cal) |

| 8. translated | (a. trans-lat-ed) | b. transl-a-ted | c. tran-slat-ed |

Classwork

Name: _____ Date: ___/___/_____ Score: _____

Lesson 20.9

Reading and Writing

Proper and Common Nouns and Adjectives

✓ **Lesson Check Point**

Directions: Read the words in the word box. Put an (X) on the line next to each word that is written incorrectly. Remember that all proper nouns and proper adjectives are capitalized. Use a dictionary or the Internet to check your answers.

路线：读单词框中的词。在书写错误的单词旁边的线上打叉(X)。记得合适的名词和形容词需要大写。用词典或通过互联网检查你 的答案。

Word Box					
X	taiwan	X	thursday	__	thousand
__	Togo	X	Today	__	Tonga
__	thunder	__	Tokyo	X	tunisia
X	Twins	__	target	X	Tomato

Directions: Read each unedited sentence and underline the word that is written incorrectly. Write each sentence correctly on the line.

路线：读每个未经编辑的句子，并给书写错误的词加下划线。在线 上写上正确的句子。

Model
On <u>thursday</u>, a tornado destroyed my hometown.
<u>On Thursday, a tornado destroyed my hometown.</u>

1. I ate tasty <u>thai</u> food at Lemongrass Thailand Restaurant.
<u>I ate tasty Thai food at Lemongrass Thailand Restaurant.</u>

2. My dentist, Dr. Tracks, <u>Takes</u> good care of my teeth.
<u>My dentist, Dr. Tracks, takes good care of my teeth.</u>

3. In <u>tanzania</u>, the townspeople have tremendous hearts.
<u>In Tanzania, the townspeople have tremendous hearts.</u>

4. I will travel to the beautiful twin islands of Trinidad and <u>tobago</u>.
<u>I will travel to the beautiful twin islands of Trinidad and Tobago.</u>

Answer Key

 Name: _____ Date:___/___/_____ Score:_____

Lesson 21.1

Reading Words with the Letter U/u

✓ Lesson Check Point

 Directions: Read each target word. Find the letter "u" and put a check (✓) in the column that identifies its position: beginning, within or end.
路线：读每个目标词。找出字母 u 在栏中打勾 (✓) 示意： 开始，中间或末尾。

Target Words	Beginning (First Letter)	Within	End (Last Letter)
1. under	✓		
2. menu			✓
3. success		✓	
4. you			✓
5. university	✓		

 Directions: Read each target word. Read the words in the row and circle the word that has a different vowel "u" sound.
路线：读每个目标词。阅读这一行的词，圈出元音 u 发不同的 词。

Target Words				
6. swum	mud	(June)	tug	sub
7. chum	(thru)	bum	cut	hum
8. snub	nut	bud	(tube)	bun
9. thug	pun	cub	nun	(juke)
10. funny	(burst)	makeup	snuff	tux

Learn To Read English With Directions In Chinese 203 Copyrighted Material

Classwork

 Name: _____ Date:___/___/_____ Score:_____

Lesson 21.2

Reading Words with the Short Vowel "u" Sound

✓ Lesson Check Point

 Directions: Read the words in the four boxes. Circle two words with the short vowel /ŭ/ sound. The anchor word for the short vowel /ŭ/ sound is up.

路线：读四个框中的词。圈出含短元音 /ŭ/ 的两个词。锚点词词含短元音/ŭ/ 为英语单词，up。

fume	(buck)	(bump)	rust	(suck)	null
June	(dull)	crude	brute	rule	truce

chute	(lush)	(drunk)	mute	dune	flute
used	(punch)	fuse	(plush)	(duck)	(buff)

 Directions: Read the words in the four boxes. Circle two words that rhyme. Rhyming words have the same ending sound, such as just and must.

路线：读四个框中的词。圈出押韵的两个词。押韵词有同样的尾音，如，英语单词 just 和 must。

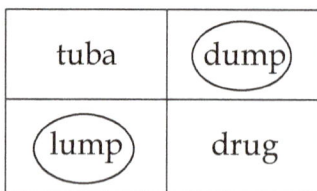 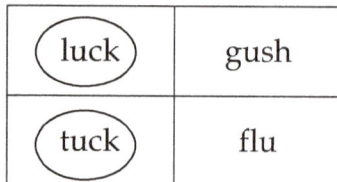

tuba	(dump)	(luck)	gush	grub	(rush)
(lump)	drug	(tuck)	flu	(hush)	use

stub	(rust)	cute	slug	super	(much)
tune	(dust)	(brush)	(crush)	smug	(such)

Name: _____ Date: ___/___/_____ Score: _____

Lesson 21.2

Reading & Writing Words with the Short Vowel "u" Sound

✓ **Lesson Check Point**

Directions: Read each sentence and underline three words with the short vowel /ŭ/ sound. Then, write the underlined words on the lines below. The anchor word for the short vowel /ŭ/ sound is <u>up</u>.

路线：读每个句子，划出含短元音/ŭ/的三个词。然后，在下面划 线处写上带下划线的词。含短元音/ŭ/的锚点词是 up。

Model

Ulysses, the <u>drummer</u>, <u>jumps</u> when he plays the <u>drums</u>.

drummer	jumps	drums

1. As Luke <u>trudged</u> in, he got <u>mud</u> on the <u>rug</u>.

trudged	mud	rug

2. The oatmeal in the <u>cup</u> is usually not <u>lumpy</u> and <u>mushy</u>.

cup	lumpy	mushy

3. The groomer <u>brushed</u> the <u>puppy's</u> fur with a soft <u>brush</u>.

brushed	puppy's	brush

4. In June, I was <u>lucky</u> to see the <u>ducks</u> and <u>cubs</u> at the zoo.

lucky	ducks	cubs

5. The <u>club's</u> members sat on the <u>rug</u> and ate blueberry <u>muffins</u>.

club's	rug	muffins

Classwork

 Name: _____ Date: ___/___/_____ Score: _____

Lesson 21.3

Reading Words with the Long Vowel "u" Sound

✓ **Lesson Check Point**

 Directions: Read the words in the four boxes. Circle two words with the long vowel /yoo/ or /oo/ sound. The anchor word for the long vowel /yoo/ and /oo/ sounds is <u>tube</u>.
路线：读四个框中的词。圈出带长元音/yoo/或/oo/的两个词。 锚点词 为含长元音/yoo/和/oo/的英语单词 tube。

guard	(June)		(brute)	junk		yucky	(dilute)
biscuit	(use)		bunch	(volume)		guest	(reduce)

stump	gulp		must	(prune)		sunken	(salute)
(nude)	(accuse)		(confuse)	quiet		lungs	(include)

 Directions: Read the words in the four boxes. Circle two words that rhyme. Rhyming words have the same ending sound, such as <u>rule</u> and <u>mule</u>.
路线：读四个框中的词。圈出押韵的两个词。押韵的词含同样的 尾音。如，英语单词 rule 和 mule。

dump	(cruel)		dusk	lumpy		(June)	duckling
Just	(fuel)		(glue)	(blue)		lucky	(tune)

(mute)	Dutch		sung	(rude)		munch	rushing
(flute)	pumps		(crude)	bumper		(excuse)	(refuse)

Answer Key

Name: _____ Date: ___/___/_____ Score: _____

Lesson 21.3

Reading & Writing Words with the Long Vowel "u" Sound

✓ **Lesson Check Point**

Directions: Read each sentence and underline three words with the long vowel /y$\overline{oo}$/ or /$\overline{oo}$/ sound. Then, write the underlined words on the lines below. The anchor word for the long vowel /y$\overline{oo}$/ and /$\overline{oo}$/ sounds is tube.

路线：读四个框中的词。圈出带长元音/y$\overline{oo}$/或/$\overline{oo}$/ 的两个词。 锚点词为含长元音/y$\overline{oo}$/和/$\overline{oo}$/ 的英语单词 tube。

Model

Bruce is going to play the tuba and drums in Uganda.

  Bruce   tuba   Uganda

1. At lunch, Lucy enjoys eating juicy fruits.

  Lucy   juicy   fruits

2. The students' blue uniforms are dull and unattractive.

  students'   blue   uniforms

3. My aunt used flowers to produce a fragrant perfume.

  used   produce   perfume

4. In June, the club's rules gradually changed for the better.

  June   rules   gradually

5. Mr. Gus Underhill refused to accept the students' excuses.

  refused   students'   excuses

Learn To Read English With Directions In Chinese

Classwork

 Name: _____ Date:___/___/_____ Score:_____

Review Lessons 21.2 & 21.3

Reading Short Vowel and Long Vowel Words

✓ Lesson Check Point

 Directions: Read the target words in the word box. In the first column, write the words that have the short vowel /ǔ/ sound, as in the word <u>up</u>. In the second column, write the words that have the long vowel /yo͞o/ or /o͞o/ sound, as in the word <u>tube</u>.

路线：读框中的目标词。在第一栏写上含短元音/ǔ/的单词，如英文单词 up。在第二栏写上含长元音/yo͞o/或/o͞o/ 的单词，如英文单词 tube。

Target Word Box				
lucky	bunch	consume	hunter	rung
using	dull	bumpers	accuse	truce
computer	tofu	lungs	commute	jumping
rushing	debut	music	dusty	uniform

Letter "u" has the /ǔ/ sound as in the word <u>up</u>

- dull
- rung
- lungs
- lucky
- dusty
- bunch
- hunter
- jumping
- rushing
- bumpers

Letter "u" has the /yo͞o/ or /o͞o/ sound as in the word <u>tube</u>

- tofu
- truce
- music
- debut
- using
- accuse
- uniform
- consume
- commute
- computer

Answer Key

Name: _____ Date: ___/___/_____ Score: _____

Lesson 21.4

Reading Words with Letter "u" Vowel Pairs

 Lesson Check Point

Directions: Read each target word. Circle the word in the column that has the same vowel "ua," "ue" or "ui" sound(s) as the target word.
路线：读每个目标词。圈出栏中含与目标词一样元音 "ua," "ue" 或 "ui" 的单词。

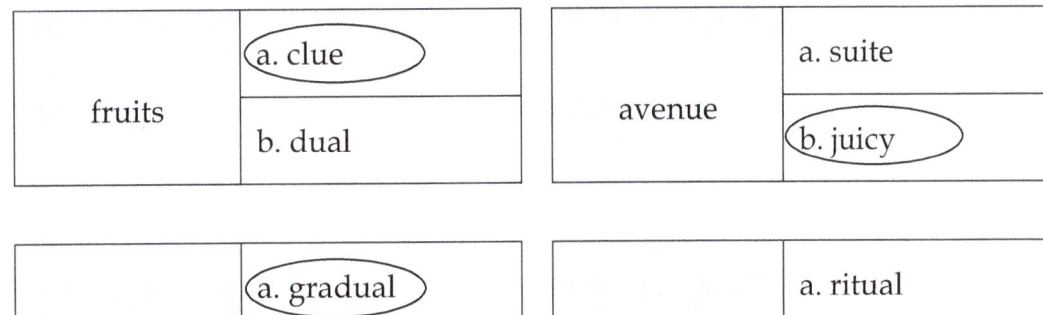

	a. clue ⭕
fruits	
	b. dual

	a. suite
avenue	
	b. juicy ⭕

	a. gradual ⭕
perpetual	
	b. recruit

	a. ritual
built	
	b. building ⭕

 Directions: Read each target word. Put a check (✓) under the correct column heading.
路线：读每个目标词。在符合要求的栏下打勾 (✓)。

Target Words	Words have the long "u" sound as in the word <u>blue</u>	Words do not have the long "u" sound
1. builds		✓
2. affluent	✓	
3. factual	✓	
4. suites		✓

Learn To Read English With Directions In Chinese

Classwork

 Name: _____ Date: ___/ ___/ _____ Score: _____

Lesson 21.5

Reading Words with the Final Letter "u"

✓ Lesson Check Point

 Directions: Read each target word. Find the letter "u" and put a check (✓) in the column that identifies its position within the syllable.
路线：读每个目标词。找到字母 u，并在栏中打勾(✓)，标示其 在音节中的位置。

Target Words	"u" is at the end of a one syllable word	"u" is at the end of the first syllable	"u" is at the end of a multi-syllable word
1. July		✓	
2. you	✓		
3. impromptu			✓
4. Utah		✓	
5. uniform		✓	

 Directions: Read each target word. Put a check (✓) under the correct column heading.
路线：读每个目标词。在符合要求的栏下打勾 (✓)。

Target Words	"u" has the /ŭ/ sound as in the word tub	"u" has the /yōō/ sound as in the word tube	"u" has the /ə/ sound as in the word circus	"u" is silent as in the word build
6. vague				✓
7. radius			✓	
8. clue		✓		
9. drums	✓			
10. survive			✓	

Unit U Lesson 21.5

Learn To Read English With Directions In Chinese

Name: _____   Date: ___/___/_____   Score: _____

Answer Key

Lesson 21.6

Reading Letter "u" Words with the Schwa Vowel Sound

✓ Lesson Check Point

 Directions: Read each target word. Circle the word in the column that has the same "u" sound as the target word.

路线：读每个目标词。圈出栏中与目标词含相同 u 音的单词。

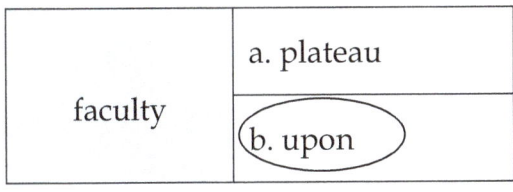
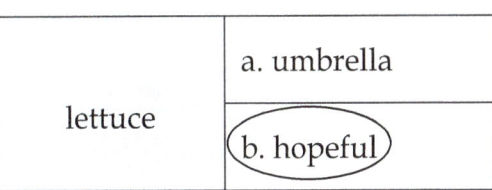
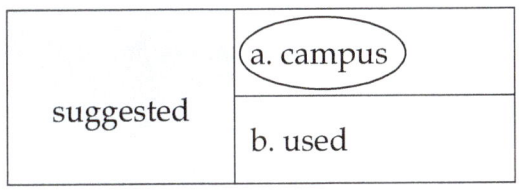
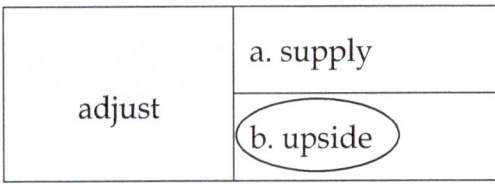

 Directions: Read each sentence and underline the letter "u" word that has the schwa vowel /ə/ sound. The anchor word for the letter "u" schwa vowel sound is <u>campus</u>.

路线：读每个句子。给含字母 u 且发施瓦/ə/音的单词加下划线。锚点词为含字母 u 且发施瓦音的英语单词，campus。

1. The umpire is not very <u>popular</u>.

2. Some of my students are very <u>playful</u>.

3. Hugo has nice <u>pictures</u> and gifts from Guyana.

4. In January, Eugene will visit <u>Portugal</u> and Uganda.

5. The <u>Museum</u> of Urban Studies is close to Pace University.

6. During class, I tend to <u>focus</u> on the bilingual presentations.

Classwork

Name: _____ Date: ___/___/_____ Score: _____

Lesson 21.7

Reading Words with the "ur" Letter Combination

Dictionary Skills/ Vocabulary

 Lesson Check Point

 **Directions:** Read each target word and its definition. Write the letter of the definition on the line of each target word. Use a dictionary or the Internet to check your answers.
路线：读每个目标词及其定义。在目标词前线上写上正确定义的 字母编号。用词典或通过互联网检查你的答案。

Target Words	Definitions
1. _b_ purse	a. the possessive form of the word, you
2. _c_ journey	b. a small bag used to carry money and items
3. _a_ Your	c. a trip; to go from one place to another
4. _e_ Failure	d. to have felt extreme sadness or sorrow
5. _d_ mourned	e. act of not succeeding

 Directions: Read each sentence and write the target word on the line that correctly completes the sentence.
路线：读每个句子和并在划线处填上合适的词。

6. My teacher shouted, "__Failure__ in school is unacceptable."

7. Jimmy _____mourned_____ the loss of his pet goldfish.

8. Grandma carries keys and money in her _____purse_____.

9. _____Your_____ brother is going to join the basketball team.

10. The characters are on a dangerous __journey__ in the woods.

Name: _____ Date: ___/___/_____ Score: _____

Lesson 21.8

Reading Words with a Silent Letter "u"

✓ **Lesson Check Point**

Directions: Read the target words in the word box. Write the words that have a silent letter "u" in the first column. Write the words that do not have a silent letter "u" in the second column.

路线：读单词框中的目标词。在第一栏中写上含不发音 u 的词。 在第二栏中写上不带不发音 u 的词。

Target Word Box				
fatigue	continuum	circuit	laughing	Guinea
guiding	avenue	Tuesday	rulers	attitude
unison	under	annual	guessing	visual
impromptu	building	tongues	biscuit	shoulder

Letter "u" is silent	Letter "u" has a letter "u" sound
fatigue	unison
circuit	avenue
laughing	Tuesday
Guinea	rulers
guiding	attitude
guessing	under
building	annual
biscuit	visual
shoulder	impromptu
tongues	continuum

Classwork

Name: _____ Date: ___/___/_____ Score: _____

Unit Review - U/u

Reading Words with Vowel "u" Sounds: /ŭ/, /o͞o/, /ə/ & Silent

✓ **Lesson Check Point**

Directions: Read each target word. Circle the word in the column that has the same "u" sound as the target word.

路线：读每个目标词。圈出栏中与目标词含相同 u 音的单词。

suggest	a. unicorn
	(b. subtract)

duckling	(a. hutch)
	b. music

student	(a. super)
	b. dumping

tongue	a. menu
	(b. guests)

Directions: Read each target word. Put a check (✓) under the correct column heading.

路线：读每个目标词。在符合要求的栏下打勾 (✓)。

Target Words	"u" has the /ŭ/ sound as in the word <u>tub</u>	"u" has the /o͞o/ sound as in the word <u>tube</u>	"u" has the /ə/ sound as in the word <u>circus</u>	"u" is silent as in the word <u>build</u>
1. suggest			✓	
2. duckling	✓			
3. student		✓		
4. tongue				✓

Name: _____ Date:___/___/_____ Score:_____

Answer Key

The Reading Challenge

Lesson 21.9

Reading Multisyllable Words

✓ Lesson Check Point

 Directions: Read and divide each target word into syllables. Write each word and place a hyphen (-) between the syllables in the second column. Write the number of syllables in the third column. Use a dictionary or the Internet to check your answers.

路线：读目标词后，划分音节。写下每个词，在第二栏中写上音 节，用 (-) 连接。在第三栏写上音节数。用词典或通过互联网检 查你的答案。

Target Words	Words Divided into Syllables	Number of Syllables
1. luncheon	lunch-eon	2
2. bunches	bunch-es	2
3. duckling	duck-ling	2
4. crushing	crush-ing	2
5. sugary	sug-ar-y	3
6. pulpit	pul-pit	2
7. bumper	bump-er	2
8. intruding	in-trud-ing	3
9. denouncing	de-nounc-ing	3
10. capsulate	cap-su-late	3

Classwork

Name: _____ Date: ___/___/_____ Score: _____

The Reading Challenge

Lesson 21.9

Reading Multisyllable Words

✓ **Lesson Check Point**

Directions: Read each target word. Circle the word in the row that is divided correctly into syllables. Use a dictionary or the Internet to check your answers.

路线：读每个目标词。圈出行中音节划分正确的词。用词典或通过互联网检查你的答案。

Model

| visualize | a. vis-ua-lize | (b. vi-su-al-ize) | c. vis-u-a-lize |

| 1. habitual | (a. ha-bit-u-al) | b. ha-bit-ual | c. hab-it-ual |

| 2. avenue | (a. av-e-nue) | b. ave-nu-e | c. a-ve-nue |

| 3. diluting | a. dil-u-ting | (b. di-lut-ing) | c. di-lu-ting |

| 4. amusing | a. a-mu-sing | (b. a-mus-ing) | c. am-u-sing |

| 5. confusion | (a. con-fu-sion) | b. con-fus-ion | c. conf-u-sion |

| 6. saluting | (a. sa-lut-ing) | b. sal-u-ting | c. sa-lu-ting |

| 7. fortunate | a. fort-u-nate | b. for-tun-ate | (c. for-tu-nate) |

| 8. truancy | a. tru-anc-y | b. tru-a-ncy | (c. tru-an-cy) |

Unit U Lesson 21.9

Name: _____ Date:___/___/_____ Score:_____

Answer Key

Lesson 21.10

Reading and Writing

Proper and Common Nouns and Adjectives

✓ **Lesson Check Point**

 Directions: Read the words in the word box. Put an (X) on the line next to each word that is written incorrectly. Remember that all proper nouns and proper adjectives are capitalized. Use a dictionary or the Internet to check your answers.

路线：读单词框中的词。在书写错误的单词旁边的线上打叉(X)。记得合适的名词和形容词需要大写。用词典或通过互联网检查你 的答案。

Word Box					
X	University	X	ukraine	__	URL
__	USSR	X	ubangi	__	upbeat
X	Universal	__	umbrella	__	Uncle
X	Ultra	__	Uruguay	X	Uncovered

 Directions: Read each unedited sentence and underline the word that is written incorrectly. Write each sentence correctly on the line.

路线：读每个未经编辑的句子，并给书写错误的词加下划线。在线 上写上正确的句子。

Model
Mrs. Ubangi usually has union meetings at a local <u>University</u>.
<u>Mrs. Ubangi usually has union meetings at a local university.</u>

1. We are studying the planet Uranus in Mrs. <u>ubet's</u> class.
<u>We are studying the planet Uranus in Mrs. Ubet's class.</u>

2. Professor Utrecht said, "The <u>united</u> Nations is very influential."
<u>Professor Utrecht said, "The United Nations is very influential."</u>

3. In 1971, <u>uzbekistan</u> became independent from the U.S.S.R.
<u>In 1971, Uzbekistan became independent from the U.S.S.R.</u>

4. I found information about two universities in <u>upper</u> Canada.
<u>I found information about two universities in Upper Canada.</u>

Classwork

👤 Name: _____ Date: ___/___/_____ Score: _____

Lesson 22.1

Reading Words with the Letter V/v

✓ **Lesson Check Point**

Directions: Read each target word. Find the letter "v" and put a check (✓) in the column that identifies its position: beginning, within or end.
路线：读每个目标词。找出字母 v，在栏中打勾(✓)示意： 开始，中间 或末尾。

Target Words	Beginning (First Letter)	Within	End (Last Letter)
1. visitor	✓		
2. travel		✓	
3. veterans	✓		
4. silver		✓	
5. Yugoslav			✓

Directions: Read each sentence and underline the words that begin with the letter "v." Write all the underlined words in alphabetical order on the lines below.
路线：读每个句子，并给首字母为 v 的词加下划线。在下面的 线上按照字母顺序写出所有下划线标记的单词。

6. My guitar case has a <u>valuable</u> <u>velvet</u> lining.

7. Samantha's <u>vintage</u> dress is <u>violet</u> and white.

8. Our <u>vice</u> president has a <u>vibrant</u> personality.

9. The character in the <u>video</u> game <u>vanished</u> into thin air.

10. Joshua plays <u>volleyball</u> for his school's team, The <u>Vikings</u>.

valuable	vanished	velvet
vibrant	vice	video
Vikings	vintage	violet
	volleyball	

Unit V Lesson 22.1

Answer Key

  Name: _____ Date: ___/___/_____ Score: _____

The Reading Challenge

Lesson 22.2

Reading Multisyllable Words

✓ Lesson Check Point

 Directions: Read and divide each target word into syllables. Write each word and place a hyphen (-) between the syllables in the second column. Write the number of syllables in the third column. Use a dictionary or the Internet to check your answers.

路线：读目标词后，划分音节。写下每个词，在第二栏中写上音 节，用 (-) 连接。在第三栏写上音节数。用词典或通过互联网检 查你的答案。

Target Words	Words Divided into Syllables	Number of Syllables
1. visionary	vi-sion-ar-y	4
2. vocalized	vo-cal-ized	3
3. vantage	van-tage	2
4. visiting	vis-it-ing	3
5. volume	vol-ume	2
6. verdict	ver-dict	2
7. vanishing	van-ish-ing	3
8. victorious	vic-to-ri-ous	4
9. vineyard	vine-yard	2
10. various	var-i-ous	3

Unit V Lesson 22.2

Learn To Read English With Directions In Chinese

Classwork

Name: _____ Date: ___/___/_____ Score: _____

The Reading Challenge

Lesson 22.2

Reading Multisyllable Words

✓ **Lesson Check Point**

Directions: Read each target word. Circle the word in the row that is divided correctly into syllables. Use a dictionary or the Internet to check your answers.

路线：读每个目标词。圈出行中音节划分正确的词。用词典或通过互联网检查你的答案。

Model

| volcano | a. vo-lcan-o | b. vol-can-o | c. vol-ca-no (circled) |

1. victory	a. vic-tor-y	b. vic-to-ry (circled)	c. vi-ctor-y
2. varsity	a. var-sit-y	b. va-rsi-ty	c. var-si-ty (circled)
3. visual	a. vis-u-al	b. vi-su-al (circled)	c. visu-a-l
4. vacation	a. va-cat-ion	b. vac-a-tion	c. va-ca-tion (circled)
5. volunteer	a. vol-un-teer (circled)	b. vo-lun-teer	c. vol-u-nteer
6. vitamin	a. vit-a-min	b. vi-tam-in	c. vi-ta-min (circled)
7. vehement	a. ve-hem-ent	b. veh-e-ment	c. ve-he-ment (circled)
8. vehicle	a. ve-hi-cle (circled)	b. veh-i-cle	c. ve-hicl-e

Unit V Lesson 22.2

Learn To Read English With Directions In Chinese

Answer Key

 Name: _____ Date: ___/___/_____ Score: _____

Lesson 22.3

Reading and Writing

Proper and Common Nouns and Adjectives

✓ **Lesson Check Point**

 Directions: Read the words in the word box. Put an (X) on the line next to each word that is written incorrectly. Remember that all proper nouns and proper adjectives are capitalized. Use a dictionary or the Internet to check your answers.

路线：读单词框中的词。在书写错误的单词旁边的线上打叉(X)。记得合适的名词和形容词需要大写。用词典或通过互联网检查你 的答案。

Word Box					
__	vision	X	vienna	X	vikings
X	Las vegas	__	Vietnam	__	velvet
X	Village	__	vehicle	__	Virginia
X	Volume	__	VIP	X	Vice president

 Directions: Read each unedited sentence and underline the word that is written incorrectly. Write each sentence correctly on the line.

路线：读每个未经编辑的句子，并给书写错误的词加下划线。在线 上写上正确的句子。

Model
In the fall, the leaves in <u>vermont</u> have vibrant colors.
In the fall, the leaves in Vermont have vibrant colors.

1. <u>valerie</u> is attending Valor Vocational School.
Valerie is attending Valor Vocational School.

2. Vince voted to go to the British <u>virgin</u> Islands.
Vince voted to go to the British Virgin Islands.

3. Washington's troops were victorious at <u>valley</u> Forge.
Washington's troops were victorious at Valley Forge.

4. This summer, I am going on <u>Vacation</u> to Victoria Falls.
This summer, I am going on vacation to Victoria Falls.

Classwork

L Name: _____ Date: ___/___/_____ Score: _____

Lesson 23.1

Reading Words with the Letter W/w

✓ Lesson Check Point

Directions: Read each target word. Find the letter "w" and put a check (✓) in the column that identifies its position: beginning, within or end.
路线：读每个目标词。找出字母 w 在栏中打勾 (✓) 示意： 开始，中间 或末尾。

Target Words	Beginning (First Letter)	Within	End (Last Letter)
1. bowling		✓	
2. arrow			✓
3. western	✓		
4. bookworm		✓	
5. shadow			✓

Directions: Read each sentence and underline the words that begin with the letter "w." Write all the underlined words in alphabetical order on the lines below.
路线：读每个句子，并给首字母为 w 的词加下划线。在下面的 线上按照字母顺序写出所有下划线标记的单词。

6. The wildcats have very long whiskers.

7. The tourists are walking along the waterfront.

8. The wilderness is home to wolves and eagles.

9. There are beautiful waterfalls in the West Indies.

10. My wife placed the clothes in the new washing machine.

walking   washing   waterfalls
waterfront   West   whiskers
wife   wildcats   wilderness
                 wolves

L Learn To Read English With Directions In Chinese   222   Copyrighted Material

 Name: _____ Date: ___/___/_____ Score: _____

Answer Key

Lesson 23.2

Reading Words with a Vowel before the Letter "w"

 Lesson Check Point

Directions: Read each target word. Circle the word in the column that has the same "aw," "ew" or "ow" sound as the target word.
路线：读每个目标词。圈出栏中含与目标词一样的"aw,""ew"或"ow"音的单词。

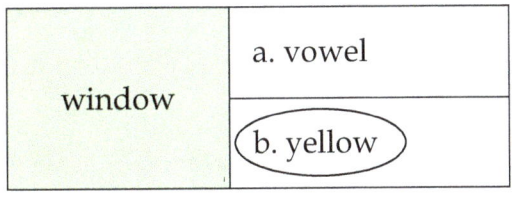
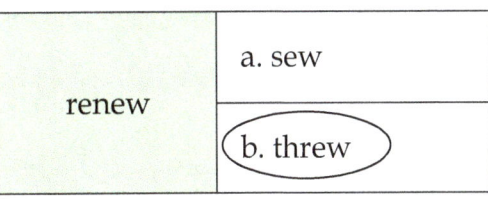
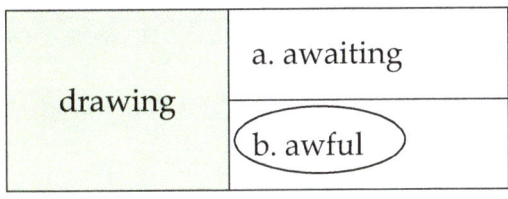
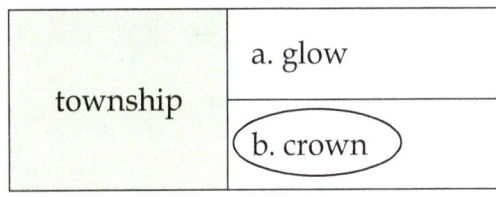

Directions: Read each target word. Put a check (✓) under the correct column heading.
路线：读每个目标词。在符合要求的栏下打勾 (✓)。

Target Words	Underlined letters have /o͞o/ sound as in the word <u>few</u>	Underlined letters have /ȯ/ sound as in the word <u>law</u>	Underlined letters have /ō/ sound as in the word <u>sew</u>	Underlined letters have /ou/ sound as in the word <u>cow</u>
1. wind<u>o</u>w			✓	
2. ren<u>ew</u>	✓			
3. dr<u>aw</u>ing		✓		
4. t<u>ow</u>nship				✓

Classwork

Name: _____ Date: ___/___/_____ Score: _____

Lesson 23.3

Reading Words with a Silent "w" and "wr" Letter Combination

Dictionary Skills/ Vocabulary

✓ **Lesson Check Point**

Directions: Read each target word and its definition. Write the letter of the definition on the line of each target word. Use a dictionary or the Internet to check your answers

路线：读每个目标词及其定义。在目标词前线上写上正确定义的 字母编号。用词典或通过互联网检查你的答案。

Target Words	Definitions
1. <u>d</u> wrap	a. to have destroyed something with intense force
2. <u>e</u> wrestling	b. a circular decoration made with flowers or evergreens
3. <u>b</u> wreath	c. the act of arguing or debating a topic
4. <u>a</u> wrecked	d. to fold in a fitted covering
5. <u>c</u> wrangling	e. a physical sport

Directions: Read each sentence. Underline the word in the parentheses that correctly completes each sentence. Then, write the underlined word on the line.

路线：阅读每个句子。在括号中选择符合句子的词，并添加下划 线。然后，在线上写出下划线单词。

6. Wendy placed a beautiful ___wreath___ on the door. (wrestling, <u>wreath</u>)

7. His house was ___wrecked___ by the tornado. (wrangling, <u>wrecked</u>)

8. The wrestler has a ___wrestling___ match tonight. (<u>wrestling</u>, wrap)

9. The mothers will ___wrap___ their babies in warm blankets. (<u>wrap</u>, wreath)

10. He was ___wrangling___ with his teacher over an unfair grade. (<u>wrangling</u>, wrap)

Name: _____ Date: ___/___/_____ Score: _____

Answer Key

Lesson 23.3

Reading Words with a Silent Letter "w"

✓ Lesson Check Point

 Directions: Read the target words in the word box. Write the words that have a silent letter "w" in the first column. Write the words that do not have a silent letter "w" in the second column.

路线：读单词框中的目标词。在第一栏中写上含不发音 w 的词。 在第二栏中写上不带不发音 w 的词。

Target Word Box				
sword	tomorrow	below	dwell	disown
winner	bandwidth	eastward	two	freewill
afterward	answer	farewell	firewall	writing
wrap	doorway	wreck	wrongly	went

Letter "w" is silent

- two
- wrap
- below
- disown
- wreck
- sword
- answer
- writing
- wrongly
- tomorrow

Letter "w" has the /w/ sound

- went
- dwell
- winner
- eastward
- freewill
- afterward
- farewell
- firewall
- doorway
- bandwidth

Classwork

Name: _____ Date:___/___/_____ Score:_____

The Reading Challenge

Lesson 23.4

Reading Multisyllable Words

✓ Lesson Check Point

 Directions: Read and divide each target word into syllables. Write each word and place a hyphen (-) between the syllables in the second column. Write the number of syllables in the third column. Use a dictionary or the Internet to check your answers.

路线：读目标词后，划分音节。写下每个词，在第二栏中写上音 节，用 (-) 连接。在第三栏写上音节数。用词典或通过互联网检 查你的答案。

Target Words	Words Divided into Syllables	Number of Syllables
1. waistband	waist-band	2
2. woman	wom-an	2
3. whistle	whis-tle	2
4. western	west-ern	2
5. wondering	won-der-ing	3
6. washing	wash-ing	2
7. writer	writ-er	2
8. worthless	worth-less	2
9. willful	will-ful	2
10. waterfall	wa-ter-fall	3

 Name: _____ Date: ___/___/_____ Score: _____

Answer Key

The Reading Challenge

Lesson 23.4

Reading Multisyllable Words

✓ **Lesson Check Point**

 Directions: Read each target word. Circle the word in the row that is divided correctly into syllables. Use a dictionary or the Internet to check your answers.
路线：读每个目标词。圈出行中音节划分正确的词。用词典或通过互联网检查你的答案。

Model

| wonderful | a. wo-nder-ful | (b. won-der-ful) | c. won-derf-ul |

| 1. waterbed | (a. wa-ter-bed) | b. wa-terb-ed | c. wat-er-bed |

| 2. wandering | a. wand-er-ing | b. wand-e-ring | (c. wan-der-ing) |

| 3. Wyoming | (a. Wy-o-ming) | b. Wy-om-ing | c. Wyo-mi-ng |

| 4. whenever | a. whe-nev-er | (b. when-ev-er) | c. wh-ene-ver |

| 5. withdrawal | a. withdr-aw-al | (b. with-draw-al) | c. with-dra-wal |

| 6. watermark | a. wat-er-mark | b. wa-term-ark | (c. wa-ter-mark) |

| 7. workable | a. wor-ka-ble | b. wor-kab-le | (c. work-a-ble) |

| 8. weekender | a. wee-kend-er | (b. week-end-er) | c. week-en-der |

Unit W
Lesson 23.4

Learn To Read English With Directions In Chinese   227   Copyrighted Material

Classwork

Name: _____ Date: ___/___/_____ Score: _____

Lesson 23.5

Reading and Writing

Proper and Common Nouns and Adjectives

✓ Lesson Check Point

Directions: Read the words in the word box. Put an (X) on the line next to each word that is written incorrectly. Remember that all proper nouns and proper adjectives are capitalized. Use a dictionary or the Internet to check your answers.

路线：读单词框中的词。在书写错误的单词旁边的线上打叉(X)。记得合适的名词和形容词需要大写。用词典或通过互联网检查你的答案。

Word Box					
X	wakefield, NY	__	wrappers	__	whiplash
X	Wealth	X	wisconsin	__	West Virginia
__	Washington	X	Wheelchair	X	white House
__	waterfall	__	Wake Island	X	Workforce

Directions: Read each unedited sentence and underline the word that is written incorrectly. Write each sentence correctly on the line.

路线：读每个未经编辑的句子，并给书写错误的词加下划线。在线上写上正确的句子。

Model

We walked along the winding path that led to the <u>Waterfalls</u>.
<u>We walked along the winding path that led to the waterfalls.</u>

1. The <u>Warden</u> works for the Wisconsin Prison System.
<u>The warden works for the Wisconsin Prison System.</u>

2. The waterfalls in the <u>west</u> Indies are breathtaking.
<u>The waterfalls in the West Indies are breathtaking.</u>

3. The new <u>Waitress</u> is from Washington, D.C.
<u>The new waitress is from Washington, D.C.</u>

4. The woodpeckers made their homes in <u>wilmington</u>.
<u>The woodpeckers made their homes in Wilmington.</u>

Answer Key

Name: _____ Date: ___/___/_____ Score: _____

Lesson 24.1

Reading Words with the Letter X/x

 Lesson Check Point

 Directions: Read each target word. Find the letter "x" and put a check (✓) in the column that identifies its position: beginning, within or end.
路线：读每个目标词。找出字母 x 在栏中打勾 (✓) 示意： 开始，中间或末尾。

Target Words	Beginning (First Letter)	Within	End (Last Letter)
1. sixty		✓	
2. oxen		✓	
3. prefix			✓
4. x-ray	✓		
5. wax			✓

 Directions: Read each sentence and underline the words that begin with the letter "x." Write all the underlined words in alphabetical order on the lines below.
路线：读每个句子，并给首字母为 x 的词加下划线。在下面的线上按照字母顺序写出所有下划线标记的单词。

6. <u>Xaria</u> has to go to the hospital for chest <u>x-rays</u>.

7. <u>Xavier</u> enjoys playing the <u>xylophone</u> at concerts.

8. <u>Xianna</u> used the <u>Xerox</u> machine to make photocopies.

9. <u>Xander</u> said, "<u>Xiamen</u> is an island of Southeast China."

10. I have worked for <u>Xola's</u> company for <u>x</u> number of years.

x_____   Xander_____   Xaria_____

Xavier_____   Xerox_____   Xiamen_____

Xianna_____   Xola's_____   x-rays_____

                       xylophone_____

Classwork

 Name: _____ Date: _____/ ___/ _____ Score: _____

Lesson 24.1

Reading Words with the Letter X/x

 Lesson Check Point

Directions: Read each target word. Circle the word in the column that has the same "x" sound(s) as the target word.
路线：读每个目标词。圈出栏中与目标词含相同 x 音的单词。

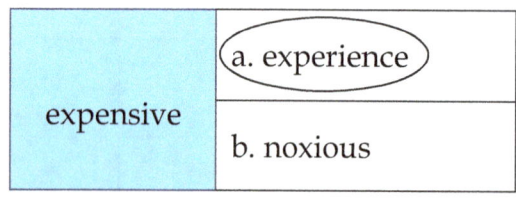

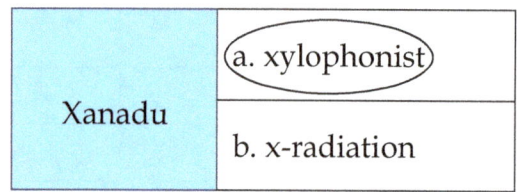
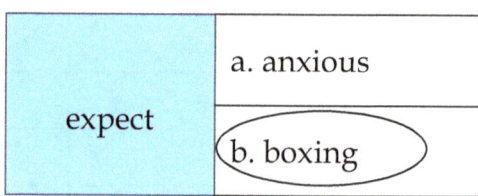

 Directions: Read each target word. Put a check (✓) under the correct column heading.
路线：读每个目标词。在符合要求的栏下打勾 (✓)。

Target Words	"x" has the /k/ + /s/ sounds as in the word <u>box</u>	"x" has the /z/ sound as in the word <u>xylophone</u>	"x" has the /g/ + /z/ sounds as in the word <u>exhibit</u>	"x" has the /k/ + /sh/ sounds as in the word <u>anxious</u>
1. expect	✓			
2. complexion				✓
3. Xanadu		✓		
4. expensive	✓			

Answer Key

 Name: _____ Date: ___/___/_____ Score: _____

The Reading Challenge

Lesson 24.2

Reading Multisyllable Words

✓ **Lesson Check Point**

 Directions: Read and divide each target word into syllables. Write each word and place a hyphen (-) between the syllables in the second column. Write the number of syllables in the third column. Use a dictionary or the Internet to check your answers.

路线：读目标词后，划分音节。写下每个词，在第二栏中写上音 节，用 (-) 连接。在第三栏写上音节数。用词典或通过互联网检 查你的答案。

Target Words	Words Divided into Syllables	Number of Syllables
1. boxer	box-er	2
2. prefix	pre-fix	2
3. saxophone	sax-o-phone	3
4. complexion	com-plex-ion	3
5. index	in-dex	2
6. textual	tex-tu-al	3
7. sixteen	six-teen	2
8. perplexing	per-plex-ing	3
9. taxicab	tax-i-cab	3
10. oxygen	ox-y-gen	3

Classwork

Name: _____ Date: ___/___/_____ Score: _____

The Reading Challenge

Lesson 24.2

Reading Multisyllable Words

✓ Lesson Check Point

Directions: Read each target word. Circle the word in the row that is divided correctly into syllables. Use a dictionary or the Internet to check your answers.
路线：读每个目标词。圈出行中音节划分正确的词。用词典或通过互联网检查你的答案。

Model

| oxidized | (a. ox-i-dized) | b. oxi-d-ized | c. o-xi-dized |

| 1. paradox | a. pa-rad-ox | b. par-ad-ox | (c. par-a-dox) |

| 2. explorer | (a. ex-plor-er) | b. exp-lo-rer | c. expl-or-er |

| 3. taxable | a. ta-xa-ble | (b. tax-a-ble) | c. ta-xab-le |

| 4. existence | a. exi-ste-nce | (b. ex-is-tence) | c. ex-i-stence |

| 5. hexagon | a. he-xa-gon | b. he-xag-on | (c. hex-a-gon) |

| 6. exciting | (a. ex-cit-ing) | b. exc-i-ting | c. exc-it-ing |

| 7. lexical | a. le-xic-al | b. le-xi-cal | (c. lex-i-cal) |

| 8. expanding | a. ex-pan-ding | (b. ex-pand-ing) | c. exp-and-ing |

Answer Key

 Name: _____ Date:___/___/_____ Score: _____

Lesson 24.3

Reading and Writing

Proper and Common Nouns and Adjectives

✓ Lesson Check Point

 Directions: Read the words in the word box. Put an (X) on the line next to each word that is written incorrectly. Remember that all proper nouns and proper adjectives are capitalized. Use a dictionary or the Internet to check your answers.

路线：读单词框中的词。在书写错误的单词旁边的线上打叉(X)。记得合适的名词和形容词需要大写。用词典或通过互联网检查你 的答案。

Word Box		
_X_ xerox Inc.	__ xylems	_X_ King xerxes I
__ xanthium	__ xenon	_X_ Xylophone
__ xylene	__ Xiang	_X_ Xanthic acid
_X_ X-ray	_X_ xavier	__ xebec

 Directions: Read each unedited sentence and underline the word that is written incorrectly. Write each sentence correctly on the line.

路线：读每个未经编辑的句子，并给书写错误的词加下划线。在线 上写上正确的句子。

Model
Xia said, "The population of <u>xankandi</u> is 33,000 people."
<u>Xia said, "The population of Xankandi is 33,000 people."</u>

1. Xia is reading about <u>xanthus</u>, the ancient City of Lycia.
<u>Xia is reading about Xanthus, the ancient City of Lycia.</u>

2. Mr. and Mrs. Xem visited the Chinese province of <u>xuzhou</u>.
<u>Mr. and Mrs. Xem visited the Chinese province of Xuzhou.</u>

3. My friend, <u>xavier</u>, is scheduled to have an x-ray at six o'clock.
<u>My friend, Xavier, is scheduled to have an x-ray at six o'clock.</u>

4. My dentist, Dr. Xu, applied a local anesthetic, <u>Xylocaine</u>, to my gums.
<u>My dentist, Dr. Xu, applied a local anesthetic, xylocaine, to my gums.</u>

Classwork

 Name: _____ Date:___/___/_____ Score:_____

Lesson 25.1

Reading Words with the Letter Y/y

✓ Lesson Check Point

 Directions: Read each target word. Find the letter "y" and put a check (✓) in the column that identifies its position: beginning, within or end.
路线：读每个目标词。找出字母 y 在栏中打勾 (✓) 示意： 开始中间或末尾。

Target Words	Beginning (First Letter)	Within	End (Last Letter)
1. galaxy			✓
2. yellow	✓		
3. hyperactive		✓	
4. strawberry			✓
5. younger	✓		

 Directions: Read each sentence and underline the words that begin with the letter "y." Write all the underlined words in alphabetical order on the lines below.
路线：读每个句子，并给首字母为 y 的词加下划线。在下面的 线上按照字母顺序写出所有下划线标记的单词。

6. Yesterday, I had a relaxing yoga class.

7. Yolanda and Nancy enjoyed my yodeling contest.

8. In Yorktown, I saw a pair of oxen yoked together.

9. The yellow car stopped at the triangular yield sign.

10. Mr. Young lives close to Yellowstone National Park.

yellow	Yellowstone	Yesterday
yield	yodeling	yoga
yoked	Yolanda	Yorktown
	Young	

Name: _____ Date: ___/___/_____ Score: _____

Lesson 25.1

Reading Words with the Letter Y/y

✓ **Lesson Check Point**

 Directions: Read each target word. Circle the word in the row that has a different "y" sound than the target word.
路线：读每个目标词。圈出行中 y 发音与目标词不同的单词。

Target Words				
1. yours	young	(candy)	year	yield
2. lyric	(myself)	gymnast	cylinders	symbols
3. Polynesia	sibyl	vinyl	(younger)	polymer
4. community	energy	baby	penny	(pyramid)
5. young	(money)	yours	yes	youth

 Directions: Read the words in the four boxes. Circle two words that have the same "y" sound.
路线：读四个框中的词。圈出两个发相同 y 音的词。

young	(belly)
reply	(city)

cylinder	(yesterday)
cycles	(yahoo)

(very)	apply
your	(jelly)

(happy)	(shiny)
ratify	years

penny	July
(syringe)	(vinyl)

(plywood)	baby
cylinder	(identify)

Classwork

 Name: _____ Date:___/___/_____ Score:_____

Lesson 25.2

Reading Words with a Vowel before the Letter "y"

✓ **Lesson Check Point**

 Directions: Read each target word. Circle the word in the column that has the same "y" sound as the target word.
路线：读每个目标词。圈出栏中与目标词含相同 y 音的单词。

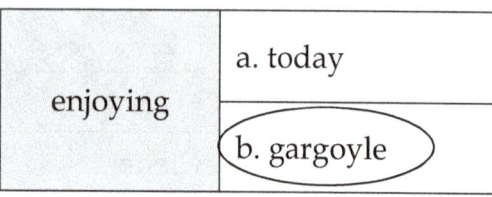

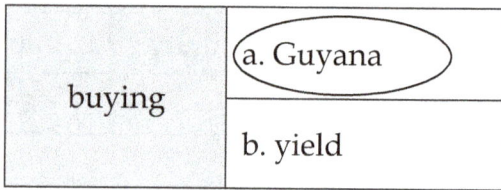

 Directions: Read each target word. Put a check (✓) under the correct column heading.
路线：读每个目标词。在符合要求的栏下打勾 (✓)。

Target Words	"y" has the /y/ sound as in the word <u>yes</u>	"oy" has the /oi/ sound as in the word <u>boy</u>	"y" has the /ī/ sound as in the word <u>by</u>	"y" is silent as in the word <u>day</u>
1. enjoying		✓		
2. chimney				✓
3. Maya	✓			
4. buying			✓	

Name: _____ Date: ___/___/_____ Score: _____

Answer Key

Lesson 25.3

Reading Words with the "cy" Letter Combination

✓ Lesson Check Point

 Directions: Read each target word. Find the "cy" letter combination and put a check (✓) in the column to identify its position in the word: beginning, within or end.
路线：读每个目标词。找到"cy"字母组合，并在栏中打勾(✓)示意：开始，中间或末尾。

Target Words	Beginning (First 2 Letters)	Within	End (Last 2 Letters)
1. Nancy			✓
2. bicyclist		✓	
3. cymbal	✓		
4. regency			✓
5. cytoplasm	✓		

 Directions: Read each target word. Put a check (✓) under the correct column heading.
路线：读每个目标词。在符合要求的栏下打勾 (✓)。

Target Words	"cy" has the /s/ + /ĭ/ sounds as in the word <u>cylinder</u>	"cy" has the /s/ + /ī/ sounds as in the word <u>cycle</u>	"cy" has the /s/ + /ē/ sounds as in the word <u>agency</u>
6. Nancy			✓
7. bicyclist	✓		
8. cymbal	✓		
9. regency			✓
10. cytoplasm		✓	

Unit Y Lesson 25.3

Classwork

 Name: _____ Date:___/___/_____ Score: _____

Lesson 25.4

Reading Words with the Final Letter "y"

✓ Lesson Check Point

 Directions: Read each target word. Find the letter "y" and put a check (✓) in the column that identifies its position within the word.
路线：读每个目标词。找到字母 y，并在栏中打勾(✓)，标示其 在音节中的位置。

Target Words	"y" is at the end of a one syllable word	"y" is at the end of the first syllable	"y" is at the end of a multi-syllable word
1. myself		✓	
2. community			✓
3. cry	✓		
4. discovery			✓
5. tycoon		✓	

 Directions: Read each target word. Put a check (✓) under the correct column heading.
路线：读每个目标词。在符合要求的栏下打勾 (✓)。

Target Words	"y" has the /ē/ sound as in the word <u>agency</u>	"y" has the /ī/ sound as in the word <u>flying</u>
6. myself		✓
7. community	✓	
8. cry		✓
9. discovery	✓	
10. tycoon		✓

Name: _____ Date: ___/___/_____ Score: _____

Lesson 25.5

Reading Words with the "yr" Letter Combination

✓ Lesson Check Point

 Directions: Read each target word. Circle the word in the column that has the same "yr" sounds as the target word.
路线：读每个目标词。圈出栏中与目标词含相同"yr"音的单词。

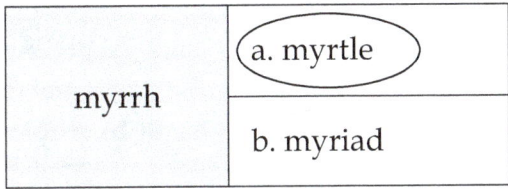
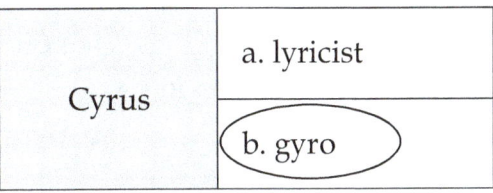

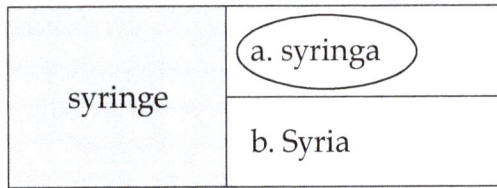

| myriad | a. lyrical (circled) |
| | b. payroll |

 Directions: Read each target word. Put a check (✓) under the correct column heading.
路线：读每个目标词。在符合要求的栏下打勾 (✓)。

Target Words	"yr" has the /û/ + /r/ sounds as in the word myrtle	"yr" has the /ĭ/ + /r/ sounds as in the word pyramid	"yr" has the /ī/ + /r/ sounds as in the word gyro	"yr" has the /ə/ + /r/ sounds as in the word martyr
1. myrrh	✓			
2. Cyrus			✓	
3. myriad		✓		
4. syringe				✓

Classwork

Name: _____ Date: ___/___/_____ Score: _____

Lesson 25.6

Reading Letter "y" Words with the Schwa Vowel Sound

✓ Lesson Check Point

Directions: Read each target word. Circle the word in the column that has the same "y" sound as the target word.
路线：读每个目标词。圈出栏中与目标词含相同 y 音的单词。

Polynesian	a. polyvinyl (circled)
	b. pyramid

sibyl	a. mandatory
	b. vinyl (circled)

nicely	a. vacancy (circled)
	b. polymerize

Pennsylvania	a. polymer (circled)
	b. younger

Directions: Read each target word. Put a check (✓) under the correct column heading.
路线：读每个目标词。在符合要求的栏下打勾 (✓)。

Target Words	"y" has the /ə/ sound as in the word <u>syringe</u>	"y" does not have the /ə/ sound
1. Polynesian	✓	
2. sibyl	✓	
3. nicely		✓
4. Pennsylvania	✓	

Learn To Read English With Directions In Chinese

Name: _____ Date: ___/___/_____ Score: _____

Lesson 25.7

Reading Words with a Silent Letter "y"

✓ **Lesson Check Point**

 Directions: Read the target words in the word box. Write the words that have a silent letter "y" in the first column. Write the words that do not have a silent letter "y" in the second column.

路线：读单词框中的目标词。在第一栏中写上含不发音 y 的词。 在第二栏中写上不带不发音 y 的词。

Target Word Box				
prey	mayor	yes	payday	playing
yeast	jeopardy	donkey	midday	yellow
abundantly	yogurt	friendly	safely	always
layer	chewy	youth	prayer	today

Letter "y" is silent	Letter "y" has the /y/ or /ē/ sound
prey	yes
mayor	yeast
payday	chewy
playing	yellow
donkey	youth
midday	yogurt
always	friendly
layer	safely
prayer	jeopardy
today	abundantly

Classwork

 Name: _____ Date: ___/___/_____ Score: _____

The Reading Challenge

Lesson 25.8

Reading Multisyllable Words

✓ Lesson Check Point

 Directions: Read and divide each target word into syllables. Write each word and place a hyphen (-) between the syllables in the second column. Write the number of syllables in the third column. Use a dictionary or the Internet to check your answers.

路线：读目标词后，划分音节。写下每个词，在第二栏中写上音 节，用 (-) 连接。在第三栏写上音节数。用词典或通过互联网检 查你的答案。

Target Words	Words Divided into Syllables	Number of Syllables
1. yourself	your-self	2
2. Yemenite	Yem-en-ite	3
3. Yorktown	York-town	2
4. yoga	yo-ga	2
5. yonder	yon-der	2
6. Yankee	Yan-kee	2
7. yardstick	yard-stick	2
8. yearly	year-ly	2
9. yodeling	yo-del-ing	3
10. youthfulness	youth-ful-ness	3

Answer Key

Name: _____ Date: ____/____/____ Score: _____

The Reading Challenge

Lesson 25.8

Reading Multisyllable Words

 Lesson Check Point

 Directions: Read each target word. Circle the word in the row that is divided correctly into syllables. Use a dictionary or the Internet to check your answers.

路线：读每个目标词。圈出行中音节划分正确的词。用词典或通过互联网检查你的答案。

Model

| yesterday | a. ye-ster-day | b. yest-er-day | c. yes-ter-day ✓ |

1. Yucatán	a. Yuc-a-tán	b. Yu-ca-tán ✓	c. Yu-cat-án
2. yarmulke	a. yar-mul-ke ✓	b. yar-mulk-e	c. yarm-u-lke
3. yodeling	a. yod-e-ling	b. yo-de-ling	c. yo-del-ing ✓
4. youthful	a. youthf-ul	b. youth-ful ✓	c. you-thful
5. Yoruba	a. Yo-ru-ba ✓	b. Yor-u-ba	c. Yo-rub-a
6. Yankee	a. Yank-ee	b. Ya-nk-ee	c. Yan-kee ✓
7. yielding	a. yield-ing ✓	b. yiel-di-ng	c. yieldi-ng
8. younger	a. you-nger	b. youn-ger	c. young-er ✓

Unit Y Lesson 25.8

Classwork

Name: _____ Date: ___/___/_____ Score: _____

Lesson 25.9

Reading and Writing

Proper and Common Nouns and Adjectives

✓ Lesson Check Point

Directions: Read the words in the word box. Put an (X) on the line next to each word that is written incorrectly. Remember that all proper nouns and proper adjectives are capitalized. Use a dictionary or the Internet to check your answers.

路线：读单词框中的词。在书写错误的单词旁边的线上打叉(X)。记得合适的名词和形容词需要大写。用词典或通过互联网检查你 的答案。

Word Box					
__	Yemen	X	yokosuka	__	yachting
__	yellow	__	Yankees	X	Yogurt
X	Young	__	yardage	__	yesterday
X	yoruba	X	Yourself	X	yorktown

Directions: Read each unedited sentence and underline the word that is written incorrectly. Write each sentence correctly on the line.

路线：读每个未经编辑的句子，并给书写错误的词加下划线。在线 上写上正确的句子。

Model
Is the New York <u>yankees</u> your favorite baseball team?
<u>Is the New York Yankees your favorite baseball team?</u>

1. Yolanda's friend loves to eat <u>yoplait</u> yogurt.
<u>Yolanda's friend loves to eat Yoplait yogurt.</u>

2. All the signs in <u>yorktown</u> are painted yellow.
<u>All the signs in Yorktown are painted yellow.</u>

3. Last year, the <u>young</u> family visited Yosemite National Park.
<u>Last year, the Young family visited Yosemite National Park.</u>

4. <u>yesterday</u>, Yusef plotted the y-axis and the x-axis on graph paper.
<u>Yesterday, Yusef plotted the y-axis and the x-axis on graph paper.</u>

Answer Key

Name: _____ Date: ___/___/_____ Score: _____

Lesson 26.1

Reading Words with the Letter Z/z

✓ Lesson Check Point

Directions: Read each target word. Find the letter "z" and put a check (✓) in the column that identifies its position: beginning, within or end.
路线：读每个目标词。找出字母 z 在栏中打勾 (✓) 示意： 开始，中间 或末尾。

Target Words	Beginning (First Letter)	Within	End (Last Letter)
1. blizzard		✓	
2. topaz			✓
3. Tanzania		✓	
4. zebra	✓		
5. zookeeper	✓		

Directions: Read each sentence and underline the words that begin with the letter "z." Write all the underlined words in alphabetical order on the lines below.
路线：读每个句子，并给首字母为 z 的词加下划线。在下面的 线上按照字母顺序写出所有下划线标记的单词。

6. Samira <u>zipped</u> up her <u>zebra</u> costume.

7. Danny wants to work at the <u>zoo</u> as a trained <u>zoologist</u>.

8. The two <u>zoom</u> lenses on <u>Zianna's</u> camera are very expensive.

9. In New <u>Zealand</u>, Abdulla wore his shirt with a <u>zigzag</u> design.

10. Valeria is studying the rich cultures of <u>Zambia</u> and <u>Zimbabwe</u>.

<u>Zambia</u>   <u>Zealand</u>   <u>zebra</u>

<u>Zianna's</u>   <u>zigzag</u>   <u>Zimbabwe</u>

<u>zipped</u>   <u>zoo</u>   <u>zoologist</u>

                    <u>zoom</u>

Classwork

 Name: _____ Date: ___/___/_____ Score: _____

Lesson 26.1

Reading Words with the Letter Z/z

✓ Lesson Check Point

 Directions: Read each target word. Circle the word in the column that has the same "z" sound as the target word.
路线：读每个目标词。圈出栏中与目标词含相同 z 音的单词。

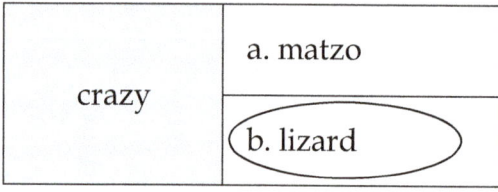

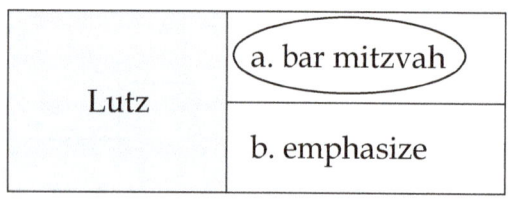   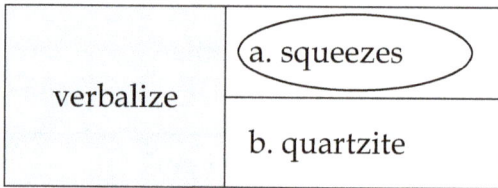

 Directions: Read each target word. Put a check (✓) under the correct column heading.
路线：读每个目标词。在符合要求的栏下打勾 (✓)。

Target Words	"z" has the /z/ sound as in the word <u>zipper</u>	"z" has the /s/ sound as in the word <u>quartz</u>
1. crazy	✓	
2. normalize	✓	
3. Lutz		✓
4. verbalize	✓	

Answer Key

 Name: _____ Date: ___/___/_____ Score: _____

Lesson 26.2

Reading Words with a Silent Letter "z"

✓ Lesson Check Point

 Directions: Read the target words in the word box. Write the words that have a silent letter "z" in the first column. Write the words that do not have a silent letter "z" in the second column.

路线：读单词框中的目标词。在第一栏中写上含不发音 z 的词。 在第二栏中写上不带不发音 z 的词。

Target Word Box				
fizzle	sizzler	Brazil	analyze	capitalize
agonize	dozen	dizziness	amazing	gizzard
cadenza	blazing	puzzling	economize	blizzard
sizzles	fuzz	centralize	drizzling	puzzle

Letter "z" is silent	Letter "z" has the /z/ or /s/ sound
fuzz	Brazil
sizzler	analyze
puzzle	capitalize
gizzard	agonize
fizzle	dozen
blizzard	amazing
sizzles	cadenza
puzzling	blazing
dizziness	economize
drizzling	centralize

Learn To Read English With Directions In Chinese   247   Copyrighted Material

Classwork

 Name: _____ Date: ___/___/_____ Score: _____

The Reading Challenge

Lesson 26.3

Reading Multisyllable Words

✓ Lesson Check Point

 Directions: Read and divide each target word into syllables. Write each word and place a hyphen (-) between the syllables in the second column. Write the number of syllables in the third column. Use a dictionary or the Internet to check your answers.

路线：读目标词后，划分音节。写下每个词，在第二栏中写上音节，用 (-) 连接。在第三栏写上音节数。用词典或通过互联网检查你的答案。

Target Words	Words Divided into Syllables	Number of Syllables
1. Zaire	Za-ire	2
2. zealot	zeal-ot	2
3. zodiac	zo-di-ac	3
4. zigzag	zig-zag	2
5. Zulu	Zu-lu	2
6. zeniths	ze-niths	2
7. zany	za-ny	2
8. zinger	zing-er	2
9. zestfulness	zest-ful-ness	3
10. Zambia	Zam-bi-a	3

Answer Key

Name: _____ Date: ___/___/_____ Score: _____

The Reading Challenge

Lesson 26.3

Reading Multisyllable Words

✓ **Lesson Check Point**

Directions: Read each target word. Circle the word in the row that is divided correctly into syllables. Use a dictionary or the Internet to check your answers.
路线：读每个目标词。圈出行中音节划分正确的词。用词典或通过互联网检查你的答案。

Model

| zoology | a. zo-ol-o-gy ⭕ | b. zoo-lo-gy | c. zool-o-gy |

| 1. Zealand | a. Zea-land ⭕ | b. Zeal-an-d | c. Zeal-and |

| 2. Zimbabwe | a. Zimb-ab-we | b. Zim-bab-we ⭕ | c. Zim-ba-bwe |

| 3. zodiac | a. zo-di-a-c | b. zod-ia-c | c. zo-di-ac ⭕ |

| 4. zoologist | a. zo-ol-o-gist ⭕ | b. zoo-log-ist | c. zoo-lo-gist |

| 5. zeroing | a. ze-roi-ng | b. zer-o-ing | c. ze-ro-ing ⭕ |

| 6. zonal | a. zo-nal | b. zon-al ⭕ | c. zo-n-al |

| 7. Zambia | a. Za-mbi-a | b. Zam-bi-a ⭕ | c. Zamb-i-a |

| 8. zestful | a. ze-stf-ul | b. ze-stful | c. zest-ful ⭕ |

Unit Z
Lesson 26.3

Classwork

 Name: _____ Date: ___/___/_____ Score: _____

Lesson 26.4

Reading and Writing

Proper and Common Nouns and Adjectives

✓ Lesson Check Point

 Directions: Read the words in the word box. Put an (X) on the line next to each word that is written incorrectly. Remember that all proper nouns and proper adjectives are capitalized. Use a dictionary or the Internet to check your answers.

路线：读单词框中的词。在书写错误的单词旁边的线上打叉(X)。记得合适的名词和形容词需要大写。用词典或通过互联网检查你的答案。

Word Box					
X	Zillion	__	zippers	__	Zealand
__	Zambia	X	Zookeeper	__	Zululand
X	zurich	__	zealous	X	Zoom lens
__	Zeus	X	zanzibar	X	Zoology

 Directions: Read each unedited sentence and underline the word that is written incorrectly. Write each sentence correctly on the line.

路线：读每个未经编辑的句子，并给书写错误的词加下划线。在线 上写上正确的句子。

Model

The steep path zigzags through the zagros Mountains.
<u>The steep path zigzags through the Zagros Mountains.</u>

1. Zoey lives in the Eastern Time zone.
<u>Zoey lives in the Eastern Time Zone.</u>

2. At noon, the Zebras at the Bronx Zoo were sleeping.
<u>At noon, the zebras at the Bronx Zoo were sleeping.</u>

3. My school, Zesty Academy, has Zero tolerance for bullying.
<u>My school, Zesty Academy, has zero tolerance for bullying.</u>

4. Mr. Zinger's new movie is a Zillion times better than his first one.
<u>Mr. Zinger's new movie is a zillion times better than his first one.</u>

Answer Key

 Name: _____ Date: ___/___/_____ Score: _____

Appendix 1.0

Introduction of the Letter A/a

✓ **Lesson Check Point**

 Directions: Circle the correct letter "a" pair: uppercase and lowercase letters.
路线：圈出正确的字母 a 对：大写和小写字母。

Ao   (Aa)   aE   Au   iA

 Directions: The uppercase letter "A" is in the first column. Look at the four letters in the row and circle the lowercase letter that matches the uppercase letter "A."
路线：大写字母 A 在第一栏。看看这一行的四个字母，圈出大写字母 A 的小写字母。

A	o	e	u	(a)
A	(a)	c	z	x
A	e	w	(a)	c
A	o	(a)	c	u

 Directions: The lowercase letter "a" is in the first column. Look at the four letters in the row and circle the uppercase letter that matches the lowercase letter "a."
路线：小写字母 a 第一栏。看看这一行的四个字母，圈出小写字母 a 的大写字母。

a	Z	(A)	V	W
a	V	C	(A)	Z
a	D	O	W	(A)
a	(A)	H	V	Q

Classwork

 Name: _____ Date: ____/____/_____ Score: _____

Appendix 2.0

Introduction of the Letter B/b

✓ **Lesson Check Point**

 Directions: Circle the correct letter "b" pair: uppercase and lowercase letters.
路线：圈出正确的字母 b 对：大写和小写字母。

    Bd   (Bb)   bF   Db   Bk

 Directions: The uppercase letter "B" is in the first column. Look at the four letters in the row and circle the lowercase letter that matches the uppercase letter "B."
路线：大写字母 B 在第一栏。看看这一行的 四个字母，圈出 大写字母 B 的小写字母。

B	(b)	f	q	d
B	g	(b)	d	h
B	f	p	d	(b)
B	h	(b)	p	k

 Directions: The lowercase letter "b" is in the first column. Look at the four letters in the row and circle the uppercase letter that matches the lowercase letter "b."
路线：小写字母 b 第一栏。看看这一行的四个字母，圈出小写字母 b 的大写字母。

b	F	D	(B)	G
b	Q	P	D	(B)
b	P	(B)	F	M
b	H	R	Q	(B)

Name: _____ Date: ___/___/_____ Score: _____

Appendix 2.0

Letter Recognition B/b

Uppercase and Lowercase Letter

✓ **Lesson Check Point**

Directions: Read each target word. Read the words in the row and circle the word that begins with a different letter.

路线：读每个目标词。读这一行的词，圈出首字母不同的词。

Target Words				
1. boy	bin	bean	(fat)	buns
2. buzz	balloon	(house)	bandit	blood
3. both	bandage	brick	(queen)	bang
4. bubbles	(drip)	bank	bag	break
5. because	(puppet)	ballot	baggage	black

Directions: Read the words in the four boxes. Circle two words that start with the uppercase and lowercase letter "b."

路线：读四个框中的词。圈出首字母为 b 的小写或大写字母的 词汇。

(bin)	win		(Bit)	sit		(Bake)	Make
tin	(Bin)		Hit	(bit)		(bake)	dare

(bat)	(Bat)		Float	oat		Wet	(Best)
hat	Sat		(Boat)	(boat)		date	(best)

Classwork

Name: _____ Date: ___/___/_____ Score: _____

Appendix 3.0

Introduction of the Letter C/c

✓ Lesson Check Point

Directions: Circle the correct letter "c" pair: uppercase and lowercase letters.

路线：圈出正确的字母 c 对：大写和小写字母。

(Cc)　　　Kc　　　Co　　　Oc　　　cS

Directions: The uppercase letter "C" is in the first column. Look at the four letters in the row and circle the lowercase letter that matches the uppercase letter "C."

路线：大写字母 C 在第一栏。看看这一行的 四个字母，圈出 大写字母 C 的小写字母。

C	o	(c)	u	g
C	v	a	r	(c)
C	(c)	g	d	o
C	q	(c)	p	k

Directions: The lowercase letter "c" is in the first column. Look at the four letters in the row and circle the uppercase letter that matches the lowercase letter "c."

路线：小写字母 c 第一栏。看看这一行的四个字母，圈出小写字母 c的大写字母。

c	Q	O	(C)	G
c	(C)	T	Q	M
c	D	B	H	(C)
c	(C)	K	J	D

Answer Key

Name: _____ Date: ___/___/_____ Score: _____

Appendix 3.0

Letter Recognition C/c

Uppercase and Lowercase Letter

✓ **Lesson Check Point**

Directions: Read each target word. Read the words in the row and circle the word that begins with a different letter.

路线：读每个目标词。读这一行的词，圈出首字母不同的词。

Target Words				
1. clip	cool	came	(poll)	color
2. cart	caramel	(open)	capture	clump
3. cent	cell	(queen)	choice	chap
4. curtain	chat	center	(goat)	city
5. church	chocolate	(engage)	chair	civic

Directions: Read the words in the four boxes. Circle two words that start with the uppercase and lowercase letter "c."

路线：读四个框中的词。圈出首字母为 c 的小写或大写字母的 词汇。

book	(Camel)
Brook	(clue)

(comb)	Octopus
(Cook)	Kite

(Cake)	keep
Goat	(capital)

(Cat)	Queen
(cow)	open

Grow	(cute)
(Cab)	float

(come)	home
Tom	(Candy)

Classwork

 Name: _____ Date: ___/___/_____ Score: _____

Appendix 4.0

Introduction of the Letter D/d

✓ **Lesson Check Point**

 Directions: Circle the correct letter "d" pair: uppercase and lowercase letters.
路线：圈出正确的字母 d 对：大写和小写字母。

    Db   Df   (Dd)   Bd   Op

 Directions: The uppercase letter "D" is in the first column. Look at the four letters in the row and circle the lowercase letter that matches the uppercase letter "D."
路线：大写字母 D 在第一栏。看看这一行的 四个字母，圈出 大写字母 D 的小写字母。

D	p	(d)	t	b
D	h	y	(d)	t
D	l	t	b	(d)
D	t	(d)	k	f

 Directions: The lowercase letter "d" is in the first column. Look at the four letters in the row and circle the uppercase letter that matches the lowercase letter "d."
路线：小写字母 d 第一栏。看看这一行的四个字母，圈出小写字母 d 的大写字母。

d	B	Q	(D)	F
d	K	(D)	P	B
d	B	T	(D)	K
d	(D)	F	B	P

Answer Key

Name: _____ Date:___/___/_____ Score:_____

Appendix 4.0

Letter Recognition D/d

Uppercase and Lowercase Letter

✓ Lesson Check Point

 Directions: Read each target word. Read the words in the row and circle the word that begins with a different letter.
路线：读每个目标词。读这一行的词，圈出首字母不同的词。

Target Words				
1. dad	day	(box)	drive	duck
2. deep	(pull)	drum	dove	dull
3. dwell	doll	dawn	dock	(peace)
4. dryer	do	dense	(queen)	dash
5. drink	(both)	den	down	deer

 Directions: Read the words in the four boxes. Circle two words that start with the uppercase and lowercase letter "d."
路线：读四个框中的词。圈出首字母为 d 的小写或大写字母的 词汇。

(date)	late		(Ditch)	Queen		Bell	Quite
open	(Draw)		(dock)	boat		(Deal)	(doll)

Quick	(dream)		Back	(dome)		Race	(drive)
quack	(Dawn)		belt	(Drip)		(Dog)	Quill

Classwork

 Name: _____ Date: ___/___/_____ Score: _____

Appendix 5.0

Introduction of the Letter E/e

✓ **Lesson Check Point**

 Directions: Circle the correct letter "e" pair: uppercase and lowercase letters.
路线：圈出正确的字母 e 对：大写和小写字母。

    eF   Ex   fE   (eE)   Ae

 Directions: The uppercase letter "E" is in the first column. Look at the four letters in the row and circle the lowercase letter that matches the uppercase letter "E."
路线：大写字母 E 在第一栏。看看这一行的 四个字母，圈出 大写字母 E 的小写字母。

E	r	(e)	f	a
E	c	a	w	(e)
E	(e)	c	x	r
E	z	s	(e)	a

 Directions: The lowercase letter "e" is in the first column. Look at the four letters in the row and circle the uppercase letter that matches the lowercase letter "e."
路线：小写字母 e 第一栏。看看这一行的四个字母，圈出小写字母 e 的大写字母。

e	D	(E)	R	F
e	G	H	T	(E)
e	(E)	F	V	D
e	F	(E)	S	X

Name: _____ Date: ___/___/_____ Score: _____

Answer Key

Appendix 6.0

Introduction of the Letter F/f

✓ **Lesson Check Point**

 Directions: Circle the correct letter "f" pair: uppercase and lowercase letters.
路线：圈出正确的字母 f 对：大写和小写字母。

    fE   Fh   (fF)   Ef   Tf

 Directions: The uppercase letter "F" is in the first column. Look at the four letters in the row and circle the lowercase letter that matches the uppercase letter "F."
路线：大写字母 F 在第一栏。看看这一行的 四个字母，圈出 大写字母 F 的小写字母。

F	l	t	k	(f)
F	j	l	(f)	m
F	t	(f)	b	h
F	(f)	l	t	h

 Directions: The lowercase letter "f" is in the first column. Look at the four letters in the row and circle the uppercase letter that matches the lowercase letter "f."
路线：小写字母 f 第一栏。看看这一行的四个字母，圈出小写字母 f 的大写字母。

f	(F)	E	K	H
f	L	(F)	J	E
f	E	K	H	(F)
f	H	(F)	D	B

Classwork

Name: _____ Date: ___/___/_____ Score: _____

Appendix 6.0

Letter Recognition F/f

Uppercase and Lowercase Letter

✓ Lesson Check Point

 Directions: Read each target word. Read the words in the row and circle the word that begins with a different letter.

路线：读每个目标词。读这一行的词，圈出首字母不同的词。

Target Words				
1. face	force	fault	(house)	form
2. fire	(pizza)	fizz	friend	flow
3. fork	frisk	(quiet)	fourth	fall
4. flirt	(love)	from	fast	fur
5. full	fright	flash	firm	(boys)

 Directions: Read the words in the four boxes. Circle two words that start with the uppercase and lowercase letter "f."

路线：读四个框中的词。圈出首字母为 f 的小写或大写字母的 词汇。

(Field)	flake
Years	take

both	(Fig)
(fond)	Hours

(fame)	teach
(Fist)	Laugh

book	Drip
(fight)	(Few)

(Flank)	tea
Pup	(fair)

happens	(fee)
Dreams	(Float)

Name: _____ Date: ___/___/_____ Score: _____

Answer Key

Appendix 7.0

Introduction of the Letter G/g

✓ **Lesson Check Point**

 Directions: Circle the correct letter "g" pair: uppercase and lowercase letters.
路线：圈出正确的字母 g 对：大写和小写字母。

yG   Gj   gJ   (Gg)   gO

 Directions: The uppercase letter "G" is in the first column. Look at the four letters in the row and circle the lowercase letter that matches the uppercase letter "G."
路线：大写字母 G 在第一栏。看看这一行的 四个字母，圈出 大写字母 G 的小写字母。

G	p	q	y	(g)
G	j	y	(g)	p
G	(g)	j	y	q
G	j	(g)	q	y

 Directions: The lowercase letter "g" is in the first column. Look at the four letters in the row and circle the uppercase letter that matches the lowercase letter "g."
路线：小写字母 g 第一栏。看看这一行的四个字母，圈出小写字母 g 的大写字母。

g	Q	O	J	(G)
g	U	(G)	O	J
g	Q	K	C	(G)
g	(G)	Q	P	O

Classwork

Name: _____ Date: ___/___/_____ Score: _____

Appendix 7.0

Letter Recognition G/g

Uppercase and Lowercase Letter

✓ **Lesson Check Point**

Directions: Read each target word. Read the words in the row and circle the word that begins with a different letter.

路线：读每个目标词。读这一行的词，圈出首字母不同的词。

Target Words				
1. gel	guest	garb	(jeep)	gown
2. grant	(pet)	goal	guard	gulp
3. game	grief	grant	(queen)	go
4. goat	glove	(ball)	glaze	grown
5. gold	(jump)	glide	gray	ghost

Directions: Read the words in the four boxes. Circle two words that start with the uppercase and lowercase letter "g."

路线：读四个框中的词。圈出首字母为 g 的小写或大写字母的 词汇。

(gold)	open
Queen	(Greece)

(ground)	Down
(Gulf)	jump

Once	June
(Graph)	(game)

Ooze	(Gone)
(greed)	jeep

year	(Grub)
Dock	(glare)

(Glee)	(gram)
joke	Day

Answer Key

 Name: _____ Date: ___/___/_____ Score: _____

Appendix 8.0

Introduction of the Letter H/h

✓ Lesson Check Point

 Directions: Circle the correct letter "h" pair: uppercase and lowercase letters.

路线：圈出正确的字母 h 对：大写和小写字母。

    Hf   (hH)   Ht   hB   Hb

 Directions: The uppercase letter "H" is in the first column. Look at the four letters in the row and circle the lowercase letter that matches the uppercase letter "H."

路线：大写字母 H 在第一栏。看看这一行的 四个字母，圈出 大写字母 H 的小写字母。

H	(h)	f	t	b
H	m	(h)	f	t
H	l	k	(h)	f
H	b	t	d	(h)

 Directions: The lowercase letter "h" is in the first column. Look at the four letters in the row and circle the uppercase letter that matches the lowercase letter "h."

路线：小写字母 h 第一栏。看看这一行的四个字母，圈出小写字母 h 的大写字母。

h	T	F	U	(H)
h	(H)	J	F	M
h	E	M	C	(H)
h	D	(H)	B	T

Learn To Read English With Directions In Chinese   263   Copyrighted Material

Classwork

Name: _____ Date: ___/___/_____ Score: _____

Appendix 8.0

Letter Recognition H/h

Uppercase and Lowercase Letter

✓ Lesson Check Point

Directions: Read each target word. Read the words in the row and circle the word that begins with a different letter.

路线：读每个目标词。读这一行的词，圈出首字母不同的词。

Target Words				
1. home	hat	(land)	heart	hill
2. head	horse	heat	hulk	(boat)
3. hatch	heel	(down)	harm	here
4. heir	hold	high	host	(love)
5. hint	half	hitch	(team)	hemp

Directions: Read the words in the four boxes. Circle two words that start with the uppercase and lowercase letter "h."

路线：读四个框中的词。圈出首字母为 h 的小写或大写字母的 词汇。

tune	love
(help)	(Hold)

(Hole)	bless
pole	(hiss)

flame	(Hint)
blink	(hence)

(hook)	(Heel)
trees	peel

(Hit)	kind
(hood)	look

dress	(hope)
(Here)	from

Learn To Read English With Directions In Chinese

Name: _____ Date: ___/___/_____ Score: _____

Answer Key

Appendix 9.0

Introduction of the Letter I/i

✓ **Lesson Check Point**

 Directions: Circle the correct letter "i" pair: uppercase and lowercase letters.
路线：圈出正确的字母 i 对：大写和小写字母。

    Ji   Ti   (Ii)   jI   Il

 Directions: The uppercase letter "I" is in the first column. Look at the four letters in the row and circle the lowercase letter that matches the uppercase letter "I."
路线：大写字母 I 在第一栏。看看这一行的 四个字母， 圈出 大写字母 I 的小写字母。

I	j	(i)	t	u
I	q	g	j	(i)
I	(i)	t	g	l
I	l	t	(i)	h

 Directions: The lowercase letter "i" is in the first column. Look at the four letters in the row and circle the uppercase letter that matches the lowercase letter "i."
路线：小写字母 i 第一栏。看看这一行的四个字母，圈出小写字母 i 的大写字母。

i	(I)	T	J	L
i	K	G	H	(I)
i	Y	L	(I)	T
i	J	(I)	Y	K

Classwork

 Name: _____ Date: ___/___/_____ Score: _____

Appendix 10.0

Introduction of the Letter J/j

✓ **Lesson Check Point**

 Directions: Circle the correct letter "j" pair: uppercase and lowercase letters.
路线：圈出正确的字母 j 对：大写和小写字母。

    Gj   Ji   (jJ)   Jl   Pj

 Directions: The uppercase letter "J" is in the first column. Look at the four letters in the row and circle the lowercase letter that matches the uppercase letter "J."
路线：大写字母 J 在第一栏。看看这一行的 四个字母，圈出 大写字母 J 的小写字母。

J	p	(j)	n	q
J	(j)	q	y	k
J	b	c	(j)	v
J	y	h	c	(j)

 Directions: The lowercase letter "j" is in the first column. Look at the four letters in the row and circle the uppercase letter that matches the lowercase letter "j."
路线：小写字母 j 第一栏。看看这一行的四个字母，圈出小写字母 j 的大写字母。

j	B	Q	(J)	G
j	G	V	F	(J)
j	(J)	U	C	O
j	Q	H	(J)	T

Name: _____ Date: ___/___/_____ Score: _____

Answer Key

Appendix 10.0

Letter Recognition J/j

Uppercase and Lowercase Letter

✓ **Lesson Check Point**

 Directions: Read each target word. Read the words in the row and circle the word that begins with a different letter.
路线：读每个目标词。读这一行的词，圈出首字母不同的词。

Target Words				
1. jaw	just	(house)	Jim	jumbo
2. jolt	(bunny)	jelly	juice	joy
3. junk	job	jam	(yearly)	jump
4. jet	(giggles)	joke	June	joint
5. just	jigsaw	(puppy)	journal	Jack

 Directions: Read the words in the four boxes. Circle two words that start with the uppercase and lowercase letter "j."
路线：读四个框中的词。圈出首字母为 j 的小写或大写字母的 词汇。

quest	(journey)
yarn	(Join)

(Jacket)	boat
gold	(just)

pie	you
(juicy)	(Jelly)

(Jumbo)	(jail)
good	yes

(junk)	great
(Job)	queen

youth	(Jungle)
(jealous)	guest

Learn To Read English With Directions In Chinese

Classwork

 Name: _____ Date: ___/___/_____ Score: _____

Appendix 11.0

Introduction of the Letter K/k

✓ Lesson Check Point

 Directions: Circle the correct letter "k" pair: uppercase and lowercase letters.
路线：圈出正确的字母 k 对：大写和小写字母。

Bk   (Kk)   kL   Mk   Kl

 Directions: The uppercase letter "K" is in the first column. Look at the four letters in the row and circle the lowercase letter that matches the uppercase letter "K."
路线：大写字母 K 在第一栏。看看这一行的 四个字母，圈出 大写字母 K 的小写字母。

K	p	h	(k)	q
K	(k)	f	b	l
K	f	b	d	(k)
K	h	(k)	p	l

 Directions: The lowercase letter "k" is in the first column. Look at the four letters in the row and circle the uppercase letter that matches the lowercase letter "k."
路线：小写字母 k 第一栏。看看这一行的四个字母，圈出小写字母 k 的大写字母。

k	B	(K)	N	L
k	(K)	P	L	B
k	B	X	(K)	C
k	P	G	L	(K)

Answer Key

Name: _____ Date:___/__/____ Score:_____

Appendix 11.0

Letter Recognition K/k

Uppercase and Lowercase Letter

 Lesson Check Point

 Directions: Read each target word. Read the words in the row and circle the word that begins with a different letter.

路线：读每个目标词。读这一行的词，圈出首字母不同的词。

Target Words				
1. keep	kale	kedge	(heal)	knoll
2. kick	(laugh)	knot	kid	ketch
3. knight	karts	(home)	kept	kick
4. know	kill	(bald)	kind	keel
5. keys	(down)	knock	keg	knob

 Directions: Read the words in the four boxes. Circle two words that start with the uppercase and lowercase letter "k."

路线：读四个框中的词。圈出首字母为 k 的小写或大写字母的 词汇。

light	house
(Kale)	(keep)

From	(Keen)
Right	(kick)

(key)	blue
low	(Kept)

(Knock)	Bold
(kid)	laugh

Rose	(kind)
(Knit)	bay

(know)	(Karts)
West	team

Classwork

 Name: _____ Date: ___/___/_____ Score: _____

Appendix 12.0

Introduction of the Letter L/l

✓ **Lesson Check Point**

 Directions: Circle the correct letter "l" pair: uppercase and lowercase letters.
路线：圈出正确的字母 l 对：大写和小写字母。

Lb   Kl   (lL)   lH   lJ

 Directions: The uppercase letter "L" is in the first column. Look at the four letters in the row and circle the lowercase letter that matches the uppercase letter "L."
路线：大写字母 L 在第一栏。看看这一行的 四个字母，圈出 大写字母 L 的小写字母。

L	h	(l)	f	b
L	(l)	k	y	p
L	f	b	(l)	d
L	h	b	k	(l)

 Directions: The lowercase letter "l" is in the first column. Look at the four letters in the row and circle the uppercase letter that matches the lowercase letter "l."
路线：小写字母 l 第一栏。看看这一行的四个字母，圈出小写字母 l 的大写字母。

l	B	K	(L)	D
l	H	F	K	(L)
l	(L)	H	C	P
l	D	(L)	V	H

Answer Key

Name: _____ Date: ___/___/_____ Score: _____

Appendix 12.0

Letter Recognition L/l

Uppercase and Lowercase Letter

✓ Lesson Check Point

Directions: Read each target word. Read the words in the row and circle the word that begins with a different letter.

路线：读每个目标词。读这一行的词，圈出首字母不同的词。

Target Words				
1. love	lace	(home)	low	lent
2. load	(tree)	laugh	lid	loaf
3. last	lip	lease	lapse	(mail)
4. learn	(hope)	lark	least	lungs
5. large	limbs	life	lamps	(boats)

Directions: Read the words in the four boxes. Circle two words that start with the uppercase and lowercase letter "l."

路线：读四个框中的词。圈出首字母为 l 的小写或大写字母的 词汇。

teach	found
(lake)	(Leave)

branch	(League)
touch	(loud)

(leech)	Trees
dreams	(Lamb)

(Lounge)	(leash)
Bold	keeps

Young	(Lean)
(lame)	drawn

(lime)	Friends
(Lawn)	deep

Classwork

 Name: _____ Date:___/___/_____ Score: _____

Appendix 13.0

Introduction of the Letter M/m

✓ Lesson Check Point

 Directions: Circle the correct letter "m" pair: uppercase and lowercase letters.
路线：圈出正确的字母 m 对：大写和小写字母。

Mn　　　　Nm　　　　Um　　　　(Mm)　　　　Mw

 Directions: The uppercase letter "M" is in the first column. Look at the four letters in the row and circle the lowercase letter that matches the uppercase letter "M."
路线：大写字母 M 在第一栏。看看这一行的 四个字母，圈出 大写字母 M 的小写字母。

M	(m)	n	v	w
M	v	(m)	w	s
M	n	x	p	(m)
M	(m)	v	n	j

 Directions: The lowercase letter "m" is in the first column. Look at the four letters in the row and circle the uppercase letter that matches the lowercase letter "m."
路线：小写字母 m 第一栏。看看这一行的四个字母，圈出小写字母 m 的大写字母。

m	N	V	Z	(M)
m	K	(M)	N	U
m	W	V	(M)	X
m	N	(M)	V	W

Answer Key

Name: _____ Date:___/___/_____ Score:_____

Appendix 13.0

Letter Recognition M/m

Uppercase and Lowercase Letter

✓ Lesson Check Point

Directions: Read each target word. Read the words in the row and circle the word that begins with a different letter.
路线：读每个目标词。读这一行的词，圈出首字母不同的词。

Target Words				
1. maid	(nose)	mud	mock	mince
2. moon	make	mixed	(used)	mouth
3. mint	(went)	moist	map	musk
4. meal	meat	(need)	mole	Maine
5. must	mix	mail	moan	(under)

Directions: Read the words in the four boxes. Circle two words that start with the uppercase and lowercase letter "m."
路线：读四个框中的词。圈出首字母为 m 的小写或大写字母的 词汇。

none	(Made)		nod	vase		night	(Mouse)
wind	(mood)		(Miss)	(mean)		(might)	wage

(mold)	(Much)		(mild)	noise		(mumps)	voice
Whose	Noun		watch	(Mane)		(Moat)	nail

Learn To Read English With Directions In Chinese   273   Copyrighted Material

Classwork

 Name: _____ Date: ___/___/_____ Score: _____

Appendix 14.0

Introduction of the Letter N/n

✓ **Lesson Check Point**

 Directions: Circle the correct letter "n" pair: uppercase and lowercase letters.

路线：圈出正确的字母 n 对：大写和小写字母。

    nM   (nN)   wN   Nu   Wn

 Directions: The uppercase letter "N" is in the first column. Look at the four letters in the row and circle the lowercase letter that matches the uppercase letter "N."

路线：大写字母 N 在第一栏。看看这一行的 四个字母， 圈出 大写字母 N 的小写字母。

N	w	m	(n)	v
N	(n)	v	w	x
N	m	b	(n)	w
N	v	(n)	c	x

 Directions: The lowercase letter "n" is in the first column. Look at the four letters in the row and circle the uppercase letter that matches the lowercase letter "n."

路线：小写字母 n 第一栏。看看这一行的四个字母，圈出小写字母 n 的大写字母。

n	S	M	(N)	X
n	C	V	M	(N)
n	(N)	M	Z	V
n	M	(N)	X	W

Answer Key

 Name: _____   Date:__/__/_____   Score: _____

Appendix 14.0

Letter Recognition N/n

Uppercase and Lowercase Letter

✓ **Lesson Check Point**

 Directions: Read each target word. Read the words in the row and circle the word that begins with a different letter.

路线：读每个目标词。读这一行的词，圈出首字母不同的词。

Target Words				
1. neck	nine	news	(milk)	next
2. noon	(used)	neat	notch	niche
3. name	nice	note	(wrong)	nip
4. numb	none	new	nod	(male)
5. notice	nerve	(unto)	nuke	Nile

 Directions: Read the words in the four boxes. Circle two words that start with the uppercase and lowercase letter "n."

路线：读四个框中的词。圈出首字母为 n 的小写或大写字母的 词汇。

Mail	van		(Noise)	under		flag	(Nine)
(Nile)	(nail)		wine	(noon)		miss	(nice)

(Noun)	(note)		(night)	mind		(news)	win
word	Mouth		(Next)	set		united	(Nod)

Learn To Read English With Directions In Chinese   275   Copyrighted Material

Classwork

 Name: _____ Date:___/___/_____ Score:_____

Appendix 15.0

Introduction of the Letter O/o

✓ **Lesson Check Point**

 Directions: Circle the correct letter "o" pair: uppercase and lowercase letters.

路线：圈出正确的字母 o 对：大写和小写字母。

Oc   (oO)   uO   pO   qO

 Directions: The uppercase letter "O" is in the first column. Look at the four letters in the row and circle the lowercase letter that matches the uppercase letter "O."

路线：大写字母 O 在第一栏。看看这一行的 四个字母，圈出 大写字母 O 的小写字母。

O	s	p	g	(o)
O	c	(o)	b	j
O	q	d	c	(o)
O	(o)	g	q	h

 Directions: The lowercase letter "o" is in the first column. Look at the four letters in the row and circle the uppercase letter that matches the lowercase letter "o."

路线：小写字母 o 第一栏。看看这一行的四个字母，圈出小写字母 o 的大写字母。

o	Q	C	G	(O)
o	(O)	D	U	R
o	C	B	(O)	D
o	G	(O)	C	E

Answer Key

 Name: _____ Date: ___/___/_____ Score: _____

Appendix 16.0

Introduction of the Letter P/p

✓ Lesson Check Point

 Directions: Circle the correct letter "p" pair: uppercase and lowercase letters.
路线：圈出正确的字母 p 对：大写和小写字母。

(Pp)   Bp   Dp   Pg   Fp

 Directions: The uppercase letter "P" is in the first column. Look at the four letters in the row and circle the lowercase letter that matches the uppercase letter "P."
路线：大写字母 P 在第一栏。看看这一行的 四个字母， 圈出 大写字母 P 的小写字母。

P	(p)	q	b	d
P	b	f	(p)	q
P	h	(p)	b	f
P	q	d	s	(p)

 Directions: The lowercase letter "p" is in the first column. Look at the four letters in the row and circle the uppercase letter that matches the lowercase letter "p."
路线：小写字母 p 第一栏。看看这一行的四个字母，圈出小写字母 p 的大写字母。

p	Q	(P)	B	F
p	H	B	D	(P)
p	F	(P)	S	D
p	(P)	F	D	B

Learn To Read English With Directions In Chinese   277   Copyrighted Material

Classwork

Name: _____ Date: ___/___/_____ Score: _____

Appendix 16.0

Letter Recognition P/p

Uppercase and Lowercase Letter

✓ **Lesson Check Point**

 Directions: Read each target word. Read the words in the row and circle the word that begins with a different letter.
路线：读每个目标词。读这一行的词，圈出首字母不同的词。

Target Words				
1. pitch	pack	(grow)	pound	purse
2. plots	(bind)	plush	proud	plight
3. peace	plate	page	(quest)	prowl
4. pale	(good)	plant	poor	pull
5. punch	prude	(quick)	pike	pool

 Directions: Read the words in the four boxes. Circle two words that start with the uppercase and lowercase letter "p."
路线：读四个框中的词。圈出首字母为 p 的小写或大写字母的 词汇。

| (Praise) | quaint |
| youth | (phase) |

| (point) | (Prince) |
| quart | group |

| grew | (purse) |
| (Prime) | quiet |

| (Pink) | quick |
| (place) | jam |

| jump | quite |
| (Paid) | (peace) |

| young | (peach) |
| guess | (Port) |

Answer Key

 Name: _____ Date: ___/___/_____ Score: _____

Appendix 17.0

Introduction of the Letter Q/q

✓ Lesson Check Point

 Directions: Circle the correct letter "q" pair: uppercase and lowercase letters.
路线：圈出正确的字母 q 对：大写和小写字母。

    Qd   Gq   Oq   (qQ)   Qp

 Directions: The uppercase letter "Q" is in the first column. Look at the four letters in the row and circle the lowercase letter that matches the uppercase letter "Q."
路线：大写字母 Q 在第一栏。看看这一行的 四个字母，圈出 大写字母 Q 的小写字母。

Q	g	h	p	(q)
Q	(q)	j	y	b
Q	p	(q)	b	d
Q	y	p	(q)	b

 Directions: The lowercase letter "q" is in the first column. Look at the four letters in the row and circle the uppercase letter that matches the lowercase letter "q."
路线：小写字母 q 第一栏。看看这一行的四个字母，圈出小写字母 q 的大写字母。

q	D	O	(Q)	P
q	(Q)	A	D	O
q	O	C	G	(Q)
q	G	(Q)	C	O

Learn To Read English With Directions In Chinese

Classwork

Name: _____ Date: ___/___/_____ Score: _____

Appendix 17.0

Letter Recognition Q/q

Uppercase and Lowercase Letter

✓ **Lesson Check Point**

Directions: Read each target word. Read the words in the row and circle the word that begins with a different letter.
路线：读每个目标词。读这一行的词，圈出首字母不同的词。

Target Words				
1. quack	quaint	quick	(please)	quiz
2. quilt	(guess)	quip	quire	quote
3. quirt	quirk	(young)	quit	quartz
4. quench	quite	quiet	(jump)	quince
5. quake	quota	quail	quest	(guest)

Directions: Read the words in the four boxes. Circle two words that start with the uppercase and lowercase letter "q."
路线：读四个框中的词。圈出首字母为 q 的小写或大写字母的 词汇。

pajamas	(Qualm)
(quality)	Orchid

jacket	peanut
(quarrel)	(Quarter)

joint	(quicken)
oxygen	(Quartz)

(quest)	jumper
(Quiver)	yours

(quote)	(Quotient)
picture	Ocean

(quick)	painter
young	(Quebec)

Answer Key

 Name: _____ Date: ___/___/_____ Score: _____

Appendix 18.0

Introduction of the Letter R/r

✓ **Lesson Check Point**

   Directions: Circle the correct letter "r" pair: uppercase and lowercase letters.
路线：圈出正确的字母 r 对：大写和小写字母。

Rz　　　(rR)　　　jR　　　rE　　　Fr

   Directions: The uppercase letter "R" is in the first column. Look at the four letters in the row and circle the lowercase letter that matches the uppercase letter "R."
路线：大写字母 R 在第一栏。看看这一行的 四个字母， 圈出 大写字母 R 的小写字母。

R	x	(r)	v	u
R	(r)	x	z	c
R	b	h	c	(r)
R	n	z	(r)	s

   Directions: The lowercase letter "r" is in the first column. Look at the four letters in the row and circle the uppercase letter that matches the lowercase letter "r."
路线：小写字母 r 第一栏。看看这一行的四个字母，圈出小写字母 r 的大写字母。

r	Y	U	(R)	Z
r	(R)	H	C	M
r	U	N	F	(R)
r	M	(R)	D	O

Classwork

Name: _____ Date: ___/___/_____ Score: _____

Appendix 18.0

Letter Recognition R/r

Uppercase and Lowercase Letter

✓ Lesson Check Point

Directions: Read each target word. Read the words in the row and circle the word that begins with a different letter.
路线：读每个目标词。读这一行的词，圈出首字母不同的词。

Target Words				
1. race	roach	reel	(match)	rains
2. rode	(nurse)	range	roam	rule
3. rinse	ranch	(mouse)	robe	reed
4. raise	rend	rock	rank	(cease)
5. ripping	(cards)	read	rack	rope

Directions: Read the words in the four boxes. Circle two words that start with the uppercase and lowercase letter "r."
路线：读四个框中的词。圈出首字母为 r 的小写或大写字母的 词汇。

(rate)	moose
Piece	(Rice)

(rob)	(Rave)
nose	mother

Part	(Roar)
mouse	(rhythm)

Pat	maple
(roost)	(Rat)

team	Price
(rope)	(Rich)

dream	(Room)
(ramp)	neck

Answer Key

 Name: _____ Date: ___/___/_____ Score: _____

Appendix 19.0

Introduction of the Letter S/s

✓ **Lesson Check Point**

 Directions: Circle the correct letter "s" pair: uppercase and lowercase letters.
路线：圈出正确的字母 s 对：大写和小写字母。

    sA   sB   Zs   Cs   (sS)

 Directions: The uppercase letter "S" is in the first column. Look at the four letters in the row and circle the lowercase letter that matches the uppercase letter "S."
路线：大写字母 S 在第一栏。看看这一行的 四个字母，圈出 大写字母 S 的小写字母。

S	c	o	d	(s)
S	(s)	c	u	o
S	o	a	(s)	c
S	u	(s)	c	o

 Directions: The lowercase letter "s" is in the first column. Look at the four letters in the row and circle the uppercase letter that matches the lowercase letter "s."
路线：小写字母 s 第一栏。看看这一行的四个字母，圈出小写字母 s 的大写字母。

s	G	(S)	O	C
s	Q	C	U	(S)
s	(S)	U	O	C
s	Z	Q	(S)	V

Learn To Read English With Directions In Chinese   283   Copyrighted Material

Classwork

Name: _____ Date: ___/___/_____ Score: _____

Appendix 19.0

Letter Recognition S/s

Uppercase and Lowercase Letter

✓ Lesson Check Point

 Directions: Read each target word. Read the words in the row and circle the word that begins with a different letter.
路线：读每个目标词。读这一行的词，圈出首字母不同的词。

Target Words				
1. smart	soft	(chart)	smith	shop
2. sail	(opens)	saw	skit	soil
3. skill	smooth	shoot	seat	(van)
4. source	soup	side	(zero)	sight
5. sky	snooze	(cake)	short	smell

 Directions: Read the words in the four boxes. Circle two words that start with the uppercase and lowercase letter "s."
路线：读四个框中的词。圈出首字母为 s 的小写或大写字母的 词汇。

| zero | (Six) |
| (shore) | cone |

| (Shield) | cup |
| (sink) | zoo |

| (shame) | (Said) |
| zap | clean |

| Cross | (slurp) |
| (Shine) | win |

| none | child |
| (soap) | (Snail) |

| camp | (song) |
| zebra | (Shake) |

Name: _____ Date:___/___/_____ Score:_____

Appendix 20.0

Introduction of the Letter T/t

✓ **Lesson Check Point**

 Directions: Circle the correct letter "t" pair: uppercase and lowercase letters.
路线：圈出正确的字母 t 对：大写和小写字母。

    Tf   tE   (Tt)   tF   iT

 Directions: The uppercase letter "T" is in the first column. Look at the four letters in the row and circle the lowercase letter that matches the uppercase letter "T."
路线：大写字母 T 在第一栏。看看这一行的 四个字母， 圈出 大写字母 T 的小写字母。

T	t	h	f	d
T	b	f	t	h
T	l	t	b	f
T	h	d	b	t

 Directions: The lowercase letter "t" is in the first column. Look at the four letters in the row and circle the uppercase letter that matches the lowercase letter "t."
路线：小写字母 t 第一栏。看看这一行的四个字母，圈出小写字母 t 的大写字母。

t	F	T	H	E
t	T	B	E	F
t	H	B	T	Y
t	R	F	S	T

Classwork

 Name: _____ Date:___/___/_____ Score:_____

Appendix 20.0

Letter Recognition T/t

Uppercase and Lowercase Letter

✓ **Lesson Check Point**

 Directions: Read each target word. Read the words in the row and circle the word that begins with a different letter.
路线：读每个目标词。读这一行的词，圈出首字母不同的词。

Target Words				
1. twin	that	(day)	trust	talk
2. tooth	tight	team	top	(face)
3. tempt	(key)	time	trash	tweed
4. torch	though	their	temp	(live)
5. treat	thick	twice	(herd)	thief

 Directions: Read the words in the four boxes. Circle two words that start with the uppercase and lowercase letter "t."
路线：读四个框中的词。圈出首字母为 t 的小写或大写字母的 词汇。

| Floor | (Trade) |
| (tear) | draw |

| horses | (toil) |
| lunch | (Track) |

| (tease) | keep |
| (Toll) | load |

| (Text) | Pie |
| (troop) | Joy |

| Egg | lone |
| (theme) | (Trip) |

| (taste) | pants |
| beach | (Think) |

Name: _____ Date: ___/___/_____ Score: _____

Appendix 21.0

Introduction of the Letter U/u

✓ **Lesson Check Point**

 Directions: Circle the correct letter "u" pair: uppercase and lowercase letters.
路线：圈出正确的字母 u 对：大写和小写字母。

(uU)　　　Yu　　　Gu　　　Uv　　　Au

 Directions: The uppercase letter "U" is in the first column. Look at the four letters in the row and circle the lowercase letter that matches the uppercase letter "U."
路线：大写字母 U 在第一栏。看看这一行的 四个字母，圈出 大写字母 U 的小写字母。

U	(u)	v	c	y
U	h	x	(u)	z
U	j	b	v	(u)
U	s	(u)	g	a

 Directions: The lowercase letter "u" is in the first column. Look at the four letters in the row and circle the uppercase letter that matches the lowercase letter "u."
路线：小写字母 u 第一栏。看看这一行的四个字母，圈出小写字母 u 的大写字母。

u	Y	T	(U)	Z
u	(U)	B	N	Y
u	C	Q	(U)	D
u	J	V	G	(U)

Classwork

 Name: _____ Date:___/___/_____ Score:_____

Appendix 22.0

Introduction of the Letter V/v

✓ Lesson Check Point

 Directions: Circle the correct letter "v" pair: uppercase and lowercase letters.
路线：圈出正确的字母 v 对：大写和小写字母。

vW   Vu   Cv   (Vv)   Wv

 Directions: The uppercase letter "V" is in the first column. Look at the four letters in the row and circle the lowercase letter that matches the uppercase letter "V."
路线：大写字母 V 在第一栏。看看这一行的 四个字母，圈出 大写字母 V 的小写字母。

V	w	(v)	x	y
V	y	w	n	(v)
V	(v)	x	y	u
V	x	z	(v)	w

 Directions: The lowercase letter "v" is in the first column. Look at the four letters in the row and circle the uppercase letter that matches the lowercase letter "v."
路线：小写字母 v 第一栏。看看这一行的四个字母，圈出小写字母 v 的大写字母。

v	X	Z	(V)	Y
v	Y	W	X	(V)
v	(V)	Y	N	M
v	W	(V)	X	C

Name: _____   Date: ___/___/_____   Score: _____

Answer Key

Appendix 22.0

Letter Recognition V/v

Uppercase and Lowercase Letter

✓ **Lesson Check Point**

 Directions: Read each target word. Read the words in the row and circle the word that begins with a different letter.
路线：读每个目标词。读这一行的词，圈出首字母不同的词。

Target Words				
1. voice	volt	(wool)	vase	verse
2. verb	vest	vow	vogue	(used)
3. vain	(west)	veil	vault	vine
4. view	void	(mouse)	versed	vile
5. vote	vex	voiced	(wig)	vein

 Directions: Read the words in the four boxes. Circle two words that start with the uppercase and lowercase letter "v."
路线：读四个框中的词。圈出首字母为 v 的小写或大写字母的 词汇。

skill	(vouch)
(Vamp)	Wrote

(vague)	(Van)
rose	name

whiz	(valve)
mail	(Vice)

(Vent)	cove
Weep	(verge)

(vane)	(Very)
must	goat

(Visit)	card
(vet)	West

Unit V Appendix 22.0

Classwork

 Name: _____ Date: ___/___/_____ Score: _____

Appendix 23.0

Introduction of the Letter W/w

 Lesson Check Point

Directions: Circle the correct letter "w" pair: uppercase and lowercase letters.
路线：圈出正确的字母 w 对：大写和小写字母。

wU   (Ww)   Xw   Vw   Wv

Directions: The uppercase letter "W" is in the first column. Look at the four letters in the row and circle the lowercase letter that matches the uppercase letter "W."
路线：大写字母 W 在第一栏。看看这一行的 四个字母，圈出 大写字母 W 的小写字母。

W	x	(w)	v	z
W	v	z	(w)	y
W	(w)	y	v	m
W	n	v	y	(w)

Directions: The lowercase letter "w" is in the first column. Look at the four letters in the row and circle the uppercase letter that matches the lowercase letter "w."
路线：小写字母 w 第一栏。看看这一行的四个字母，圈出小写字母 w 的大写字母。

w	V	(W)	Y	M
w	X	Y	V	(W)
w	(W)	V	X	M
w	Y	F	(W)	X

Learn To Read English With Directions In Chinese

Answer Key

Name: _____ Date: ___/___/_____ Score: _____

Appendix 23.0

Letter Recognition W/w

Uppercase and Lowercase Letter

 Lesson Check Point

 Directions: Read each target word. Read the words in the row and circle the word that begins with a different letter.
路线：读每个目标词。读这一行的词，圈出首字母不同的词。

Target Words				
1. wind	west	(vacuum)	whole	waste
2. wrote	(night)	wink	wolf	wish
3. which	wrap	whom	were	(vessel)
4. wept	whale	(card)	whose	wide
5. wash	wrench	watch	word	(zebra)

 Directions: Read the words in the four boxes. Circle two words that start with the uppercase and lowercase letter "w."
路线：读四个框中的词。圈出首字母为 w 的小写或大写字母的 词汇。

crow	(Work)	(wheat)	nerve	Village	cars
visitor	(wave)	zoom	(Wax)	(wild)	(Wheel)

(will)	x-rays	(Worth)	(when)	corn	(ways)
(Would)	Nile	violet	Never	(Wine)	vintage

Classwork

 Name: _____   Date: ___/___/_____   Score: _____

Appendix 24.0

Introduction of the Letter X/x

✓ **Lesson Check Point**

 Directions: Circle the correct letter "x" pair: uppercase and lowercase letters.
路线：圈出正确的字母 x 对：大写和小写字母。

    Xw   xY   (xX)   Sx   Kx

 Directions: The uppercase letter "X" is in the first column. Look at the four letters in the row and circle the lowercase letter that matches the uppercase letter "X."
路线：大写字母 X 在第一栏。看看这一行的 四个字母， 圈出 大写字母 X 的小写字母。

X	k	(x)	y	z
X	v	w	(x)	m
X	(x)	z	e	s
X	v	z	h	(x)

 Directions: The lowercase letter "x" is in the first column. Look at the four letters in the row and circle the uppercase letter that matches the lowercase letter "x."
路线：小写字母 x 第一栏。看看这一行的四个字母，圈出小写字母 x 的大写字母。

x	K	(X)	Z	M
x	W	K	V	(X)
x	(X)	M	K	Y
x	V	Y	(X)	Z

Answer Key

 Name: _____ Date: ____/ ___/ _____ Score: _____

Appendix 24.0

Letter Recognition X/x

Uppercase and Lowercase Letter

✓ Lesson Check Point

 Directions: Read each target word. Read the words in the row and circle the word that does not contain a letter "x."
路线：读每个目标词。读行中的单词，圈出不含字母 x 的词。

Target Words				
1. fix	wax	excite	(sing)	flax
2. box	taxes	expo	foxes	(cold)
3. flex	ox	(night)	taxi	exalt
4. exam	toxin	axle	sixty	(loving)
5. text	vex	(young)	next	coax

 Directions: Read the words in the four boxes. Circle two words that start with the uppercase and lowercase letter "x."
路线：读四个框中的词。圈出首字母为 x 的小写或大写字母的 词汇。

vogue	(xylems)
(Xanthine)	kid

youth	voiced
(xanthone)	(Xenograft)

kept	(Xanthous)
one	(x-axis)

(xylem)	voiced
(Xerox)	keys

(Xyster)	know
yes	(xylan)

(Xylene)	(xylose)
moose	view

Classwork

 Name: _____ Date:___/___/_____ Score:_____

Appendix 25.0

Introduction of the Letter Y/y

✓ **Lesson Check Point**

 Directions: Circle the correct letter "y" pair: uppercase and lowercase letters.
路线：圈出正确的字母 y 对：大写和小写字母。

Yx   (yY)   Yz   Ky   Vy

 Directions: The uppercase letter "Y" is in the first column. Look at the four letters in the row and circle the lowercase letter that matches the uppercase letter "Y."
路线：大写字母 Y 在第一栏。看看这一行的 四个字母， 圈出 大写字母 Y 的小写字母。

Y	v	(y)	b	x
Y	x	z	(y)	u
Y	(y)	x	z	w
Y	x	z	v	(y)

 Directions: The lowercase letter "y" is in the first column. Look at the four letters in the row and circle the uppercase letter that matches the lowercase letter "y."
路线：小写字母 y 第一栏。看看这一行的四个字母，圈出小写字母 y 的大写字母。

y	V	X	Z	(Y)
y	(Y)	V	X	Z
y	W	(Y)	X	M
y	U	M	(Y)	X

Name: _____ Date: ___/___/_____ Score: _____

Appendix 25.0

Letter Recognition Y/y

Uppercase and Lowercase Letter

✓ Lesson Check Point

Directions: Read each target word. Read the words in the row and circle the word that begins with a different letter.
路线：读每个目标词。读这一行的词，圈出首字母不同的词。

Target Words				
1. yield	(grown)	yogurt	yam	yeast
2. yacht	(jeep)	yolk	yucca	yawn
3. yuppie	yodel	young	(quick)	your
4. yellow	yelp	(please)	yummy	yoga
5. yourself	yank	yes	yo-yo	(game)

Directions: Read the words in the four boxes. Circle two words that start with the uppercase and lowercase letter "y."
路线：读四个框中的词。圈出首字母为 y 的小写或大写字母的 词汇。

gum	jump
(yelp)	(Youth)

(Yarn)	quill
paint	(yells)

jet	(You)
globe	(yaw)

jog	(yak)
(Year)	grace

(Yet)	(yams)
judge	glow

(yawn)	June
(Yeast)	peach

Classwork

 Name: _____ Date:___/___/_____ Score:_____

Appendix 26.0

Introduction of the Letter Z/z

✓ **Lesson Check Point**

 Directions: Circle the correct letter "z" pair: uppercase and lowercase letters.

路线：圈出正确的字母 z 对：大写和小写字母。

(zZ)　　　Nz　　　Zn　　　zM　　　zA

 Directions: The uppercase letter "Z" is in the first column. Look at the four letters in the row and circle the lowercase letter that matches the uppercase letter "Z."

路线：大写字母 Z 在第一栏。看看这一行的 四个字母，圈出 大写字母 Z 的小写字母。

Z	n	x	(z)	t
Z	v	(z)	x	w
Z	m	w	s	(z)
Z	(z)	v	w	n

 Directions: The lowercase letter "z" is in the first column. Look at the four letters in the row and circle the uppercase letter that matches the lowercase letter "z."

路线：小写字母 z 第一栏。看看这一行的四个字母，圈出小写字母 z 的大写字母。

z	B	V	(Z)	N
z	W	(Z)	X	U
z	(Z)	S	W	V
z	A	N	X	(Z)

Name: _____   Date:___/__/_____   Score:_____

Appendix 26.0

Letter Recognition Z/z

Uppercase and Lowercase Letter

✓ **Lesson Check Point**

 Directions: Read each target word. Read the words in the row and circle the word that begins with a different letter.
路线：读每个目标词。读这一行的词，圈出首字母不同的词。

Target Words				
1. zebu	zap	zebra	(cage)	zoo
2. zones	(seals)	zany	zeal	zest
3. zip	zing	zero	zinc	(flesh)
4. Zhan	zoom	(moon)	ziti	zonal
5. zest	(sung)	zone	zoos	zebra

 Directions: Read the words in the four boxes. Circle two words that start with the uppercase and lowercase letter "z."
路线：读四个框中的词。圈出首字母为 z 的小写或大写字母的 词汇。

cents	(Zeta)
(zing)	sea

mix	(zap)
(Zip)	sick

(Zoom)	(zit)
index	wind

(zinc)	remix
(Zipper)	cents

nice	Plant
(ziti)	(Zone)

rest	(Zoo)
eggs	(zoom)

Classwork

**Your Next Step:
Learn To Read English Vowels With Directions In Chinese**

www.ingramcontent.com/pod-product-compliance
Lightning Source LLC
Chambersburg PA
CBHW080800300426
44114CB00020B/2767